LIFE ON THE
FRINGE

For all my dear family and friends,

who have made my life's journey this much

fuller, tastier, and more fun to take on

Co-published in 2024 by

MCCM Creations
10B, Sing Kui Commercial Building
27 Des Voeux Road West
Sheung Wan, Hong Kong

www.mccmcreations.com

and

Hong Kong University Press
The University of Hong Kong
Pok Fu Lam Road, Hong Kong

https://hkupress.hku.hk

Editor: Madeleine Slavick
Illustration Artist: Peter Suart
Cover Designer: Peter Suart
Layout Designer: Lie Fhung

ISBN 978-988-8842-95-7 (Paperback)

Illustrations © Peter Suart 2024
Photographs © the authors

©Benny Chia 2024
Benny Chia has asserted his right as the author of this work.
Every effort has been made to obtain the necessary permissions with
copyright material, both quoted and illustratve. We apologise for any omissions
and will be pleased to make appropriate acknowledgements in future editions.

All rights reserved. No portion of this publication may be reproduced or
transmitted in any form or by any means, electronic or mechanical, including
photocopying, recording, or any information storage or retrieval system, without
prior permission in writing from the publisher.

British Library Cataloguing-in-Publication Data
A catalogue record for this book is available from the British Library.

10 9 8 7 6 5 4 3 2 1

Printed and bound by Regal Printing
Hong Kong, China

BENNY CHIA

LIFE ON THE FRINGE

THE ~~almost~~ NAKED MEMOIR

mccmcreations

邊渡四十年

謝俊興

*'I always get to where I am going by
walking away from where I have been.'*

Attributed to Winnipeg-the-Pooh

CONTENTS

	Prelude	6
	Prologue	9
CHAPTER 1	Into the Arts by Hazard	15
CHAPTER 2	Taking it from the Top	29
CHAPTER 3	Sleepless in Paradise	43
CHAPTER 4	Flying Solo by Night	65
CHAPTER 5	A Meteor Shower	93
CHAPTER 6	The Morning After	109
CHAPTER 7	Opening Bells	137
CHAPTER 8	Up and Running	149
CHAPTER 9	Romping Away	163
CHAPTER 10	Look to Windward	191
CHAPTER 11	Spin It Again	225
CHAPTER 12	Looking Away	237
CHAPTER 13	Turning Around	245
CHAPTER 14	Venice Calling	293
CHAPTER 15	Learn • Play • Lead	311
	Epilogue	349
	Acknowledgements	360
	Index	363

PRELUDE

I ALWAYS LOOKED FORWARD to conversations with Benny Chia at the Fringe Club. Often, I would deliberately walk up the steep hill instead of taking a cab, because it allowed me time to leave the hectic workaholic pace of Central behind to prepare me for what was always a meeting of minds, creativity, and ideas as well as little anecdotes on life and personal discoveries.

The best days were those spent on the balcony of Colette's over lunch or tea, our backs to the humdrum, our faces to the quieter hills, sun streaming between buildings, and trees above us. The past and present stood still, as we entered our chat like two travellers walking in the same direction, believing in hope and possibility, and comparing notes on the paths we chose in the arts world that led to these intermittent intersections and encounters.

When Benny asked me to read this manuscript, I was at once perplexed and curious, given that in the grander scheme of the arts world in Hong Kong and internationally, his experience and expertise was substantial, whereas my role has been minute. I felt there were many other more suitable candidates for the task. I felt this was something close to his heart, and my stepping up was an act of faith in our friendship, not knowing if this would place it on unsettled ground. You see, his request also came at a time that the Fringe Club, Benny's creation and lifeblood, had reached the end of an era.

Would a memoir be a tell all? Would it be a hard read, a slog along the debate-worn road on the struggle of the arts and missed opportunities? What tone or viewpoint would Benny take? What would I say if I didn't quite take to it, given that we have always spoken quite candidly in our discussions?

As soon as I read through the first few pages, I smiled. I entered the moment that was so familiar, for Benny writes with honesty, hope, and humour.

We journey with Benny through his childhood in a cramped flat with no artwork or music, yet through his curiosity, he discovers a love for stories, books, and comics. Accompanying his mother to the cinema, he comes under the spell of movies and musicals – they offer escape to a world of story and possibility beyond the confines of his surroundings. At school, Benny discovers music and eventually an appetite for travel and adventure that draws him into a life in the arts. Benny's creative search for meaning, as expressed in the many facets and modes of the arts, has taken him to all corners of the world – to meet, learn from, and to work together with artists from all walks of life.

This is the Benny I know, who like the Fringe Club and its stories, stands like a welcoming beacon on a city hill – representing the creativity, resilience and commitment of Hong Kong over the past 40 years, and creating and facilitating artistic encounters that do not always fit convention, only because he's quietly one step ahead, waiting for us to catch up.

MARISSA FUNG-SHAW

Mrs. Fung-Shaw is a former Trustee, Asian Cultural Council and Member, member of M+ Board of Directors, and Co-Chair of The Absolutely Fabulous Theatre Connection

PROLOGUE

A CHANCE CONVERSATION in an elevator changed the direction of my life. It was a summer morning forty-four years ago when I stepped into that lift. About two minutes later, I had an offer for a job at the Hong Kong Arts Centre that would take me on a magical journey, meeting a host of good people who would rescue me in cliffhanging moments, friends who would show me a way forward, and artists who taught me to live by my ideals even when the going gets tough.

Over the decades, I have witnessed – and played a part in – our city's sea changes from a cultural desert into a fertile art habitat. I wanted to put all that in writing. The idea came to me when I was waiting for a long night to pass. I had found myself keeping watch on the bedroom ceiling and listening for the sounds of the early morning traffic to return. I wanted Hong Kong to return as I'd known it. I never knew life could be like this, waking up to the same Groundhog Day, the same drill, and stepping into the same muddy puddle, over and over again. Except, in this plot of ours, unlike in the movie, there was no ultimate redemption. At the time, there seemed no end in sight.

Sometimes, my mind harks back listlessly to that long weekend when millions of people – otherwise docile homebodies – took to the streets to protest against the government passing laws that would eventually change the city for good. Overturned garbage cans, shattered glass, dismantled railings. Shop windows boarded up for their protection. Hordes of angry protesters barricaded themselves at road junctions. MTR stations closed – their drawn shutters battered, rammed, fire-bombed. Phalanxes of police in riot gear confronting the angry mob. Teargas canisters smoking where they hit the ground. Guns fired. Passing through the streets in Central, it was the closest I've ever been to a war zone. I can still feel the acrid smoke rasping in the back of my throat.

The last time I saw Hong Kong looking so desolate was in photographs of Christmas 1941, when the Japanese army invaded our city. It's disconcerting to juxtapose these two periods of history. I felt the need to cling to some sense of normality. Central District has always been a gauge of Hong Kong's cardiovascular health, fast-paced, hectic but peaceful. And then, without warning, the COVID-19 pandemic visited us; like a hostile and deadly sniper taking random aim at people, it kept them off the streets. The double blow floored us, well and good.

I opened the doors of the Fringe Club – set up in a disused cold storage warehouse – to the public for the first time in January 1984, after launching the Fringe Festival the previous year. Almost forty years later, at the height of the pandemic, it ran out of steam. We had to call it quits. As a financially responsible operator, we scraped the bottom of the barrel to pay what we owed the staff, all the outstanding bills, and disbanded. After immersing myself

PROLOGUE

in it from the day of its conception, nurturing it, taking care of it through sickness and health, having to part with it was like a limb being torn off.

I had to do something to settle myself, so I went about digging up old work diaries, press clippings, photos, newsletters, files, and spent all day rifling through them. I wanted to hold on to something, put past events on record: I didn't want the Fringe as I remembered it to slip from my grasp. The next day, I took out my treasured Montblanc pen from its case, filled it up with the turquoise ink that I like, and proceeded to write.

Months later, I had diligently filled up several notebooks with some satisfaction. One night after dinner, I sat myself down in an easy chair to read them but soon got up to rummage through the fridge for snacks. Filled with dates of events, names of people and places, it read like a series of timelines with self-important annotations. It lacked the flavour of a page-turner, or any flavour at all. It was then that I decided to write it as a memoir, a cross between a work journal and an autobiography. I thought this would create at least some voyeuristic frisson if nothing else. I picked up Mary Karr's *The Art of Memoir* from an online bookstore and other similar books to get some idea of how to go about it. Ms Karr, for one, was for telling it like it was, warts and all.

How far should I go? Should I knock on those forbidden doors, or was it better to keep things under lock and key? I am by nature a private person. Little is known about me outside of work, and I am comfortable that way. Also, it's a cultural thing. Where I come from, we feel shy about revealing too much of ourselves and what we're really thinking, especially about something considered inappropriate, disrespectful, or disgraceful, not just about ourselves but to people related to us. Yet, at the same time, I knew I didn't want to bore anyone by being overly proper and polite.

The story of the Fringe has never been told from start to finish. Some episodes are so uncanny – things happening the way they did, problems seemingly unsolvable resolving themselves, and the chance encounters of people – that they read like fiction.

Many of those events occurred when the mere thought of Hong Kong's future was enough to keep people up at night. The uncertainty, instead of being a deterrent, sent artists into an overdrive of activity. Let it out. Make a splash before the curtain was brought down on them. Social and political matters were the main focus, what people talked and worried about. The Fringe, considered an outlier and a mere diversion, was left pretty much to its own devices. The media loved to write about it. It made good headlines. Grungy and wacky, it provided the levity against the grim news of the day in the lead up to handover. It adopted the motto made famous by Voltaire, the French freethinker: 'I don't agree with what you say, but I defend your right to say it.' It became a barometer of freedom of expression.

I was handed the keys to a building, an ice depot so full of history and character, that I could own, even for just a month and despite its rundown condition (now a selfie destination every bride-to-be and taxi driver knows about). There I was given the chance to launch three unique festivals, try my hand at scriptwriting, produce original and critically acclaimed dance and mime theatre pieces, and make friends with arts practitioners around the world in Bergen, Kaiping, Melbourne, San Francisco, Singapore, Sydney, Seoul, Shanghai, Taipei, Venice, and Vienna.

Like looking at paintings and photographs, I am engrossed in observing human faces in their multitudinous expressions. I try

PROLOGUE

to portray the *personae dramatis* in my stories captured in those 'decisive moments', as Cartier-Bresson might call them. In so doing, I might have taken some poetic freedom in recalling conversations and rearranging the furniture. My intention has been to bring past events into sharp focus. For those who have passed on – sadly, there have been a few – I remain truthful to their loving memories.

In the end, I didn't make much use of the usual memory aids or archived materials. I simply let memories come and float to the surface. Sometimes the act of remembering can be like birdwatching: you don't always find what you've come for, but you may find another species. In some cases, when I had doubted the veracity of my recall, I contacted those persons of interest for a cross-check or a comparison of subjective truths.

During those long, interminable years of the COVID pandemic, we commissioned Osbert and Sheryl, a couple of urban farmers, to create what the French call *jardin sauvage*, a naturally wild garden of herbs and edible flowers, on our roof. They grew mint, pandan, lemongrass, rosemary, thyme, calendula, nasturtium, dill, sweetgrass, and many other varieties. We used them to create a tisane – a fresh herbal tea – taken with Madeleines that once helped revive Marcel Proust's childhood memories.

Vivian, our bar manager, baked and served them in the room where Dairy Farm used to sell cold milk and ice cream over a long marble-topped counter. Sometimes, in an unearthly moment, alone there, I swear I could still smell the buttery and vanilla aroma transfusing the room and hear the faint echo of the crowd applauding and cheering from the roof where we once had Benjamin Zephaniah rapping and ranting in verse against political, social, and racial injustices; the timeless Jane Birken, insouciant as always, coming from her Valentine's Day concert to chat with her fans; the pyrotechnic erth performing Gargoyles and setting fire to a scaffolding; and showing off-beat movies to an audience who came dressed up in fancy costumes for fun. Now, only the willowy dill and slender eucalyptus were there taking bows from a phantom crowd in the wind – a silent coda to those rhapsodic nights haunting my memory.

What we choose to remember tells a lot about who we are. For those of you who already know me, I hope you'll know me somewhat better after reading this. For those I haven't had the pleasure of meeting, I hope this will arouse enough interest for you to want to know more about someone who has chosen a life in the arts and made a career of it. I hope every reader will enjoy hearing these stories, when the arts first took root in our soil, unafraid and full of hope for the future.

BENNY CHIA

chapter 1

INTO THE ARTS BY HAZARD

I DON'T REMEMBER my mother ever owning a book, or even reading one. Maybe prayer books, for she was a devout Catholic. She didn't think I should read any books other than schoolbooks. Yet I was addicted to all kinds of storybooks and comics and would read them after everyone had gone to bed, under my blanket with a flashlight if necessary.

You wouldn't have called my mother an arts person. Where I grew up, in a tenement, there was not a single painting on the wall, not even a reproduction; only a framed picture of Jesus wearing a crown of thorns, his pierced hand on his bleeding heart. To this, we knelt every night to say our rosaries and beg forgiveness for our sins.

And no music either. The only times we'd hear music played was on the second-hand gramophone Mother had picked up from Cat Street, along with a stack of scratchy 78 rpm singles. We'd use the music to drown out the insults and complaints thrown at us nightly from the landlady: she and Mother had an ongoing feud.

LIFE ON THE FRINGE

Mother entrusted me with the task of winding up the gramophone and playing cheery hit songs such as 'Goodnight Irene' and 'Bye Bye Blackbird', one after another.

I have to start with talking about my mother because, though she passed on a long time ago, it is she who got me where I am today, steeped in the arts like a Madeleine in a cup of Proustian tea. She hadn't wanted this for me; quite the contrary.

My mother's baptised name was Philomena, but nobody ever called her that. She met my father at her graduation dance or something and fell for him. Father was quite a handsome devil in his day. She eloped to start a life with him in Singapore and, in due course, gave birth to four sons, two of whom survived, the eldest and the youngest. Joe is the eldest and I, the youngest, six years between us. Eventually, she left my father and brought us back to Hong Kong to raise us here, working as an outpatient nurse and administering vaccinations and inoculations against smallpox, polio, and diphtheria, all dangerous infectious diseases at the time.

For many years, we lived in a windowless rented cubicle in an old three-storey building on Mosque Street, with a communal kitchen and a portable can for toilet. To give our home a bit of colour, we pasted Christmas wrapping paper on the walls. It wasn't an easy life, but Mother was as hardy as she was stubborn: she stuck it out.

For relief, she went to the movies, and when I was old enough, I would queue up for tickets for the Saturday matinees. Her favourite cinema was Queen's Theatre in Central, and her favourite films were Hollywood song-and-dance movies with happy endings. She would often take me with her, as I could go for free, while Joe would have needed another ticket. Mother was frugal.

Benny in the arms of his mother,
with brother Joe, and father

St Joseph's Building in early 1980 when
the building was about to be torn down. This was where
Mother, Joe and I stayed with Grandmother upon
returning to Hong Kong from Singapore circa 1950.
Photo by Andrew E. Tse.

INTO THE ARTS BY HAZARD

I came under the spell of MGM musicals. Watching these movies, cocooned in the dark of the cinema, led me to believe that there was a world out there, other than mine, that's always happy, beautiful, and in Technicolor, and I wanted to be part of it. Only later would I become aware that my work in the arts sprung from this longing for ever-elusive happiness.

Over time, I developed a taste for tuneful song-and-dance music. On some Sunday evenings, I'd eavesdrop on a programme on the radio that our neighbour regularly tuned in to; we couldn't afford one. I'd put my ear to the paper-thin partition wall and listen to Eileen Wood's *Down Memory Lane*. Miss Wood loved Broadway musicals and would play excerpts or the entire score, from overture to finale. She'd take the listener through the stories – *Oklahoma, South Pacific, The King and I* – a long list of titles. Sometimes the music would bring me back to a scene from the movie version I'd seen. It would be many years later that I sat in a plush theatre in London's West End, thrilled to bits, the orchestra transporting me to paradise with the overture of Lerner and Loewe's *Camelot*.

Like a good Chinese parent, Mother put great stock in our education. She enrolled me at the brand-new St. Peter's Primary School. It had a music room, the nicest room in the whole school, bright and airy with a jet-black upright piano polished to a shine, and a cabinet brimming with percussion instruments.

We looked up to the music teacher, Wong Hay, even though we were almost the same height. He was different from other teachers: he dressed dapperly and always smelled nice. He preferred paisley scarves to dull ties, and a light-coloured jacket with a silk kerchief over the nondescript suits other teachers wore.

He taught us how to play the Chinese recorder, or Shepherd's Flute. Handmade, they were of varying quality; you might pick one up that didn't sound right. I was lucky with the instrument I'd bought from a music store; it had a pleasant and delicate tone. Wong Hay formed a band with the better players. I was in this band, and sometimes I'd be given a solo passage to play. Our band went on to win some competitions and played for *Rediffusion*, a popular radio station by subscription. After the performance, he'd treat us to a meal in a proper restaurant – such a high that would keep me up all night. To this day, I try not to leave performers alone to stew in their own adrenaline after a show, especially if it has bombed; you'd want to be there for them.

The class mistress took a strong dislike to me for no reason that I knew of and made sure that the other teachers would feel the same about me. It was Wong Hay *laoshi* who got me through those long, punishing years unscathed, for he not only taught music but also art. He would pin up our paintings on the notice-board, and nothing would make me feel better about myself than to see my work exhibited in the classroom, which was often.

When I was old enough, I got myself a summer job working for Miss Daisy, who ran the box office for Harry Odell Productions in Holland House (now gone) at the foot of Ice House Street. I had no idea that one day this street would mean so much to me.

Harry Odell was Hong Kong's last impresario, and in the bloodline of the legendary Sergei Diaghilev and Florenz Ziegfeld. Mr Odell had the physical similarities. Portly and probably born in a dark suit, vest, and bow tie, he made himself known upon entering a room with a cloud of cigar smoke, a frizzy head of silver hair, and a booming baritone voice. He liked to tell people that he'd once been a nimble-footed tap dancer in Nagasaki. Locally, he presented first-rate concerts in venues such as the

State Theatre in North Point, and Loke Yew Hall at the University of Hong Kong, whose decor and acoustics often did not do justice to the artists. When the purpose-built City Hall Concert Hall opened, he took to it like a swan to a pond presenting some of the most illustrious names in classical music and dance.

Miss Daisy ran the office like a Mother Superior. Nothing escaped her. She once caught me skulking in the back of the concert hall, craning to catch the act on stage. She told me not to make a nuisance of myself but to scram for a seat in the far-end corner of the first row, usually left unoccupied because of poor sightline.

From that vantage point, I watched Arthur Rubinstein put the audience under his spell before settling down to play the piano; I saw the nervous flicking of the wrists of a prima ballerina, probably Margot Fonteyn, waiting in the wings backstage; and I listened to Frank Sinatra in a rare afternoon performance. I think that was probably the only time he sang in Hong Kong. He was about to start his second set with his signature ballads. To get in the mood, someone offstage handed him what was supposed to be bourbon in a teacup. He took the cue, loosened his black tie, and cracked a suave self-deprecating joke. This went completely over the heads of the bemused audience, mostly students, I among them, who'd been given cheap tickets to paper the house. We had no idea who this middle-aged *gweilo* singer was.

My stint as an errand boy for Miss Daisy ended when school term began again. I had to concentrate on studying and passing exams and could no longer afford the time for concerts, the school band, or art classes. I gradually lost touch with Miss Daisy, and Harry Odell was slowly edged out as City Hall began to present its own shows.

My love for the cinema persisted through my school years. Even in the thick of preparing for exams, I seldom let a week pass without going to a movie. By the time I entered Hong Kong University to study comparative literature, I would choose arthouse films. In the year Mr Ackbar Abbas joined the faculty, he introduced us to French Nouveau Roman writers like Robbe-Grillet and Marguerite Duras, showing us a firmament of newly discovered literary stars. We promptly shunned the old standards such as Racine and Molière.

Protests were in the air: the student movement in Paris against De Gaulle and what he stood for; the Civil Rights movement in the US; and the Anti-Vietnam War demonstrations worldwide. I'll never forget the National Guard shooting of unarmed students at Kent State University. Here in Hong Kong, my buddy Raymond Liang joined a protest in front of the US Consulate on Garden Road; it was there that he met Klaus, a German professor and fellow protester. Raymond and I house-sat for Klaus when he went home that summer. On his return, he was notified by Immigration to clear out of Hong Kong. He was given two weeks to wrap things up and was summarily deported.

Raymond played in the band The Willows — that had come first in a song contest — and tried composing protest songs. One went like this: 'You gave us examinations. And more examinations . . .' He wanted to sing them in solidarity with other students to change the world, so he roped me into starting the Friday Beer and Song Club. I was the beer in this combination. We made posters using old newspapers and plastered them all over campus. We set up our gig in the Student Union after class on Fridays and served beer on tap. Unbeknownst to us, most of the Hong Kong students didn't drink alcohol, nor did they truly believe in abolishing exams. The turnout was abysmal. As we didn't want the beer to go to waste, we made an effort to down as much of it as we could the next morning at breakfast. Not exactly the best way to enjoy a pint. But this experience with the Friday Beer and Song didn't make me any wiser or deter me from launching the Fringe Club later on.

I became drawn to the oeuvres of some of the French New Wave movie directors such as Marguerite Duras, François Truffaut, and Claude Lelouch. They transported me to a land of romance. How could I resist titles such as *Hiroshima Mon Amour*, *Baisers Volés*, and *Un homme et une femme*?

At the time, I was a sucker for anything French-sounding. The mere thought of languishing in a garret, writing love poems on the Left Bank to Anouk Aimée (Claude Lelouch's *A Man and a Woman*) or Dominique Sanda (Vittorio de Sica's *The Garden of the Finzi-Continis*), was enough to get me into a state. As for my romantic notion of Paris, blame it on César Vallejo, who has made the prospect of dying there seem irresistible. Listen to this canto in his poem, Black Stone on a White Stone:

> *I will die in Paris while it rains,*
> *On a day which I already remember.*
> *I will die in Paris and I do not run away.*
> *Perhaps in the Autumn,*
> *On a Thursday that I write these lines,*
> *My bones feel the turn.*
> *And never so much as today in all my road*
> *Have I seen myself alone.*

> (Translated by Carlos Castaneda)

The Penguin paperback edition of Ernest Hemingway's *A Moveable Feast* that came on sale in the Swindon Bookstore had an old photograph of Place de la Contrescarpe on its cover. I bought it and have kept it on my bookshelf. He reminisced about his time in Paris when he was a struggling young writer. Misguidedly I thought by going to Paris and following his footsteps I could somehow end up a writer. I'd overlooked the fact that I wasn't very good at it. I found writing excruciating and still do. But I became spellbound right from the opening chapter: 'A Good Café on the Place St-Michel'. He described how he'd become oblivious to the outside world, writing his story in a café on Place St-Michel, except for the beautiful woman who sat by herself near the window who made him very excited.

I wanted to get away from Hong Kong. I felt stifled there. So I made a pact with someone dear to me to meet in Paris where I could live out my dream as a writer. When I finally made it to the café on Boul Mich, it wasn't at all like the one in which he composed the stories that would make him famous. Instead, it's rife with tourists and kerbside traffic. I retreated to a neighbour-hood cafe to find peace and quiet. Before I could whip out my notebook and pencil to write, I saw someone inserting a coin into a pinball machine. Comic book drawings of intergalactic spaceships were lit up on the glass screen. He proceeded to play and shoot a steel pinball that collided and bounced off the pumpers noisily. He was soon joined by his friends in his play. They jostled and cheered. It wasn't the best place for the solitary act of writing and agonising over next sentences.

When I got too distracted by pinball machines, I'd traipse around Paris. I followed Walter Benjamin's suggestions to play the flâneur to get to know the city. I stumbled upon a bistro on Pont Neuf where you could order a carafe of new Beaujolais wine from the patron's cousin's vineyard to go with a plate of country pâté and strong-tasting andouille. I discovered picturesque squares and secret alleyways that belonged only to me. This way, I lifted myself from the inescapable mundaneness of living too close to one's dream.

On cold winter Sundays, I'd find refuge in the Louvre. Admission was free and the heating profuse. I kept visiting favourite paintings as I'd do old friends. I learned to say their names correctly, and enumerated them for the sake of it: the three Bellinis, three Brueghels, and the three Italian monks with the same prefixes of Fra. This went on uneventfully, until one Sunday morning when a man removed a Bellini from the wall that could fit inside his overcoat and walked away, not before asking a couple if they would mind. By the time the alarm was raised, he had disappeared.

Paris had become a demanding mistress. I felt I needed a change of scenery. I wanted to find happiness elsewhere. So I moved to Leuven in the Flemish-speaking part of Belgium and enrolled at the Katholieke Universiteit Leuven (KUL). I traded ritzy bright lights for green-shaded lamps in library corners.

Leuven, also known as Louvain in French-speaking Wallonia, had saved its finest architecture for the universities. The rest of the town was row upon row of indistinguishable townhouses. I shared one of those with Margaret, Gerald, and Viola from Hong Kong. Later, Margaret and I moved to Guido Gezellelaan in the part of town referred to as de Blauwe Boot that, in olden days, was used to transport the mentally unsound and heretics out to sea to perish; nowadays, it's called that derogatorily because of the large number of non-white people living there. Guido Gezelle was a Flemish poet and Catholic priest who, it is said, was once romantically linked with a merry English widow. He wrote:

I dream even now of you...
Of Happy days when we two will together with
Tempers mild – pass days, pass days
In tempo wild – we'll share
Times good and ill

Everyone went about on bicycles. Riding in the old cobble-stoned part of town could be treacherous in the rain. The first joke that greeted us on our arrival: we've got beautiful weather here. It only rains twice in a year, each lasting 160 days.

Yet, the students didn't seem to mind. We flocked from all corners of the world to come here for the studies of phenomenology, at the source. This had come about with Edmund Husserl, the Austrian philosophy professor from the University of Freiburg who'd taken the trouble to look into the meanings of things and had a Eureka moment: the meanings of things, he said, were, in fact, in the things themselves. The Nazis didn't like this sort of thinking at all. Upon his death, they intended to seize his books and notes to make a bonfire. A prolific writer, Husserl left behind some 40,000 pages of handwritten script. A monk scholar risked his life to salvage and deposit them with KUL – not only for safekeeping but for transcription even though his handwriting was atrocious and almost indecipherable. Thus the revered Husserl Archive was established.

Yet, it was enshrouded in secrecy. Nobody on campus seemed to know much about it. I recently asked my friend and fellow student John Lauricella, who wrote back: 'From memory, I think the archive was on the second floor near the Philosophy Library which was in the same building as where our lessons were given. I recall Husserl's manuscripts were stored in a plain, grey

INTO THE ARTS BY HAZARD

steel cabinet.'

The periodic publication of a Husserl paper would set alight conversations in the university bars and cafes. It ranked in excitement right next to a rare treat of steamed mussels and frites with the students. One of them we held in awe. I think he was from Gdańsk, Poland. As if possessed, he vowed to complete his PhD thesis in record time. He glued himself to his desk and lived only on coffee. He even gave up his head-turner girlfriend; he was an extreme case. The atmosphere on campus was that intense.

I wrote an outline for my proposed thesis on poetry translation. I intended to argue that cultural nuances are intrinsically not translatable, using T. S. Eliot's *Four Quartets* as an example to illustrate that. This might not offer a solution to improve the lives of the 360 million people living in poverty at that time, but I was prepared to give it four or more years of my life to prove it.

Professor Herman Servotte, Jesuit priest and Vice-Rector of the University, agreed to be my supervisor. The Jesuit Order believes that God is in all matters, and we can find Him through learning. An authority on T. S. Eliot, Professor Servotte kept a beautiful penthouse apartment overlooking a beautiful square. There was a wall shelf of classical and jazz music records and a serious hi-fi system to play them. I was puzzled at how he could live in this fashion as an ordained priest. Later I found out it's that he hadn't taken a vow of poverty. I didn't know one could have a choice in these things and misguidedly thought academic pursuits could lead me to such a plush life.

I had nothing much to show Professor Servotte in proven scholarship, or any future promise of it. Still, he was most helpful and kind. This is my future, my chosen path, so I thought, and it was in this frame of mind that I returned to Hong Kong to pack the rest of my belongings for a long stay in Belgium. Before I left Leuven, I was given a farewell dinner and a reading from the *I Ching, The Book of Changes*, for a lark. It predicted a brilliant future for me in academia as well as success in my application for a full scholarship.

Back in Hong Kong, I read about the new Arts Centre that had just opened on the Wan Chai waterfront. I picked a date for a visit. Had it been any other day, I might not have met Gregory Leong in the elevator, and my life wouldn't have taken this unexpected turn.

chapter 2

TAKING IT FROM THE TOP

THE HONG KONG ARTS CENTRE was erected on a long stretch of land reclaimed from the Hong Kong harbour – now called Harbour Road – lest we forget. Before it was built up like it is today, it was one of the two solitary buildings built on one side of the road. The rest was forlorn land that was fenced off or left unattended to gather weeds. Developers that owned the land were waiting for the topsoil to settle so they could build on it. All this was before the Academy for Performing Arts, the Convention Centre, the two luxury hotels, and roads for dual-lane traffic were there.

It was the summer of 1978. The Arts Centre facade still bore the new sheen of dark charcoal on its rough-hewn claddings. Its bold industrial look took first-time visitors by surprise. Inside, the foyer and atrium shone in loud traffic yellow on the doorframes, handrails, and exposed ductwork. An outsize cone-like object for ventilation with connecting tentacles of steel cables and ducts was hung from the ceiling. They screamed industrial chic. In contrast, the floors, landings, and stairs, all four storeys of them, were carpeted in a melange of maroon, sage green, and plum. Purple, I was told, was the favourite colour of the architect's young bride.

His name was Tao Ho and he was among the first batch of home-grown architects to leave a mark on the Hong Kong skyline. His masterpiece design for an eighteen-storey arts complex built on a measly 100" × 100" site had spunk and flair: everywhere one turned, it was look-at-me, look-at-me. Compared to City Hall, the only game in town for a long while and already showing signs of premature greying, this new kid on the block was almost a brash show-off.

Earlier that year, I had had a first-hand look at the ground-breaking Centre Pompidou. Its industrial inside-out *jolie-laide* design – so ugly it's almost beautiful – had everyone talking. This used to be the *quartier* for the well-heeled, after-concert crowd. They'd have *soupe à l'oignon* and pig's knuckle served with sauerkraut in a bistro unmistakably called *Pied de Cochon*. They were thrilled to be rubbing shoulders with butchers and market vendors who got off work around midnight to have their first meal of the day there.

I caught the Pompidou's opening exhibition entitled Paris/Moscow and was blown away. If only I could be part of this bold future, I thought. Even better, if I could get a job here. Those memories were going through my head as I entered the elevator of the Hong Kong Arts Centre. Maybe they were triggered by the traffic yellow paint I saw.

I took the elevator. Gregory Leong stepped in as the door was closing. He spotted me right away. He was my English tutor at university for a semester. Greg, as he likes to be called, is half a head shorter than me. On that day he was wearing a pair of dual-tone sunglasses, a choirboy haircut, and *soupçon* of eye makeup. He spoke in a beautifully mellow baritone voice that he used to good effect. He seemed glad to see me and told me this was where he was working. I told him I was on a summer break from my studies. He asked if I'd have time to help him out. 'I'm snowed under, simply desperate,' he said, making an exaggerated gesture. I liked the idea of a stop-gap summer job, and I liked the look and smell of this place, so I said yes. That's how it started.

Greg asked me to chat with the big boss, Neil Duncan, a tall, bearded, soft-spoken Scot with a receding hairline, kindly eyes, and a welcoming smile. After some small talk on my background and interests, he asked why I wanted to work there. I said the first thing that came to my mind, that if I were living in Paris and given a chance to work in the Centre Pompidou, I'd jump at it. He seemed pleased with that answer.

Neil had been headhunted from London. His previous job was with the Arts Council there. He'd come to Hong Kong with his tall and bonny wife, Kathleen. They were housed in a tranquil corner apartment in Shouson Hill. Neil's specialty was classical music and opera. When he talked to you, he had a way of looking past you into the distance, and you could almost hear music playing in head – Poulenc, Messiaen, Shostakovich – the kind that's full of existential angst, not quite in tune with his sunny exterior.

He liked theatre, too. Neil was hands-on with those two. As for the visual arts and Asian arts, he left them in the hands of Alan Wong and Helga Berger. Alan, who had a reedy voice and frail build, was firm in his resolve and ran the Pao Galleries his own way, not bending to pressure from anyone, except perhaps to the gentle persuasion of Neil. Helga was Head of Programme.

LIFE ON THE FRINGE

Her interests and areas of expertise were in Asian arts, and she liked to fly solo.

Neil seldom spoke harshly to anyone. He led his team with a soft touch, sometimes too soft, especially when it came to quelling the power struggles among his senior staff.

On my first day, I took the elevator to the eleventh floor, where Greg went about showing me around. The offices were partitioned by clear glass panels; everyone could see what everyone else was up to. I would be sharing an office with Greg. On entering the glass cage of a room, I caught sight of a tall, gangly young man clearing his desk. He put on a brave face and nodded at me. Greg told me aside that I was replacing him 'because he's more disorganised than I am.' His desk was indeed super messy: loose papers everywhere, mint candy wrappers, piles of leaning files. I said I wasn't very organised myself either.

My job was to look after the venue bookings. I started by clearing the shelves and putting things back in place. The chap before me left in a hurry and wasn't given time for a proper handover. In those days, things around the office were done pretty much by hand. A paper chart was used to *pencil in* the bookings; the digital age had yet to arrive. Documents were typed out manually with typewriters. The telephone had a number dial and a handset to listen and speak to the person on the line. Making a trunk (long-distance) call overseas was a big deal. To do so you had to book it in advance with Cable & Wireless in Mercury House and make the call from a phone booth there. Before the fax machine and PC became standard office equipment, a contraption called Telex was used to receive short messages by noisily typing them out like a Morse code receiver.

Greg took me on a tour of the building and joked that I would pass probation if I could find my way out from the maze of staircases and back corridors. We started from the penthouse apartment on the roof, where Business Manager So Hau Leung, second-in-command, was lodged. With him in residence, on-the-spot decisions could be made over any emergency outside office hours.

The top floor housed the Members' Club. On entering, as you stepped off the elevators, there was a well-stocked bar to order your drinks to be taken into the generous lounge area with comfy seating facing out to the harbour. A book-lined arts library was tucked away in the back. Few of us knew about this treasure trove of art books, theatre plays, and a complete set of the *Grove Dictionary of Music and Musicians*, which was absolute gold for classical music buffs before Google. It was kept ship-shape by a diminutive and reclusive librarian who'd probably read and indexed all the books and manuscripts there undisturbed (until sometime later, when some bean counters came along, couldn't see any real value in it, wrote it off as a liability, and promptly turned it into a rentable space). The lounge's bandstand – the panoramic sea view windows as backdrops – was equipped with electric keyboards, a drum set, and its own PA system. At weekends, the house band with guest singers attracted an audience drawn largely from some fourteen constituent member organisations made up of amateur drama, music, dance, and art movie groups. In the early days, it was they who supported the Arts Centre as the first independent, local arts community-initiated project.

One night, Yvonne Chow was spotted in the crowd. She'd just come off from playing the lead in *The City of Broken Promises*, an original musical that the producer was hoping to take to the West Coast and then to Broadway. Yvonne was my colleague who had joined the Arts Centre around the same time as I had. She'd have made it to New York – with any luck, her name in lights on the marquee – had she not chosen a different path. And on that night, the crowd pleaded: everyone wanted to hear her sing. She picked a showstopper from the new Broadway musical called *Evita*, bringing the house to its feet. As Yvonne took her bows, you could see the Hong Kong harbour awash in glittering lights, confident and proud of its future. We were not to know that there would be no other night like this and that life doesn't always keep its promises.

The floors below, from the twelfth to the fifteenth, were leased to other arts organisations. One of the offices there, occupied by an organisation called I.I.E., was to become the site of a grisly murder that gave Andrew Welsh, the General Manager who succeeded Neil, the shock of his life.

The two restaurants, on the sixth and seventh floors, serving European and Cantonese cuisine, were unaffordable for us junior staff. We ate our lunches at a makeshift canteen across the road, by a large building site that would become the Academy for Performing Arts. The canteen catered for the construction workers. It was built like a squatter hut with thin, corrugated metal sheets for a roof. In the noonday sun, it could get as sizzling hot as the fry-ups served. Over sweaty lunches, I got to know the stagehands at the Arts Centre, electrical and mechanical workers, and front--of-house clerks. From them, the frontline workers, I learned the ropes of the workplace double quick.

Greg walked me through the Pao Siu Loong galleries on the fourth and fifth floors, remarking archly that this was Alan's fortress. And then he took me into the Shouson Theatre, a 400-seat auditorium. He was in his element there. With a flourish, he showed me the control room with its Rank Strand lighting console. Only engineers flown in from London could fix it if anything went wrong.

And then we went backstage. I had never in my life seen a fly system, all its blocks, bars, and counterweights, webs of ropes suspended from what looked like a futuristic Gothic tower. He demonstrated how to turn on the working lights – which I learned to do right away – and went on to show me what to do in an emergency, like how to lower the safety curtain.

He pulled down a lever that's used to stop a fire from spreading into the auditorium. 'But you must never, never touch this one,' he said, pointing to the lever in fire-engine red. 'This will release the water curtain, and tons – yes, six tons of water – will come crashing down. We don't want that, do we?' I shook my head gravely to show that I agreed with what he said and totally got it.

He continued to take me through the orchestra pit, the green room, and the three below- ground venues: rehearsal studio, recital hall, and studio theatre. Each space still smelled of the sea that it had just displaced.

I was in charge of hiring, a department of one, the first line of defence against hordes of visitors that turned up every day to check out the new arts space. Very soon, I got the hang of it. I could even show off the little I knew.

One Saturday morning, a group of Christian brothers and sisters from a seminary came to visit. They wanted to hire the Shouson Theatre for a religious ceremony. I took them on a by now expert guided tour of the backstage. I flicked on the lights, turned on the PA system, tapped on the microphones like an old pro, while doing a running commentary. I also wanted to demonstrate with some pride how the safety curtain operated. I pulled on the lever but it wouldn't give. I pulled again. Nothing happened. The Christian brothers and sisters were looking at me questioningly, so I put my full body weight on it and this time

LIFE ON THE FRINGE

it gave. An avalanche of water came down on the stage and the orchestra pit.

This must be how it feels before a plane crash. I stood there, my eyes closed. I didn't want to believe that it had actually happened, and that it had happened to me. This can't be real, I thought to myself. When I open my eyes again, it'll all be well again. I closed and then opened my eyes and looked around. A little voice inside me cried for help. I turned around. My Christian friends had gone without saying goodbye, and at no other time had I needed God's help more.

The stage was covered in a sheet of water. I stared in horror as it slipped into the orchestra pit and cracks in the floorboards. What was I supposed to do? Mop it up? Soak it up? I hurried back to my desk and made a call to Henry in E&M. I must've sounded like a house on fire. He rushed to the rescue with a suction apparatus. I asked Rowena in marketing for all the newspapers she had been hoarding and ran to the disaster scene to scatter them all around. Luckily, the much-treasured Steinway wasn't there that day; the stage had been cleared for a tribal music concert that evening by a hill tribe from the Philippines.

After getting all the help I could, I could see the place just looked very wet but no longer a catastrophe to run away from. I broke the news to Neil and Helga, and it was Helga who ordered that all the air conditioners be turned to full blast to dry out the theatre.

The performance went ahead. The musicians in their loincloths sitting on their haunches endured the evening. I heard that some caught a chill afterwards. The tribe explained that they didn't have air conditioning in their rainforest homes.

I didn't get fired. Maybe it was because I had managed to do some damage control before running to them in tears. In the days

TAKING IT FROM THE TOP

that followed, however, when the muddied water slowly reappeared down the hatch and through cracks, I felt I ought to be.

Yet, other than this mishap, I must have been doing okay. I even passed probation with some favourable comments. I got along with my colleagues and somehow became a conduit between *Upstairs and Downstairs*: Head of the Stage Department Michael Outhwaite was fond of using this popular London weekend television drama series to mock the management whose offices, ensconced on the eleventh floor, enjoyed city and harbour views, whereas his was a hole in the wall next to the loading bay. Michael had reason to be disgruntled; so did the front-of-house and E&M staffers whose offices were also storeroom-sized and windowless.

The preferred mode of communication was by 'memo'. A constant stream of them, going back and forth between Programme and Stage Department, ended up in Michael's in-tray. He mockingly called himself and all those not working downstairs, footmen and galley maids. They were to serve the lords and ladies upstairs in Management. He could make life difficult for you, which he routinely did. Unlike those in Management, I carried no real authority, yet I was at the receiving end of all kinds of demands from hirers and artists. Often I'd find myself being grilled on both sides. I learned customarily the hard way not to treat my fellow worker as an in-tray but a person. I accepted that Michael and his backstage crew were customarily grouchy and prone to say no to requests. So would you, if you had to work in dim light all the time.

I tripped up a few times by expecting my memos to be followed like court orders, so I changed tack. I started to hand-deliver them and talk the memos through, make everyone feel that we're all in this together. I spent time gabbing with them when we weren't busy. Michael, who reminded me of the

LIFE ON THE FRINGE

serpent in Eden, would say things like, 'You know what; you're overqualified for your (lowly) job. That lot, they've got a cushy life; they'll never budge. Better take your chances elsewhere, or you'll be stuck here forever.'

Stationed in the foyer behind the yellow counter, front-of-house was manned, or rather womanned, by three beautiful women: Deborah, Katherine, and Mabel. They're the frontline, the faces, the first impressions visitors made of the place. They took a lot of flak from customers coming in to buy tickets or passersby asking for directions to the toilets – the top Q&A in any art establishment. I had no reason to be unfriendly with them. We worked on every show together, and all being new to our jobs, made our fair share of mistakes. I found that exchanging memos to explain and apportion blame never settled any dispute; it just made things sticky and unpleasant. Instead, coming face to face, sometimes with a *mea culpa* and a smile, nearly always worked wonders, But, as Elton John sings, 'Sorry seems to be the hardest word.'

I found out soon enough that there are draughts under every chair. I received a letter from Belgium that I wasn't awarded the scholarship I'd been so sure of getting. That night, I dreamt that I was all set to travel, my suitcases all packed with painstaking care. I took them to a checkpoint where someone in a grey uniform asked me for identification. I showed him a handwritten document, but he said it wouldn't do. I needed something with my name on it, in print. Even a credit card would do. I went through my pockets, knapsacks, and suitcases but could find nothing. Sweating, I got into a panic. Time was running out. I ran to the pier, and the ship I was supposed to board had already set sail. I waved at it like an unrestrained string puppet and then

38

TAKING IT FROM THE TOP

dived into the water to swim frantically after it. Then I sat bolt upright, fully awake.

By that time, I was married to Margaret, and we were expecting our first baby. I couldn't afford to return to my studies without a full scholarship. I was left with no option but to buckle down to a job to bring rice to the table. My entry-level pay wouldn't be adequate anymore, and I couldn't ask for a raise, still green. Instead, I went for a job interview for the position of a film censor, whose duties were to watch and vet movies and pick out the unsavoury bits to cut – pornographic mainly. All very straightforward. I would report to the chief censor, a disrobed Catholic priest named Pierre, who was known to be rather liberal-minded. The salary offered was triple what I was earning, and no unsociable working hours either.

It would have been irresponsible of me not to accept the job. I told Greg of my dilemma, that I really liked what I was doing but needed more money to support my new family. Also, I was showing symptoms of the first stage of work addiction.

At that time, we were living in a rundown two-storey beach house with a neglected garden in Ting Kau, Tsuen Wan, outside the city. It was rumoured that some guy had killed himself there, so our rent was low. My day began with the first light of dawn. I left early so I could arrive at work early, parking my rusty old Volvo in one of the few free spots.

Every morning, I climbed those few steps into the building, still groggy from working late the night before. By the time I finished work, it would be dark. It didn't feel good to short-change my family like this. I wrote in my diary at the time that I felt I was slipping into my work routine like a warm bath in a cold winter – easier to stay in than get out.

Left to right: Po Yang, Margaret and Chi Kay in Macau (circa 1995)

Greg told Neil, who said he'd like to have a word with me about my situation. He said I should stay on and promised me a raise if I did but couldn't quite match what I'd been offered. He put it to me in a very nice way. I'm not practical in making life's decisions, always heeding the heart over the head.

It was September. I took an afternoon off on a wonderfully bright day and walked through Chater Garden in Central. I was treading on clouds; insulated from the sweltering heat and loud traffic, I was possessed by euphoria. My first son, Po Yang, was born that morning. Two years and two months later, my second son, Chi Kay, came into the world. They were both adorable and exasperating by turns; it seemed that the winding road to happiness was sign-posted for me. But as a father, I felt inadequate and remorseful as those tied to their work in the theatre are prone to feel, knowing they ought to be home for dinner, or by their children's side on Christmas Eve.

I wrote to Professor Servotte to put my thesis on hold. He wrote back, advising me not to, but to keep chipping away at it, after work, and at weekends; 'That's what I did when I couldn't do it full-time,' he said. I knew my limitations. It was either one or the other, and I even gave up the idea of being a writer.

Greg wasn't one to hide his feelings. We shared an office. We both smoked and drank like two kamikaze pilots on their last mission. He had a way with words and could talk me under the table anytime, whereas I was likely to choke, especially doing phone-in radio interviews every Monday morning, after I'd been promoted to the position of Programme Organiser (Western Arts).

Greg had finally ousted Helga Berger and become Head of Programme. He'd been openly critical of her for only looking after her own patch and not supporting what others were doing. He moved into her corner office. His old desk was filled by Sze Suk Ching, a Taiwanese lady, recruited to take over Helga's Asian Arts portfolio. Things were not quite the same with this change. His swashbuckling days seemed to be curtailed: he took to his new responsibilities with the sobriety of a reformed AA member.

chapter 3

SLEEPLESS IN PARADISE

THERE WAS A MOVEMENT to decriminalise homosexuality in Hong Kong. Neil, for some reason, had taken an interest in it and became a torchbearer. A leading figure in the arts, Neil was happily married by all accounts and in the good books of the Government, whose head was Sir Murray MacLehose, a fellow Scot, who showed an understanding of the value of arts and culture as a means to engage with and rein in society. Neil had a direct line to the Protocol Office, staffed by the *aide-de-camp* of the Governor, to avoid crossing any red line that might cause embarrassment to the Government.

It was a worrisome time for gays, who were facing stigma, witch-hunts, and the dire consequences of being found out – especially within the expatriate community: a small village rife with gossip, where everyone knew everyone, with no place to hide. All this could have gone unnoticed if not for the death of an expatriate police officer who was found with multiple gunshot wounds in his own room locked from the inside. A forensic investigation followed. Given the improbability of repeatedly shooting oneself, the secret life of an expatriate law enforcement officer, and all the other things that were enshrouded in mystery, the media had a field day but stopped short of mentioning the unmentionable. (This could well have been the tipping point that brought about a law reform to decriminalise gay sex between consenting adults in 1991.) Later, Neil said on record that he'd been warned off from heading the movement; without a proponent, it was dead in the water, and wouldn't be revived for a decade.

Despite everything that was going on, Greg, who's openly gay, was flaunting it. He didn't seem to be too concerned to be caught out and ratted on. Sometimes when we needed a chitchat to kick off the working week, he'd go freely into his weekend escapades over a smoke and mug of Lipton tea. I was a good listener. He loved the opera – the convoluted plots, the grand gestures, and intrigues. In the power struggle to dispose of Helga, he could be relentless.

It must be said that Helga had introduced a plethora of Asian artforms, including those tribal musicians from the rainforest of the Philippines; Bharata Natyam dance from Southern India; Gagaku and Nōh Theatre and Kabuki from ancient Japan; Gamelan music, Balinese dance and Shadow Puppets from Indonesia, and Yashagana from Karnataka, India.

The Arts Centre wasn't as accessible as it is now. There was only a single flyover, a kind of footbridge, connecting with the part of Wan Chai that came alive after dark, with topless bars and late-night revelry. At night, Harbour Road was empty of traffic, and the street lamps were so far apart that they seemed to have disappeared into their own shadows. The staff on night duty would band together to find safety in numbers on their way home.

Regarded as esoteric and an acquired taste, Asian arts programmes were often not big at the box office. Asian countries were places you flew over on your way to London, New York, or Paris. For your culture fix, you looked to the West. Helga was unintimidated by this cultural bias; she showed no interest in the Western arts – primarily imported from Britain and the United States – that made up a big part of our programme which drew the attention of the English-language press such as the *South China Morning Post* and the *Hong Kong Standard*.

One morning in December, the queue at our box office went around the block. Usually, the foyer at this hour was about as busy as churches on weekdays. Today it was packed with animated expatriate homemakers with their kids. They're lining up for tickets to *Aladdin* – a popular Christmas pantomime show performed alternatively by Garrison Players and Hong Kong Players, the two competing am-drams (local British amateur dramatic societies) that dominated the local theatre scene at the time.

I had a chance to play a plum part in Garrison Players' production of *The King and I* in the Hong Kong Arts Festival. Rehearsals were held inside the Victoria Barracks, where Pacific Place, a clutch of luxury hotels and the British Consulate are now located. This area was usually out of bounds to civilians. Even if you were provided a special entry permit, you had to pass through checkpoints staffed by armed British soldiers. For a month or so, I went there every evening to rehearse my part as Lun Tha, the Burmese emissary and lover of Princess Tup Tim, who's offered to the King of Siam as concubine and peace offering.

This Broadway musical was directed by Peter Chapman, whose lovely wife, Carol, played Anna, the leading lady. They made a picture-perfect couple from Mid-Levels – a high-end residential area favoured by expats. Peter was obviously very much in love with his wife. In rehearsals, Carol was all he would see or hear, for he was completely oblivious to the mess I was making with my singing and acting.

I had two of the most beautiful and romantic show tunes in musicals to myself: 'We Kissed in the Shadow' and 'I Have Dreamed'. No way you could muff it. You just had to sing passably and act a little. The lovely music would carry you through. I looked the part, being Asian. Other than that, it's quite obvious that I shouldn't be allowed to sing, not on stage in any case. That I was weaned on musicals wasn't quite enough.

The show opened in the Hong Kong Arts Festival at Shouson Theatre, Arts Centre. Waiting for my turn in the wings, I began to blanch with stage fright. I am myopic. I went on stage. The spotlights shone right into my eyes. I could hardly see where I was going. I got into a trance-like state. I sang when I was supposed to, went offstage, came back on, and sang again. I heard applause, opened my eyes and caught a sea of blurred faces. By then I'd got used to the blinding light and wasn't afraid anymore. After the curtain calls, I was rather pleased with myself. I thought I had done well enough considering, until the music director Mr Himmler (his real name) came at me and dressed me down for not following his cues and the orchestra in the pit. I told him I was as blind as a bat on stage. He told me to go get myself some contact lenses, which I promptly did, the next day.

The following evening, with my brand-new lenses, I went on stage. What horror! A sea of faces all staring at me, some of them looked as though they knew me! I felt awfully self-conscious of the heavy stage make-up on my face and the tremors rising from my legs and through the culottes I was wearing for the character.

My mind instantly went blank. I croaked. Lynn Yau (currently CEO of the Absolutely Fabulous Theatre Connection, a pioneering arts-in-education organisation) who played Princess Tup Tim opposite me was rock solid and a real angel, sparing me the hard looks I well deserved.

There was a sense of camaraderie among the cast, and selfless fortitude among the crew. No one gets paid in am-drams. They do it for the sheer love of it. Harry, who played the King, once told an anecdote during rehearsal break. It took place in a POW camp in Sham Shui Po during the Japanese Occupation, where living conditions were hellish, and everyone interned was starved to a bag of bones. Christmas time came, and the inmates, British no doubt, wanted to stage *Twelfth Night* to revive their spirits and take their mind off things.

After the Japanese camp commandant gave them the green light, they called for an audition. This worked like a defibrillator on a heart patient. People turned up in droves. During the casting, the actors vying for the part of Sebastian came to blows. This made me understand why Andrew, working backstage, would willingly perch on the fly tower above the stage to do the scene changes for the entire run. How seriously they took to it, just so they could lift themselves from the humdrums of everyday existence, albeit fleetingly. While it lasted, they made me feel I was a part of the team though I wasn't invited back for another role.

The am-drams had a good run with the Arts Festival, having done three full-length productions three years in a row, and they took the Arts Centre as their home base. The concept of bringing arts to the community in less densely populated areas by providing the facilities came about in 1960s Britain. Now it had transmigrated to Hong Kong, whose population was predominantly Cantonese-speaking Chinese with a different cultural outlook. The question waiting to be asked was: If drama was the art form to be promoted, what language should it use? English, the official language, or Cantonese, which is a Chinese dialect spoken by the majority in Hong Kong? Andrew Leigh from London's Old Vic Theatre was invited to Hong Kong to review this situation and write a paper, whose recommendations would be used to inform the Government on how arts funding should be allocated for future development.

Andrew came to call on Neil for his opinion. And Neil asked me to join them, thinking that, because I speak Cantonese, I was an authentic source of information. What seems a simple enough question now wasn't so simple then. Political and economic power rested with the expatriates in the higher echelons of society. Events of any importance were not real until they were written and read about in the *South China Morning Post*, the *Hong Kong Standard*, or a tabloid called *The Star*. These, as well as radio and lifestyle magazines, wouldn't miss a beat in reporting on and reviewing shows and events with expatriate content. The amount of media attention they attracted often blew things out of proportion.

Local Cantonese-speaking theatre was still in its infancy. Even if it wasn't, it wouldn't have been of much interest to the reporters on the arts beat of the English press, for most of them did not speak Cantonese. No one seemed to have minded, and the feelings were mutual. Of the 150 or so publications in Chinese, none would have been caught dead doing a review of an am-dram production. To change this, someone at the British Council came up with a brilliant idea.

Peter Day and his wife, coming from a theatre in education background from the UK, were tasked to create a bilingual ensemble by the name of Chung Ying Theatre Company. This was an attempt to amalgamate the two languages through the medium of theatre. This seemed quite an improbable proposition. Cantonese – the underweighted local dialect – wasn't even considered as a form of written language, whereas English, the language of Shakespeare and West End hits, was also that of the ruling class. Chung Ying, literally translated as 'Chinese and English', proceeded to audition actors from Hong Kong and London. The founding director was Glen Walford, who was succeeded by Colin George, followed by the indefatigable Bernard Goss. The 'Chung' actors, due to their scarcity at the time, had to be culled from various sectors. They were Carmen Lo, Lee Chun Chow (aka C.C.), Sherman Chow, Dominic Cheung, Cheung Tat Ming, and others. The 'Yings', picked from a pool of seasoned actors, were Martin Clarke, Michael Harley, and Nick Owen.

Bernard decided early on that his potential audience was not his compatriots but the Cantonese-speaking locals. Since his repertoire was rooted in Western theatre, he wanted to look for someone to translate his scripts into Cantonese, with the aim to bridge the chasm between the two very dissimilar languages and bring them to life. He was introduced to Rupert Chan by Hardy Tsoi, a talented budding theatre director back then. Bernard and Rupert hit it off. Together they created a partnership spanning over three very productive years, with a string of hits – *Hobson's Choice* (1984), *Twelfth Night* (1986), *Spring Fever Hotel* (1987), *A Midsummer Night's Dream* (1988) and others – performing to a Cantonese-speaking audience.

Chung Ying played at the schools during the day and drew an audience to the theatre at night. Bernard began to reduce the use of English dialogues to a minimum. For the first time, Shouson

LIFE ON THE FRINGE

Theatre was no longer an expatriate stronghold. You could see and hear the young local audience enjoying themselves heartily. Theatre had never been this much fun. He made it both entertaining and invigorating. Soon he'd built up a loyal following. He liked the freshness and raw energy of the local cast. Some of them have gone on to successful theatre and film careers as actors and directors, winning accolades and awards.

It's hard to pinpoint when Canto drama began to take centre stage. For me, it must have been somewhere around the time when *I am Hong Kong* (1985) premiered at the City Hall Theatre. It was an original Chung Ying Theatre production, directed by Bernard Goss, script by Raymond To Kwok Wai with Hardy Tsoi, music by Hugh Trethowan. The story is about the cultural awakenings of a group of young people stepping out from Hong Kong's colonial past into a new-found confidence and hope for the future. Set against the backdrop of the Sino-British talks going on at that time – fearful and uncertain of what was to happen – it hit a chord among the audience. Coming out of the theatre, I found myself on Queen's Pier, puffing on a cigarette and staring into the night over the shimmering reflections of my city. And tears welled up in my eyes uncontrollably.

Bernard gave his all. His last production was *A Midsummer Night's Dream*, which Rupert translated ominously as *Midsummer Nightmare*. Without warning of any kind, Bernard fell ill. His condition turned critical in a matter of days. A man of the theatre until the end, he put the finishing touches on the script, even on his deathbed. The night the show opened; everything went beautifully. I like to imagine that, to thunderous applause from the audience, Bernie went on stage and took his bows, and as the curtain descended, he faded into a blaze of onstage lights.

The expat actors weren't shipped back to their home country but stayed on and did different things. Martin became Head of Radio 3. Nick carried out his research into *dai pai dong* (local street stalls), before taking up English teaching. Michael became a choleric theatre critic.

Backtracking to a summer morning in 1980, I got an urgent call to meet in Neil's office. By that time, I'd taken over from Greg as Programme Organiser (Western Arts), and he'd taken over Helga's office to head the Programme Department.

Neil and Greg were both in high spirits and excited. They have received a telex message from the Boston Ballet Company, offering to perform in Hong Kong after their historical tour in China. The Boston Ballet was front-page news as the first American company invited to perform in post-Mao China, following US President Richard Nixon's ice-breaking visit. A huge deal. Half the world was holding its breath for the bamboo curtain to lift and open to the world. The Boston Ballet had taken on this mission, on the coattails of Nixon's ping pong diplomacy, and offered us a chance to present them. We hadn't yet had a chance to present a ballet troupe of this size and scale and this hot.

It was a last-minute decision on their part, and they proposed to do two programmes: Sir Frederick Ashton's *Cinderella* set to Sergei Prokofiev's music, and a double-bill of *La Fille mal gardée* and *Les Sylphides*. They asked for a stage with a proper sprung floor, after their experience dancing in venues not purpose-built for dancing in China and staying in patriotic hostels. All they asked for were decent hotel accommodation and payment of per diem for the dancers. Sounded easy enough. But as with all good deals, there is always a catch – we had only a week or so to set this all up.

Shouson Theatre was just too small for a full-sized ballet company. City Hall would be the obvious choice, but it was already kind of booked right up to the millennium. Lee Theatre in Causeway Bay, built for Cantonese opera, would do but was also unavailable at such short notice. We would have to let this opportunity go if we couldn't find the right venue. Then the name of a little-known cinema in North Point, next to the tram lines came up in conversation – Sunbeam Theatre. Besides showing movies, it's a popular venue for song-and-dance shows and operatic troupes from China. These shows, celebrating friendship and the greatness of the nation, were presented by United Arts, the unofficial cultural arm of Xinhua News Agency. Sunbeam Theatre looked far from grand. Street food hawkers crowding the entrance offered roasted chestnuts, dripping curry fish balls, and pungent grilled squid to the moviegoers.

I met with the house manager of the cinema, a middle-aged man in short sleeves and sandals. He took me into the empty auditorium, which looked drab in the fluorescent house lights. It was begging for a fresh coat of paint, and the seats were a worry – they're the kind that would snap back into position the moment your bum left them and make a loud noise.

I wasn't sure the stage floor was sprung or any good for dancing. Noticing my concern, he took me into the orchestra pit. I looked up to see thick timber floorboards propped up by massive wooden beams. What he said next clinched the deal, 'Margot Fontyn was here. She approved.' What's good enough for Dame Margot should be good enough for the Boston Ballet. When do you want to book it, he asked. I told him next week. He shook his head. How about next year? It turned out that United Arts had booked it the whole time.

Then I remembered meeting someone by the name of Wong at a reception. He introduced himself as a Xinhua News Agency researcher and we'd become quite friendly over time, but for all I knew, he could have been a commissar undercover. I gave him a call and explained our situation. He was well informed about the Boston Ballet, referring to them as the 'envoy of friendship from the people of America'. I told him we needed help with the venue, and he said he'd look into it. The next thing I knew, we were given the dates we asked for. It was going to happen.

The second item on the list was to find forty-two hotel rooms. The corps de ballet and the technical crew were to bunk up two in a room and the rest in singles. The Furama Inter-Continental Hotel in Central, famous for its revolving restaurant, had a new Marketing Director, Daniel Dayaram. On the day of their arrival, he gave them a top-brass welcome with bouquets of flowers and welcome drinks, complete with the fanfare of autographing the guestbook. Press photographers in droves were snapping away in the hotel foyer. After an extended tour and lodging in red-flag hotels, known for their proletarian amenities, they found the Furama was one step from heaven. Daniel, an Omar Sharif double, charmed the beautiful and handsome dancers as only he could.

I borrowed the company yacht from Dow Chemical, the sponsor of our summer school, and took the dancers to Sai Kung Beach for a dip, while the crew were setting up for the evening performance. It was a perfect Hong Kong summer day and the sea was warm and inviting, but the ballerinas dressed in their pretty swimsuits kept well away from the sun and the water. They'd been told not to get tanned or leave strap marks on their bodies, on pain of suspension. The prima ballerina who played Cinderella had a flawless pearly white body with well-proportioned legs that ended on a pair of feet gnarled and scarred from years of hard training and dancing on pointe. After our brief interlude at sea, we were transported to the Sunbeam Theatre. That evening on stage, the dancers were a picture of elegance and grace, without as much of a hint of ever suffering discomfort and pain.

At times, we'd book the City Hall Concert Hall for performances that would draw a larger audience. By then, the Harry Odell Productions had walked into the sunset. Concert hall legends such as Arthur Rubinstein, Vladimir Horowitz, and Pablo Casals, advanced in years, were not always keen to take long-haul flights to come here to perform, so we presented younger performers like Malcolm Frager, Melvin Tang, and Mischa Maisky. Presenting classical music was still very much our thing. Before the curtains came down on that golden era, we brought the incomparable Pierre Fournier from his lakeside home in Switzerland to do two cello recitals at City Hall. No-one before or after him could play with such eloquence and elegance.

The Furama Hotel once again rose to the occasion, laying down the red carpet for him and his Japanese wife, who was travelling with him. Daniel gave them a warm reception and escorted them to the best suite decked out with fresh-cut flowers, a pot of green tea for madame and coffee for monsieur, and fresh-baked petites fours for both of them to snack on.

The maestro, a gentleman of the old school, had beautiful manners. He took time to first settle his wife down, who seemed a bit agitated. I put that down to the long plane travel. Full of apologies, he explained that Madame was feeling delicate with a touch of migraine, and the wallpaper in the suite seemed to have brought it on. My immediate response was to ask Daniel for a room change. Looking at me even more apologetically, he said he was afraid that wouldn't help either. He could see from the frozen look on my face that my mind was stuck – he was pulling out of the deal, but the concerts had already sold out. What was I to do?

Somehow, I learned that Madame et Monsieur preferred the hotel they had stayed in on their previous visit. By his description, it turned out to be the Mandarin Oriental. After such royal treatment and a generous offer of a complimentary suite, I found it easier to administer seppuku than to own up to his hotel host that their honoured guests couldn't stand the sight of their wallpaper and would rather stay in a rival hotel. To this day, I'm grateful to Daniel that he let us off the hook simply saying that these things happen and he'd arrange to have their bags sent over.

I learned valuable music lessons from M. Fournier - aside from sticking to one's guns no matter what - at a master class. He explained to the students: 'Let the neck of the cello rest in the bend of your arm. Hold it as though you're having an intimate conversation with someone you love.' He preferred his Maucotel over his other two equally famous cellos, because it has a shorter endpin that could attach the instrument to the floor and enable a firm yet gentle embrace. You can always tell how well musicians can play from the way they relate physically to their instruments.

Soon after he'd displaced Helga, Greg talked about leaving. No one had expected that. He had fought tooth and nail for the position. Over a pint and a smoke, he told me that his mother had arranged for him to immigrate to Australia and had been pressing him hard. Later that day, his partner came and took him out for lunch, and when Greg came back, he looked all flushed in the face as though he'd had too much to drink. He plopped down on his desk, and then, all of a sudden, exploded in fury, sweeping everything – in-trays, papers, ashtrays, picture frames, teacups – to the floor.

He wasn't the first of the top-tier managers to go. Business Manager So Hau Leung, a fine classical pianist, took the lead. He'd been lodged in the penthouse apartment gorgeously decked out for him, like a stylish bachelor pad on Park Avenue in New York – soft cream-coloured leather and dark wood furniture and a Steinway grand piano as the centrepiece. The only catch was that he had to be on call twenty-four hours to deal with the kind of emergencies that new builds are prone to.

'Something always went wrong,' he recalled. 'Always at the wrong time. One night there was a blackout when a show was going on in the theatre. Just imagine. Panic. Panic. I called E&M. They came. They looked in all the dark corners with their flash-lights. Finally, before the fire trucks got here, they found, inside the power substation across the road a stray cat. Poor thing, it got electrocuted and short circuited the whole building, including the theatre.'

Penthouse notwithstanding, I guess it's a bit much if you have to be welded to your job. He was given a low-key send-off, the way he preferred. After he was gone, his apartment was turned into a rehearsal studio. Greg wanted to do a farewell bash in his usual flamboyant style. There was plenty to drink, and the speeches were in turn funny and moving. Two months later, Neil also bade farewell. Bill Bailey, Committee Chairman, and other honoured guests lavished praises on him as the founding General Manager of the Arts Centre and his contribution to the nascent arts scene in Hong Kong.

Their departures, one followed by another, had a hollowing effect on me. It reminded me of the boy who arrived late at the bazaar in James Joyce's story *Araby* and was frustrated by his innocence of the ways of the world. Like him, I felt betrayed by my own expectations; the good times as well as the lights were switched off without forewarning, leaving me stranded and directionless in the gathering darkness.

Neil went on to Brisbane to run a new opera house. He didn't stay long in his new position. I met up with him after he had returned to London. We had drinks in a pub behind St. Martin-in-the-Fields. I noticed that he'd lost his tan and the sparkle in his eyes; he seemed to agree, saying he was back with the Arts Council and it wasn't that good this time. 'It's a hatchet job,' he said – he was responsible for axing some regional orchestras – 'which could be rather awkward.' After we tossed back our drinks and said goodbye, I watched him merging into that grey mass of London commuters, hurrying home. That was the last time I saw Neil. Soon afterward he died in a car accident. I can't express the numbing shock I felt then and the sadness that washed over me – of what I remember about him, and those days when the world was new, and everything seemed possible.

Andrew Welch succeeded Neil Duncan as the Arts Centre's second General Manager. He was also recruited from the UK. Before coming to Hong Kong, he'd been with Theatre Royal in Plymouth, a tranquil seaport in southwest England. Flora Chan, who'd worked previously with the Arts Council of Peterborough, outside London, took over from Greg. I was promoted to a new position as Deputy Programme Manager.

Andrew was relocated to Hong Kong with his family. He was looking for a change from living in a low-density city with a small population and one day wasn't much different from the next. Unbeknownst to him, the Hong Kong he landed in was boiling over with people, noise, and traffic, and was about to face a future rife with political uncertainties; nobody could predict that it was also on the brink of a property and stock market meltdown. To make matters worse, a suicide and a brutal murder were going to happen under his watch. You can't really blame him for quitting before completing his contract. He made his way home with his family, never to return.

By default, I took over the in-tray of New Music that had been piling up in a corner of Greg's old desk. More wide-ranging than the label suggested, it included contemporary music of all kinds, bundled up with Nanyin storytelling, Cantonese opera, and chamber music recitals. Despite their differences, they had one thing in common – sluggish box office sales and low attendance. But for some unknown reasons, there had been a surge in the proliferation of chamber music ensembles. Their promoters were a relentless lot. They kept sending in proposals, and I kept shuffling them to the bottom of the tray. Some of them even eschewed the staple diet of Mozart, Beethoven, and Brahms for the challenging works of avant-gardists, such as Terry Reilly, Philip Glass, Steve Reich, and John Cage. This was made trendy by Kronos Quartet – the phenomenally successful hipster quartet from San Francisco, whose recordings had made it to the pop charts. Unfortunately, Hong Kong audiences hadn't quite caught up with it. Chamber music recitals were considered somnambulistic at best. The New Music that you couldn't hum in your shower was about as easy to sell as yesterday's newspapers. That became my big challenge.

A lightbulb moment came to me while reading *The Empty Space* by Peter Brook, theatre director and author, who'd converted an abandoned comic opera house into a performance space full of character and malleability. It became the base from where he produced spectacular dramatic works of epic proportions, such as *Mahabharata* (1985) and *Conference of the Birds* (1979), that shaped and expanded the parameters of contemporary theatre. In the book, he recounted how a simple change of setting could bring about a mood change in a class of students. Noticing how the cold fluorescent lights and prison-grey-colour walls in the lecture room had made them reticent and unresponsive, he then moved the class into a room with warm lighting and walls painted in a soft colour. Soon enough, the students perked up and became more attentive and engaging. This led me to think perhaps we also needed a change of milieu, away from the conventional, vanilla-flavoured recital hall setting.

I went fishing for those extraordinary places, making cold calls. You'd be surprised how helpful people could be sometimes, to strangers with unusual requests. I landed two great catches – the banking hall of the Hongkong & Shanghai Bank (rebranded as HSBC), and Flagstaff House (now housing Museum of Tea Ware) – and others. I was able to put together a series called Soirées in Historical House, or something catchy like that.

On the night of the concert at the HSBC banking hall, we arrived just as the bank was closing. We promptly set up a podium for the string quartet, did sound and lighting checks, laid down rows of folding chairs, and let the audience in. They light-footed in, looking like a bunch of complicitous trespassers who had no right to be there.

We played the concert under the grand barrel-vaulted ceiling of Venetian mosaic that depicted scenes of mercantile activities in the mythical Orient. Embedded in the centre of the dome was a gilded starburst motif. I can't recall how the music sounded, probably as wafting as in a cavernous cathedral. For an hour or so, we had this money palazzo under a dazzling Venetian mosaic dome – which later ended up in some landfill – all to ourselves. Throughout the concert, only one person walked past, and that was Sir Michael Sandberg, the taipan of the bank. He gave us a cursory look and continued on his way. If he was wondering what we were up to, he didn't bother to pause and ask.

Tickets for the recital held at Flagstaff House were snapped up the moment they went on sale. Nestled in a garden planted after the British colonised Hong Kong in 1842, Flagstaff House was built for the commander of the troops billeted in what was to be called Victoria Barracks. The two-storey mansion had a deep and wide colonnaded verandah and a reception hall spacious enough to hold banquets and dance balls. Built on a bluff, it was well positioned to monitor the movement of ships in the harbour.

Before the military handed the mansion back to the Government before the handover, Chief Justice Sir Denys Roberts was housed there temporarily. He didn't object to our holding a chamber concert there during his residency. That evening, while we were setting up, he emerged from his rooms above the reception hall in a silk dressing gown. I showed him the house programme and sheepishly invited him to the evening recital. He pored over it like a piece of legal document, raised his signature knotty eyebrows, looked over my head and said, 'Think I'll pass.'

Not wanting to overstay our welcome, we kept the concert short and sweet, skipping the intermission. After the recital, the audience seemed in no hurry to catch the bus home as they used to do. Instead, they hung around to soak up the ambience. Some wandered into the garden, where a roost of yellow-crested white cockatoos had been kept as pets by the commander; he had set them free just before the Japanese had invaded Hong Kong. Since then, the birds have been living and breeding freely in the wild, and Hong Kong has become their second-largest habitat in this part of the world. On fireworks nights, they'd flock around Hong Kong Park by the hundreds, squawking boisterously and swooping into each iridescent explosion like a bunch of unsupervised kids at a picnic.

This series of chamber recitals caught the attention of Keith Statham. Keith had been in marketing for a well-known recording company in London, before being headhunted to run the Hong Kong Arts Festival as its first full-time director. Before him had been Charles Hardy, who'd operated it more as a booking agent than a festival director, dividing his time between London and Hong Kong. Apart from a selection of overseas acts, the festival programme had read like a broadsheet of community arts news: full of earnest attempts by well-meaning amateurs.

Keith had other ideas in mind for his festival. He wanted to transform it into an international arts festival like the one in Edinburgh. However, the amateur groups in the colony had a lot of social clout. They insisted on being included in the festival, as a matter of course, under the pretext of promoting local culture. These groups couldn't be fobbed off easily, especially the ones whose members were found among the top brass in Government, or the wives or mistresses of the taipans. Keith thought if he could diplomatically point them to where they could take their acts, they would stop pestering him for the prime-time slots. Setting up a festival fringe was his solution.

Keith was in his forties. He had the swarthy good looks of

an Ian McShane in the TV series *Deadwood*, maybe a tad fuller in the jowls and midriff. Mentally, he had the moves of a chess player. He asked me out for drinks; with Keith, they're always in multiples. We met in the Foreign Correspondents' Club (FCC), located then in Sutherland House, down in Central.

The Central District, the city's commercial heartland, was in the grip of Thatcherite development frenzy. Many grand old buildings had been torn down in quick succession to make way for modern glass-and-chrome blocks. The FCC was located on a high floor that looked out on the harbour. Walking into the wood-panelled bar, I was blinded by the bright sunlight from the windows on that June afternoon. A table or two were still finishing their liquid lunches at this watering hole for journos and marketer types. A poor cousin to the nobby Hong Kong Club next door.

I had never been there before; I looked nervously around for a familiar face. Keith was standing by the bar with a fresh-drawn pint, cigarette in hand. He was in his element. Short-sighted, he'd rather be half-blind than wear eyeglasses, yet he managed to see me, even if he had to squint through clouds of cigarette smoke. He quickly settled me down with a pint and offered me a smoke from his Dunhill pack. We stood shoulder to shoulder, staring ahead at nothing in particular. Keith was not a smiler; he was not to be messed with. After some stiff chitchat, he got to the point: 'I've got an offer for you. A most exciting opening. The Arts Festival is launching a festival fringe, and I'd like you to head it. You'll be the first one to do it.'

It's a known fact that all the top jobs in the arts had always gone to British appointees. I'd be the first home-grown person to break the glass ceiling. Thinking in this way, I was ready to swallow my own vanity bait. It made no difference to me that this

SLEEPLESS IN PARADISE

new operation had no office, no staff, and no long-term financial backing. Sink or float, no one knew. Sent up like a weather balloon with just enough gas to stay airborne for two years. Keith didn't seem to mind that I knew nothing about how to run a festival. What's more, I had never flown solo; everything I'd done so far was with the support of a capable team.

The next day I told Andrew, my boss, about this meeting. He said Keith had already told him. He said this was a great opportunity and I shouldn't give it up, but he didn't really want to let me go. He proposed to second me to my new job: if it didn't work out, I could always get my old job back.

I'm usually not very good at thinking on my feet. But this time I was able to come back with a reply on the spot. I told him how grateful I was, but if I did well, I wouldn't want to come back; and if I botched it, he probably wouldn't want me back.

I didn't wait until the next day to tell Keith that I'd accepted the offer. I was chomping at the bit, as they say, to have a go at it. It was all new to me, and I was flattered that he'd asked.

chapter 4

FLYING SOLO BY NIGHT

IT WASN'T PART of Keith Statham's plan to have the Fringe find its own orbit in just two years. It was supposed to be a satellite encircling the mothership festival and called into action once a year. Keith was a strategist. Without his smart manoeuvring inside and outside the boardroom, the Festival Fringe wouldn't have got off the ground in the first place. He knew there would be roadblocks. He knew his board members would question him on this untested and probably unsound idea. 'What'd you know about Hong Kong?' they would ask. 'We're a far cry from Edinburgh. There's just not enough going on to support something like the Fringe here.'

How could he get them to approve the spending and sign the cheques? Besides coughing up the set-up costs, there was the tricky part of giving continued funding to support the unwieldy Fringe after it was spawned. Who's going to pay?

At this juncture, the Honourable Mr E. Barrie Wiggham, commissioner for Recreation and Culture (now Culture, Sports and Tourism Bureau), came into the picture. He was on the festival board, and his opinions carried weight and could sway decision making. He'd make a powerful ally. Keith knew that and very much wanted him to side with his cause.

LIFE ON THE FRINGE

Barrie was more a maven than a briefcase-carrying government official in a pinstriped suit. He'd raised many eyebrows, riding a motorbike to work instead of being chauffeured like the other bigwigs. He had this handsome shock of wavy silver-grey hair (still has, I believe) that he liked to preen back with his ringed fingers. He was friends with Kris Kristofferson when they boxed for their college at Oxford, or so he said. Good-looking with a touch of the Latino, he could charm and disarm the local dignitaries, equally at home with chatting up the ladies or holding court in a peer group discussing government policies.

Keith detected a fun-loving side to him and went about setting up a fact-finding trip to Australia. He contacted a buddy from his student days in Cambridge, Anthony Steel, the Adelaide Festival director, who was more than happy to help. At Keith's behest, Tony invited Barrie and another board member, Andrew Welch, to attend the Adelaide Festival opening. Tony offered to put them up, show them around, arrange ringside seats for them at the Fringe Parade, a Mardi Gras event held on Hindley Street – in short, show them a good time.

Keith also wanted Tony to introduce them to the young man who ran the Adelaide Fringe. Peter Tregilgas, freckled-faced, ginger-haired, and quick with a joke, was by all accounts a mover and a shaker. He was also a protégé of Don Dunston, the colourful premier of South Australia, who made Adelaide a hip and exciting city to visit. Keith knew that both Barrie and Andrew had never been to Adelaide. He made sure that the trip would make them see things his way and that their cups wouldn't run dry.

When they came back, anyone could see that they were now buddies, sharing in jokes like frat brothers. They were especially impressed by how the Fringe could light up the city that typically shut down early at night; they also felt that the straight-laced arts scene in Hong Kong could do with something offbeat and zany.

At the next board of directors meeting, the item for setting the Festival Fringe was high on the agenda. Barrie led the discussion and made a convincing case of it, speaking from first-hand experience. Andrew spoke in support, followed by a few supplementary questions from other board members to which Keith gave succinct answers. The motion was carried. On Keith's recommendation, they agreed to my appointment, bypassing the usual recruitment procedures. The board also approved a budget to cover costs for the initial two years, as well as paying for Peter Tregilgas to fly to Hong Kong to give me a quick fix on 'How to Mount and Operate a Fringe Festival 101'.

That was July 1982. I was given six months to launch. A very tight, eyeballs-busting schedule. I needed to find and set up an office and recruit an assistant right away. Andrew came to my aid and offered to rent me a small office next to the copy room. Now to get myself some office furniture and a telephone and I'd be on my way to a bright future.

I put out a hiring ad in the *South China Morning Post*, and Emma Li turned up. Capable and presentable, she didn't seem to mind that we had to share an office the size of a shoebox. Every now and then, some noise of someone pulling the plug came through. Once I was on the phone with an arts editor known for his frankness. 'What's that noise?' he asked. 'You talking to me in the loo?'

It transpired that the office was previously a toilet, and the ones above and below us were still in good working order. Apart from that, everything else was just dandy. I could still use, as before, the photocopier, telex machine, and the pantry where we made our morning cups of tea. When Peter flew in from Adelaide and turned up at the office, Emma and I looked everywhere for a chair so that he didn't have to lean.

Peter and I would spend the next twelve days together, during which time he was supposed to empty the Fringe contents in his head and upend them into mine. Doing this in an office cubicle might feel like we're cellmates serving out prison sentences together. I wanted to put Peter in a good mood and generous frame of mind. This was his first visit to Hong Kong, after all. No reason why I shouldn't take him sightseeing. I'd done a summer job as a tourist guide and could put together an itinerary for him: the beaches, the Peak, and other scenic spots, with frequent stops for coffee and beer, so that we could rest our feet and talk. And talk a lot we did; I was relentless with questions on as much as I needed to know.

In the evenings, we hit the shows. First up: Chung Ying Theatre at the Arts Centre, where we met Stage Manager Camilla Hale, who would be the first angel to come to our aid. Camilla was very engaging. When she talked with you, her large, greyish-blue eyes would draw you in, as though you're the only one in the world that matters; the rest of the world can wait.

I asked Camilla to join us on our sightseeing tour the next day. I wanted to show them my childhood haunts. We got there by midday. It was in July and sweltering. I walked them around the block, regaling them with fond memories of having ice cream in this shop house with cool, vanilla-scented, white-tiled walls, known to every kid in the neighbourhood as Dairy Farm.

We came down the steep slope of Glenealy and saw a rundown, two-storey, brick-and-stucco building, squatting at the junction of Wyndham and Ice House Street. Looking like the hull of a cargo ship, its bow pointed towards Victoria Peak, its stern towards the harbour. On its bulkhead – a chimney stack at the tip of the roof – was the year 1913 inscribed in black paint. There were stubs of banyan trees clinging to the burst downpipes, and spiky wild growths everywhere on the roof. Its windows and doors boarded up, it looked abandoned. The building was divided into two blocks connected by a very slim fire escape. By climbing up this staircase, I took Peter and Camilla into the Dairy Farm ice depot for the very first time.

I had learned from my summer job as a tourist guide that Dairy Farm, founded in the late 1880s, was the brainchild of a young, enterprising physician from Aberdeen, Scotland. He combined medical knowledge with new technology to start a business that has endured to this day. He was Dr Patrick Manson. Among other things, he was the one who introduced pasteurisation to Hong Kong.

Cow's milk was the expatriate households' staple diet. But it was also a health risk; contaminated by the deadly tuberculosis bacteria due to unhygienic handling, consuming it could be fatal. The good doctor shipped in herds of Ayrshire cows from Scotland and reared them for their milk in a farm on the hillside of Pok Fu Lam. In conjunction with this, he built a cold-storage warehouse in Central for vending and distributing milk. It was on this very site that we were now trespassing. I proceeded to tell Peter and Camilla that I often dreamed about this place.

We climbed to the top of the stairs of the old fire escape and found ourselves standing in front of a weather-beaten door. The doorknob was a bit skewed, so I gave it a twist and a shove and eased it open. Pitch dark inside. The floor felt squidgy to step on. The air smelt acrid and pungent. We couldn't see a thing at first, then accustomed to the darkness inside, we saw some clusters of

These doors and steps of the former Dairy Farm premises (1984) led to upstair spaces which had, at different times, served as Fringe Studios offices, rehearsal studio, Upstairs Theatre Colette, ArtBar, exhibition spaces, and Roofgarden.

ghostly lights. Then a swoosh of furry things rushing over our feet. Terrified, we screamed and swore. It was a swarm of wild cats dashing for the door. Even after they're long gone, their residual scent keeps the rodents away.

Afterwards, over several cold beers, Peter tried not to douse my hopes and enthusiasm for this derelict warehouse. He changed the subject and started talking about his own future prospects. The Adelaide Festival was a biennial event. Dame Edna, the best-known Aussie cross-dressing comedian, wisecracked: 'So they could keep it out of their minds for two years.'

Peter was unsure himself whether to sit out the time gap between two festivals or find something else to do. He warned me not to get stuck in the same job for too long. Job-hopping is the smart thing to get to the top faster. I countered that I wanted to create an ideal job for myself instead of hopping from one to another. He smiled at me indulgently and changed the subject.

Camilla asked what I saw in this pile of ruins. The future home of the Fringe, of course. I made my case. Everyone knows where to find this place. It's a landmark. There's plenty of room, and nobody is doing anything with it. Besides, you don't have this kind of ceiling height in a new build. You could put a theatre up in one of the spacious rooms. So far it was just a pipe dream. For all I knew, there wasn't a ghost of a chance to get my foot in the door, but it felt good talking to them about it. Camilla said she hoped I'd get it and that she'd come help clean it up if I did.

She was as good as her word. What's more, in January 1984, with the help of the British Council and British Airways, Camilla returned with two buskers from Covent Garden Piazza in London, where she worked with Alternative Arts that helped make street entertainment into an art form. A comedy duo, they called their act Mike and Dave – The Amazing Mendezies.

They performed in our first Sunday Arts Fair in Chater Garden (Fringe Festival was the first to pedestrianise Chater Road in Central), Mike playing the straight guy and Dave, the stooge. They tried to lure the curious yet restless street audience with spoof magic, circus acts, mime, and all the tricks in the bag to keep them from walking away. It was something to watch: two down-and-out white guys wearing Salvation Army specials, making fools of themselves to get a laugh, and money from the crowd. Nobody had seen anything quite like this. My sons, Po Yang and Chi Kay, six and four years old at the time, pushed their way to the front and were thrilled to bits. When they were baptised years later, they chose to christen themselves as Mike and Dave.

The idea for an Arts Fair came out of the twelve days spent with Peter. He painted it with the kind of excitement that a carnival brings to town, calling it the kingpin of his programme. I was hooked. It brought back memories of the touring Shum Sheung Fook's Big Circus Troupe that used to come around Chinese New Year to perform. It rigged up a big striped tent with pennants flying on top like a pirate junk. It was billeted on reclaimed land by the Sheung Wan waterfront. And, on the inside, troupes of clowns, jugglers, acrobats, trapeze artists, fire-eaters, knife throwers, sharp shooters, and growling tigers and their trainers took their turns in the arena. The circus felt like a magic mountain to us kids. As though we were given a get-out-of-jail-free card from school detention, we'd promise our parents anything just to be able to go. That's what the Arts Fair had got me thinking about.

In my two weeks with Peter, he was more than generous sharing what he knew. We also had loads of fun, laughing at the same kind of silly jokes. After we said our goodbyes, he invited me to visit him in Adelaide. The lyrical name of the city was music to my ears.

Three years later, I landed on a blistering hot day at Adelaide Airport. By then, I already had three fringe festivals under my belt; I was almost a veteran with worry lines on my forehead to show. Peter picked me up, dropped my bags at my hotel, and took me to Hindley Street, where the action was.

And so was the wind. A sirocco was whipping up the litter and blowing like a giant hair dryer. We slowly made our way upwind along the sidewalk. When the going was tough, we took refuge in an air-conditioned pub. Catching our breath, we stood there looking at each other – our hair and faces dusty from the red sandstorm. We laughed at each other like a couple of pranksters that had got away.

At nightfall, temperatures dropped, the evening sky cleared up, and the city just as I'd imagined emerged. We checked out a fringe show staged in a church hall on the outskirts. Here, unlike Edinburgh, where most of the venues were within walking distance, you have to drive everywhere. We left behind the bright lights of the city and drove into quiet streets extending into the distances like long pauses in a conversation. I told Peter about the old ice depot and how incredible it had been that it had fallen into my lap like pennies from heaven and that I was able to hold onto it against all odds. None of that seemed real anymore, now that I was finally here in Adelaide where it all began.

We held our first press conference to announce the launching of Festival Fringe in a little cafe tucked away near Lee Gardens in Causeway Bay. Antonio Mak, a talented young sculptor I had befriended, had done some striking drawings which we used as key images for our publicity bumf. From the word go, we caught the media's attention because we were new and different, and our name made easy headlines – invariably referring to us as 'the lunatic fringe', or 'fringe with benefits'.

Where did the term 'fringe' come from anyway? How has it grown to be the outlier it stands for today? Since the day I'd broken into the old Dairy Farm depot, I'd had this inexplicable feeling that I had been tailed by what the Scots call bogles – pesky but benign spirits. They brought in people with Scottish connections in our hours of need.

The word 'fringe' was first used in a theatre review of a local Edinburgh newspaper. That year, eight local theatre companies had gatecrashed the Edinburgh Arts Festival. They banded together and performed shows at any venue available to them, one of which was in an abbey some twenty miles out of the city. The reviewer wrote ruefully that 'it was a shame the show was so far on the fringe of the Festival.' The name stuck.

The Edinburgh Fringe has since then grown to be the world's largest festival, and its idea of an open-access festival has spread far and wide, to the four corners of the world. When it landed in Hong Kong, I had to find a Chinese name for it; there wasn't any equivalent. Coming up with a catchy title for a show, or an endearing name for a newborn baby, can't happen on demand. For days, I searched my mind for a term or words that might fit. Nothing that came to mind felt right. Then one night I had a dream. I dreamt of myself in the middle of a wheat field. It was harvesting time. The sun was shining on the sea of wheat, whose spiky heads were bobbing in the wind like a pop concert crowd. The next day, recalling the dream, a word popped up like a rabbit from a magician's hat – 穗 (Sui), which has a number of meanings. The one that fits is the word for the spiky part on the kernel of a wheat stalk. I put it in the middle of two other Chinese characters to form the term 藝穗節 *Ngai Sui Jit* which actually sounds like 'arts festival' in Cantonese.

The initial response to our festival wasn't all positive. Nobody thought it'd stand a chance here in Hong Kong. 'How can you just let Tom, Dick, and Harry put on a show, without first checking how good they are?' they asked. 'Why would anyone want to go watch a show of questionable standards? Also, how can you expect any decent players to perform without being paid? Mainstream arts were still finding their footing, and now this fringe nonsense.'

In about six months, I'd exhausted all my contacts to string together a thin programme of forty-three acts. But we hit the right notes and kicked off with a dance show called *Soar Like a Bird* by Diana E. Marto from California. It was performed at two locations: above a skating rink in Cityplaza, a shopping mall in Taikoo Shing, and on a hilltop in Lamma Island at sunrise. The performance involved sacred chanting, Isadora Duncan-inspired dancing in white tunics, and trailings of toilet rolls. It also included collaboration with Jim Shum, video artist, and a newfangled theatre group called Zuni Icosahedron. Marto's show made for good photo shoots and drew enough attention to announce the arrival of the zany Fringe.

Keith Statham sent an altogether different gig our way. Yvonne Bryceland, lead actress from the British National Theatre, who performed *A Woman Alone* – a series of monologues written by Dario Fo and Franca Rame, and directed by Michael Bogdanov, who had just escaped being prosecuted for staging explicit gay scenes in *Romans in Britain*. Bogdanov made front-page headlines,

Painting in oil by Yeung Tung Lung

Graphic design by Freeman Lau

Collage/painting by Peter Suart

Acrylic on wood; painting in four parts by Peter Suart

Painting in mixed media by Lo Sze Lim, Chris

Painting in oil by Wong Chun Kit

Painting in acrylic by Caroline Fok

Mixed media works by Leung Mee Ping

Charcoal on paper by Esther Liu

Mixed media 'assemblage' by Kith Tsang Tak Ping

Painting in oil by Yuen Nim Chi

Posters of Fringe Festival 藝穗節 from 1983 to 1998

Mike and Dave at Arts Fair, Festival Fringe 1989, Chater Road.
Photo by Tse Ming Chong.

At the Arts Fair, Festival Fringe 1984.
Benny Chia face-painting Danny Yip, the first Fringe Club bartender who later launched The Chairman — voted No 1 Asia's 50 Top Restaurant 2024.

Nickelodeon, a performance duo (Mark and Chrissie), in *Boxing Clever* (1985); the production was voted 'Best Theatre Performance' at the Time Out Street Entertainers Festival, London, 1984. Photo by Osbert Lam.

Aslan, clown from Turkey

Philip Fok performed at an outdoor fair in Happy Valley Racecourse in 1986 after returning from mime training with Desmond Jones in London. Governor Edward Youde (*second on the right*) and Lady Youde (*fourth on the right*) were also present.

and Bryceland was at the height of her fame. For the Fringe, she played Medea, the murderous queen who kills her children and destroys her family in revenge for her husband's infidelity. She performed to a full house at the Arts Centre.

We had after-show drinks with Ms Bryceland in the Member's Lounge. We were joined by Richard Rodney Bennett, composer and pianist, who came along with the National Theatre production of *Hiawatha*. He had beautiful manners and made delightful conversations. When Yvonne joined us later, I learned how ignorant I was. Serious actors don't just come off stage and switch back to their normal selves. She stayed in character with all the fury of a woman spurned. Some years later, we had a chance to present her husband, Brian Astbury, in his production of *The Guise*, by David Mowat, a satire about censorship. Brian was an inspirational teacher and a kind soul, and I told him about my bumbling role as a Fringe host on that night. He nodded with understanding. *The Guise* would be the last production they would work on together. Yvonne passed on soon afterwards.

It wasn't easy by any means. I had just lost my mother to cancer. On the work front, I was facing a steep learning curve. I was getting by with the help from former colleagues at the Arts Centre, but I knew I would have to cut the umbilical cord, or no one would even notice that I was no longer working there.

I started to look for my own base. The budget for renting an office only allowed for something small and out of the way. I should always be practical, but I wasn't. I only had eyes for an office that anyone could get to without hassle. I knew how important that was, after years of crossing that long footbridge to get to and from the Arts Centre.

The property market was heading for a meltdown. One tabloid headline read 'Speculators of shop units in World-Wide

House stampede for the exits', so I went to take a look. This new commercial block was built on the ruins of the General Post Office, a grand Edwardian edifice much mourned for its swift and heartless demise. The lobby was deserted, flyblown, posters offering discounted sales plastered everywhere. Units had been reduced to cubicles and corridors squeezed down to the last inch, all in the name of profit.

Across the tram lines, a stone's throw away, was another commercial block in a different universe – The Landmark. The new mall, airy and bright, with light limestone walls, generous walkways, and art on display on any available wall space. This was what I'd been searching for, which led me to Jennifer Davies, another angel ready to lend a hand when the going was tough.

The Landmark was the flagship mall of Hongkong Land, the biggest landlord in Central, and Jennifer was in marketing. They rented us an office on the twelfth floor of Prince's Building, a prime address in Central. The new Mass Transit Railway (MTR) rolled up to our doorstep.

Then came the time we had to put tickets on sale for our shows. Jennifer suggested we use the counter in the lobby as our box office and made space available in the Landmark for our exhibitions. I believe she did that for no other reason than out of the goodness of her heart.

We stayed in Prince's Building for a good twelve months. The Fringe office on the twelfth floor didn't look anything like its neighbours – lawyers, accountants, auditors, and stock traders – proper and not a hair out of place. Our office looked as if its contents were giveaways from an Oxfam store. We made an attempt to cover the mismatched old furniture with a new coat of paint. Artist types milled around in the corridor looking for us.

LIFE ON THE FRINGE

One of them was Philip Fok, not yet recognisable as a mime artist. He turned up at our door one afternoon. We were all busy, so Catherine Lau, who'd just joined as a Fringe volunteer (forty years on, steadfast as ever, she's known to everyone here as Cat), talked with him. He told her he was a painter and wanted to show his paintings. She went through the bookings chart. The only slots still available were for clowns, balloon twisters, and face painters for our Sunday Fair at Chater Garden. Not one to be deterred, Philip said he could perform mime, and he'd done it one time, at a friend's birthday party, just for fun.

Philip said had learned to do mime by watching Marcel Marceau playing Bip at City Hall. He was quite sure of that, and we weren't going to turn away anyone who wanted to perform. What's more, he looked the part with a very expressive face. That's how he got his start performing at the 1984 Arts Fair at Chater Garden.

At the time, his day job was government chauffeur. He'd come to us because he saw the poster on our door calling for entries. He was curious, and he had nothing better to do, while waiting for his boss to finish his meeting next door. That knock on the door would change his life.

Cat recalled that and her own visit to the Fringe office vividly. I had been looking for volunteers to help with the paperwork that had been piling up. After a slow start with just forty-three acts, the Fringe shot up 500% to 200 acts in the second year. It was more than Emma and I could handle. I looked around for help. By chance, I came across a write-up in the papers about Sara Beattie and her excellent secretarial training school. I wrote to her, offering her students a chance to practise their skills and learn to adapt to an office environment. I don't think she knew what the Fringe did or who I was, but she obliged and sent us her best students: Cat had won the Best Student of the Year Award. (The following year she sent Susie and Vivienne. Together they made the best team there was in an arts outfit.)

Cat talked about that day, many years later.

'I'd thought I'd be going for an interview in a large corporation with a grand office and lots of people working together. I expected to be told to wait outside, in a long line. When I pushed open the door of the Fringe office, it looked to me more like an elevator lobby. The lift doors and push buttons were all there. All the while I half expected the lift doors to spring open and people to walk out. There were only two people at work. I was handed a form by a young secretary. She asked me to fill in my personal details. And then I was interviewed by a youngish man. He looked nothing like the sort of business bosses I had in mind. He was in casual clothes, no jacket and tie. He talked a lot, trying to explain to me the nature of his work. I knew nothing about the Fringe then. I wasn't that much into the arts.

'Many of the things he said went over my head. But he made them sound very interesting. So, I signed up. I wasn't thinking much. I just wanted a chance to practise what I'd learnt – taking shorthand and typing. I was very good with filing. Looking around the office, I thought they could use some help from me.

'Before this, I'd been an air stewardess with British Airways. After flying for ten years, I can officially retire. I wanted a job on the ground, regular hours, and not having to pack a suitcase every time I go to work. And preferably not too demanding.

'I started as an intern then volunteered, before I became a paid staff. I'm now the administrator of the Fringe Club. Everybody calls me Cat. I'm the Fringe cat that keeps the mice away. I keep track of everything. Unfortunately, these days, I can't keep regular hours, especially during the festival or doing a production. It's more like 24/7. Not what I'd bargained for.'

After my forced entry into the ice depot with Peter and Camilla, I couldn't help thinking about it. I'd become obsessed – I couldn't get it off my mind – even though I had been telling myself to be sensible.

The night Mother passed away, I left Canossa Hospital on Old Peak Road. Driving down Glenealy, my mind was totally blank, not knowing how to feel. Then the Dairy Farm building loomed on the windscreen and I had a flashback of a summer afternoon. Mother was taking Joe and me into the shop there. We came out each with an ice cream cone in hand. We made our way slowly to Queen's Theatre at the bottom of Wyndham Street. It was heavenly.

My mother knew about her cancer. She decided to spend her remaining time travelling to places she'd always wanted to go, instead of going in and out of hospitals. She took off without telling us where, and two years later returned with just a few photographs to show us. One stood out for me: Mother holding the hand of a cherubic girl in a park.

'I babysat her,' she said proudly, 'in Old Gold Mountain [San Francisco]. I was there.'

Mother and I had been at odds with one another during my university years. I'd thought she would be proud that I was the only one in the family to go to uni, not knowing that she'd only wanted me to be a teacher or nurse, to follow in her footsteps. She didn't want to lose me to a world beyond her grasp. I hadn't understood this properly at the time.

On the last leg of her life's journey, she checked herself into Tung Wah Hospital in Sheung Wan. Joe and I took turns visiting her. She put on a brave face, but we could see that she was getting thinner and weaker by the day. The hospital prescribed bags of pills to ease her pain.

One evening, the head nurse in the ward pulled me aside and told me that Mother had been hoarding the painkillers 'We caught her trying to swallow a whole bag of them. I'm sorry. We can't look after her like this anymore. We have to ask you to take her home or to a private hospital.'

We transferred Mother to a quiet room at Canossa Hospital on Old Peak Road. They put her on morphine drip. Mother had made peace with herself and no longer wanted to talk. She was resigned to go, determined as always.

She and Father had come together again at my wedding. After so many years of not knowing much about him, he and I had little to say to each other. I think Mother had reconciled with him in the end. They had spent a year living together before Father returned to Singapore, a cordial parting. Mother was used to living the way she wanted and didn't seem to mind not having someone by her side.

After Mother's passing, I broke the news to Father. I also wanted to know why they had broken up at a time when it was uncommon to do so and why they hadn't tried to patch things up. He replied:

'I missed her a lot after she'd left. I wrote many times pleading with her to come back. At last, she replied with a letter written in classical Chinese. I didn't understand everything she wanted to say, so I took it to the parish priest who was also a school principal. He read it. He told me she was through with me – as final as "cooking the crane and torching the lute". When I heard this, I was angry and hurt, so I didn't write back.'

Later on, I looked up the meaning of the sayings Mother had written. It wasn't what the parish priest had made them out to mean. They're used as metaphors of unacceptable social behaviour. They express disapproval rather than what someone would say to end a relationship. It had all been a big misunderstanding. But by this time, everything that had mattered so much to their lives, our lives – all the heartbreaks and sleepless nights – was no more than a lingering regret.

Sometimes, after work, I'd walk from my office on Des Voeux Road, up Ice House Street, to the junction of Wyndham and Lower Albert Road, just to make sure that the Dairy Farm depot was still there and hadn't been torn down without anyone noticing. That's what happened to the General Post Office – one day, it was wrapped up in hoardings and, the next day, it was gone.

I couldn't see how obsessed I was. I was turning into a building stalker. I refused to accept the fact that she would never be mine, for she'd been betrothed to a rich and powerful lord of the land who, in this scenario, happened to be the Senior Civil Servants' Association (SCSA).

Only in a fairy tale could the pauper win over the princess with pig-headedness. It was my friend Bernard Halley who'd alerted me to the fact that SCSA had already leased the building for five years from the Government, the de facto landlord. Their plan was to turn the ice depot into a private club for high-ranking government officials. Their headquarters were just a stroll away at Central Government Offices. The location was perfect, but the timing was off. The crash of the financial markets had brought many projects to a halt or early demise, especially those that needed to raise capital.

Berny, as he likes to be called, came into the picture as a fresh-off-the-boat administrative officer, known as AO, with the Recreation and Culture Department. He had been recruited from the UK to join the Colonial Service in Hong Kong. Unlike the other colonial types who liked to lord it over the locals, Berny always wanted to side with the underdog and fight for social justice. I still see him like that in my mind, with his toothy smile and an impish glint in his eye. Every time someone asked if he was related to Edmond Halley of Halley's Comet, he always said yes unequivocally. He was never tired of it.

Instead of waving a rule book, he would work the bureaucratic system and become very good at getting around it. So, when I told him about our plan to set up the Fringe Club in the ice depot, he said he'd raise the matter at the next District Council meeting. He didn't think those old codgers would object to our using the place temporarily for a good cause, especially if they had no immediate plan themselves. I told him I'd asked a million times, on the phone and in writing, and they'd turned me down every time.

'They would, wouldn't they?' Berny said. He didn't seem deterred.

What really happened on that day? I asked Berny over the phone. This was years later, and by that time, he'd left government and moved to Tokyo, but I was hoping he'd remember. I reminded him that the year was 1983. It could've been the very last District Council meeting before Christmas recess. With lots of agenda items to get through and ours not considered that important, it might have been put near the end. There wouldn't have been much time left for discussion and deliberation.

What had actually happened at that meeting? I imagine Berny making a brief and succinct presentation to the council, representing the Government, in support of Hong Kong Festival Fringe's request for temporary use of the old Dairy Farm Cold Storage Warehouse to set up a social club for their audience and artists to get together during the festival. I also imagine him as the genie of the magic lantern who came up with three questions which he put to the SCSA to clinch the deal.

'Does the association have any immediate plan to develop the old Dairy Farm building?' No, we don't.

'In that case, is there any objection to letting Hong Kong Festival Fringe use it for a month during the festival?' No, there isn't.

'Would you also allow them some extra time to move in and get ready?' Yes (a bit hesitantly).

A few weeks later, before Christmas 1983, we received a call from SCSA, telling us to pick up some keys. They came in a large manila envelope with 'On Her Majesty's Service' printed on it. There was a whole bunch of them. One with a tag with the words: 'Door key 18th floor'. Cat has kept it to this day. The depot is a low-rise with only two-and-half-storeys and a basement. 'What's it for?' we wondered, thinking about stories of haunted houses. 'Could there be phantom floors invisible to us?' That evening, a fistful of keys in hand, we found ourselves at the entrance to the old depot.

We were accompanied by a group of volunteers who had answered our appeal on the radio. We promised them adventure and a once-in-a-lifetime opportunity to bring an old building back to life. In those days, volunteer work was mostly about looking after sick people and helping poor people; volunteering for the arts was novel and unusual.

Some forty people had responded, and about half of them showed up that evening. We hadn't met each other previously. After a quick round of introductions, I approached a large sliding door with the sign 'No Parking' painted on it. A metal chain tied the door with a chunky Yale lock. The winter evening was growing dark, and Cat's flashlight came in handy. I fumbled in the large envelope for the right key. I must've been trembling in my excitement; everyone was eager to jump to my help.

Several clumsy attempts later, the right key turned in the lock and we pushed aside the heavy door. We stood there, hesitating, when a man in a black-and-white, tong cheong sam fu (Chinese-style top and trousers) appeared out of nowhere. He turned out to be an off-duty waiter from the Foreign Correspondents' Club next door. He asked what we were doing there. I told him we were moving in.

'Nobody comes here at night, don't you know?' he said. I asked him why.

'It's haunted. That's why.'

It wasn't the welcome we were expecting, but ignoring the warning, we stepped inside. A cold gust of clammy, musty air, and black soot everywhere. The faint glow from the flashlight was sucked up by the dark. We stuck together for warmth and courage. Suddenly someone screamed, 'What's that?' She stepped on something that squelched, breaking the spell of silence, everyone suddenly talking all at once. I put on a brave face, blocking out any doubt that I might have about this place.

The next day, while I was working late alone in the office, Barrie Wiggham dropped in, a crash helmet in hand. I told him about our visit to the depot.

'That's what I've come to talk to you about,' he said. 'Don't touch the place. It's not safe.'

chapter 5

A METEOR SHOWER

I FOUND MYSELF sitting next to a stranger at a dinner party, who introduced himself to me as Nick. The house-warming party was thrown by Liz Block, a journalist from New York, who had volunteered to help with copywriting and marketing. She'd just moved into her Leung Fai Terrace apartment, a quaint old garden square in Mid-Levels, which has since been replaced by blocks of high-rises.

Liz is the kind of person who makes friends just by crossing the road. The dinner guests were friends she'd gathered during her short time in Hong Kong. We were all meeting for the first time, and I remember the evening went swimmingly after we'd all had a few drinks and broken the ice.

Nick Ratcliffe was his full name. He was witty and easy to talk to and could hold his end of a conversation on any topic. We hit it off right away. After a few more glasses of wine, I started to tell him about this amazing new festival that I was organising and that he must come to see some shows in this old building which was in danger of collapsing. Nick didn't seem alarmed at hearing this.

'I'm a structural engineer,' he said evenly. 'I'll take a look at it for you, if you like.' I couldn't believe my luck. I must've looked ridiculously grateful in accepting his offer!

Nick kept his word. He arrived the following weekend at the depot with a brawny workman who carried a drill and a heavy toolbox. I took them up to the roof, where he picked out some spots to hammer and drill down on. This arduous work I learned was called coring. They took out chunks of concrete samples from the floor slab and sent them to a lab to test for their condition and strength. Based on the test results, Nick would estimate if the structure of the building was still safe and sound.

The roof was a shambles. Covered in Canton tiles as old as the building itself (rebuilt in 1913), they had been wrecked by years of exposure to harsh weather. I could see wild, wiry weeds pushing up from the cracks. I took a closer look at the interior. In broad daylight, it felt like inside the hold of a ship that had been scuttled, gutted, and left to rot. Roots of the wild plants had pierced through the cracked roof and were hanging down from the ceiling. The place smelled of decay.

Soon enough the lab results came back, in numerical terms and technical language I couldn't decipher. I telephoned Nick. He came promptly, as he did on every occasion requiring his expertise and help, and blithely gave his verdict.

'It looks far worse than it really is. The core examination shows that the structure is in no imminent danger of collapse.'

This was the starting gunshot that we'd all been waiting for. In the weeks that followed, we ploughed on with our long task list. Volunteers, who turned up on weekends to help, were given brooms, brushes, and pails of water. We raced against the opening deadline. Morale was high, for we could see the results of the work

we put in each day. We only did up the rooms we were to use —
a makeshift black box, a bar with a bandstand, and a box office.
Other rooms were left untouched.

It was plain to see that the spalling walls and ceilings needed
more than one coat of paint. Our board member Mabel Lui got
us the paint we'd been hoping for. By sheer coincidence — like me
sitting next to Nick at a dinner party — she was seated next to a
guest who happened to be the boss of Camel Paint, a household
brand in Hong Kong. By the end of dinner, he promised her a
donation of seventy gallons of black and white paint. With the 150
yards of ash grey fabric donated by Margaret's trade suppliers, we
managed to create a cool industrial chic look to the place.

Time was pressing on; only a few weeks left. The centrepiece
for the bar had to be the bar counter itself. A bold statement, not
just an afterthought. I had met Mel Tobias through the *The King
and I*; he played the stern-faced Palace Chamberlain. But in real life,
he couldn't be a friendlier chap. The fact that he was the marketing
representative for San Miguel Brewery was not overlooked. I asked
him if we could have a bar counter built in time for the opening
and showed him the space that had once been used for clearing
cold meats and dairy products.

'Usually this takes months,' he said, 'but let me see if I can
fast-track this for you.' Mel got things done. Besides marketing
for San Miguel, he reviewed films for the *Hong Kong Standard*,
was a contributing writer for Variety magazine, and an actor in
his spare time.

As if by a magic wand, the bar counter appeared on the
opening night, complete with beer taps polished to a shine, beer
mats, and mugs by the hundreds. Later, after Mel and I became
friends, I asked him how he had made it happen.

'I could rush it through because your Chairman is our major shareholder.'

Our Chairman was a young banker when Barrie invited him to head the Fringe Board, which started him off on the social ladder. This was how things worked back then. You began with serving on arts or charity boards as a way of contributing to the community. He probably had no idea what he was getting into. Mr David K. P. Li: before he had earned all his honorific titles you could almost presage the making of his future by the way he signed his name – always legibly, with a controlled flourish – on his black, rotund, Montblanc fountain pen. During his four years as the Fringe Chairman, he never once missed a meeting.

Unfailingly well mannered, he always insisted on seeing me off to the lift after our briefing sessions in his office, no matter how busy he was. We communicated mainly by letter. He'd give well-considered instructions and always catch me out for my spelling and half-baked ideas. I couldn't have learned more on how to conduct board meetings which are important for the operation of any arts organisation. What's more, having his name on the letterhead lent clout and gravitas to the 'lunatic fringe'. It certainly made cold calls a lot easier, like getting a brewery to build a bar for us double quick.

To be ready for the opening night, we drew up a long shopping list: stage lights, a sound system, a demountable stage, lots of tables and chairs, a baby grand piano, a drum set, guitar amps, electrical appliances, office furniture, and countless other fixtures. Plus an equally long to-do list: reconnect water and electricity, redo wiring and plumbing, get the latrines working again, set up a box office and a theatre control desk, and install extractor fans before we were gassed to death by all the tobacco smoke (smoking indoors was permissible then).

There was a catch. We hadn't budgeted for any of this. When there's no money to throw at a problem, you have to become creative. We also learned to make do. Instead of proper stage lighting, we used shop window spotlights; we figured out a way to dim them by installing household dimmer switches on the back wall of the control desk. To operate them, we stood facing the stage with our hands to our backs and controlled the lights by fiddling with the switches. Crude and basic, but it served the purpose.

For a temporary stage, we used eight 8" × 4" rostrums fastened by steel clamps. We borrowed the rostrums from South Island School's gym and later from Frank Drake, as chivalrous as his namesake, who was manager of the Queen Elizabeth Stadium. The bandstand we put up in the bar was in need of a drum set, an electric keyboard, and a couple of guitar amplifiers. Stanley Pong, an amateur musician who dropped in one night, lent them to us on a whim. It turned out to be a permanent loan.

Thomas Lee of Tom Lee Music rented us a Yamaha baby grand for a small fee. Used furniture turned up by the truckload or was hand-delivered by kind strangers. Photographer John Fung picked up from the street a carpet the size of a room and slogged it up Ice House Street to our door. These items weren't always what we were asking for but were given as an act of kindness. People cared and wanted to help. A shot in the arm when things get tough.

Safety was a concern. We were wary of the floors giving way or the ceilings crashing down on us. Nick, maybe the safest structural engineer this side of the equator, brought in a truckful of steel props. He also helped build a metal stand sturdy enough to park a Sherman tank for an industrial aircon unit, as well as

LIFE ON THE FRINGE

inserting H-beams to hold up the ceiling of the theatre. With Nick around, we always felt safe.

And Barrie, reassured and impressed by all the work we'd done in keeping the building safe, stepped in to help. To start, he got us registered as a members' club. There were many hoops to jump; the hardest one was to prove that we had no ties with the local triads. The investigation was carried out by the police, normally taking three to six months. I joked that the only triad members I knew were the ones in movies. Barrie could vouch for us that the Fringe Club had no intentions of ever becoming a criminal organisation, and we got our club licence in time for our opening. I'm almost certain that we broke some kind of record for police clearance. Barrie was our man of the hour.

The Fringe Club opened its doors to the public on 21 January 1984. I remember it was a very cold evening. I stood there waiting for the guests to arrive. The two street lamps across the road were much too dim to throw a shadow. Overwhelmed by self-doubt, I thought: What if nobody comes? What if they came and turned their back on us? Look what you've done to this place. Just look: not even a decent piece of furniture and equipment. What am I going to do next? If nobody comes, who's going to finish the beer?

Peak hour traffic was thinning out. Temperatures dropped. Back then, Lan Kwai Fong was just a couple of back streets with flower stalls and warehouse shops selling tablecloths and antimacassars from Swatow. There were only two joints where you could go and get a drink: Gordon Huthart's Disco Disco, and Christian Romberg's 1997.

After a while, the guests started to arrive. In a steady stream. The Fringe Club took them by surprise – you could tell by the tentative expressions on their faces. It wasn't the usual kind of hotel ballroom for an arts festival opening. Far from it. We were raw. We were rough and ready. There wasn't any other art space quite like this.

We put on entertainment for the night. Aslan, a clown juggler from Turkey who had shown up at our door. The Amazing Mendezies from the streets of London. Hong Kong's own Chung Wah Acrobatic Troupe doing their version of Acrobatic Disco. We couldn't have had a more international mix if we'd planned it. It was a far cry from the mandatory string quartet in black tie.

People poured in, the temperatures in the ice depot rose, and the San Miguel and Lowenbrau beers were going fast. Barrie, Keith, and Andrew took up one end of the bar drinking and enjoying themselves just as they'd done in Adelaide not so long ago. David came with his elegant wife, Penny, whose silk and leather heels showed off the grey, dust-encrusted concrete floor. The Fringe Club started to swing.

The next day, two groups of performers flew in, one after another. One from Barossa Valley outside of Adelaide called the Tanunda Brass Band. The other one – Performance Exchange – came from London. I went to Kai Tak Airport to meet the brass band, winegrowers of German descent who played the kind of music you hear at beer fests. It turned out that about seventy of them flew in on the same plane. I hadn't expected this many in a brass band. It turned out that quite a few family members and friends had tagged along. I'd thought I'd be able to squeeze them all in a couple of taxis and take them to their hotel! What they needed was at least two large coaches and a welcome team of helpers to sort out their load of luggage. I don't remember how I got out of the situation, but every time I think back, I feel hot and sticky under the collar.

Later, having settled them and their family members, I got back to the office to hear the phone ringing. Someone on the line whose name I didn't quite catch: 'We're Performance Exchange from London. Just arrived. We're at the airport now. Could you tell us where we're going to stay tonight?'

Performing at the Fringe, one is supposed to take care of one's own travel and lodgings. That's how it goes. This arrangement was written down somewhere. But at that hour of night, after such a long flight (it took more than thirty hours and six stopovers to fly from London then), I thought the caller might not respond well to my waving the rule book and telling him to sort this out by himself. So I called up the hotel nearest the airport, the Regal Airport Hotel, and asked if they had rooms for eight persons.

'We're all booked up,' the receptionist said, but instead of hanging up immediately, she paused, 'except for the Presidential Suite; that's still available. It should be large enough.' She offered it at half-price due to the lateness of the booking. Relieved, I told Daniel Foley (I finally got his name) that I'd found a room for him and his players. I was very pleased with myself. The next day Daniel called. 'We're checking out. Who shall I tell them to send the bill to?'

Transylvania Six Five Thousand or One of Our Monsters Is Missing was the show that Performance Exchange brought to the Hong Kong Festival Fringe. We'd lined up six performances at The Front Page, a restaurant popular with the US Navy on shore leave, and the journos, whose club – the Press Club – was in the same block. The Front Page shared the staircase with a warren of sex dens and topless bars in Suzie Wong's Wan Chai.

It was Russell, owner of the restaurant and a former US Marine, who took care of the hotel bill that turned out to be rather large, even at half-price. After shows, he'd serve the actors burgers and drinks, and shoot the bull with them until late. I could see he really enjoyed having the show on. It's a horror spoof played energetically by the cast, with lots of shouting and chasing around in his cosy restaurant that wasn't designed for dinner theatre.

I went to see it one night. Just as the show ended, I slipped out by the back door. I went down some steps leading to a dark corridor and a fire exit door. I pushed it open and was immediately blinded by torchlights. I heard someone shout, 'Stop where you are! Don't move! Put your hands up!' I squinted to see a gun pointing at me. Police in uniform and in plainclothes standing in the dark alley were staring at me. One of them ordered me to turn and face the wall, patted me down, shoved a torchlight to the side of my face and announced, 'Wrong guy! This one is four-eyed!'

We didn't do very well in hosting overseas artists. There weren't enough of us to look after them. Also, it's too much for the artists to foot their own hotel bills. It wasn't cheap, hotels in Hong Kong, unlike homestay or Bed & Breakfast in Edinburgh or Adelaide. Something had to change if we wanted to attract international acts. We could solve this problem by throwing money at it, but we had none; even if we could, we wouldn't be a resourceful Fringe anymore, just a watered-down arts festival.

Tapping fingers for ideas, Blanche Dubois's famous last line in A Streetcar Named Desire rang out in my ears: 'Whoever you are – I have always depended on the kindness of strangers.'

But how many times had we been told that Hongkongers wouldn't take strangers into their homes? We didn't even bring friends home. For what it's worth, why would anyone want to put up artists anyway? Cat and Ms Dubois would prove them wrong.

LIFE ON THE FRINGE

I had good reason to think that Dan Foley would write us off after what we'd put him and his company through – that involuntary night in the Presidential Suite, and their debut in 'sinful' Wanchai. That was before I got to know him better. Dan could always play the bad hand dealt him better than most people. He has since performed at the Fringe every year since 1984, solo or in ensemble – undeterred by snake bites, swindles, voice loss, and other nightmarish mishaps. I once compared him to a migratory bird, the Fringe a stop on his flight to escape the northern winters.

Before he went nomadic, Dan was with Royal Lyceum Edinburgh for thirty-seven weeks in eleven productions. He has the looks and build of a classical actor or a matinée idol and could have stayed put. I imagine his epiphany came when he realised that the life of a travelling actor – choosing where to visit and what roles to play – was what he preferred and not the sedentary existence in a repertory theatre. Since then, Dan has performed in over 160 cities and dined in over 2,537 restaurants, and still counting. He has cemented professional partnerships with Risako Aoki in Tokyo and Nigel Kingsley-Thomas in London. While his current homebase is in Donegal, Ireland, his thespian roots are Shakespeare and Beckett.

While in Yogyakarta, Indonesia, of all places, walking down the street, I caught sight of a stencilled poster: 'An Evening with William Shakespeare, by Daniel Foley, Performance Exchange from London'. It was posted above a sign with a skull and crossbones to warn tourists about the smoking volcanoes. In Edinburgh I saw him perform a fifteen-minute monologue of Mozart and Salieri, in a cul-de-sac, to a small, complicitous audience.

After a couple of box office draws – *Last Tango in Hong Kong* (1985) ; *Frankenstein and Friends* (1986) – he brought *Billy*

A METEOR SHOWER

Bishop Goes to War (1987), a musical drama which he performed with Steve McArthur on piano. It's about a young Canadian's rite of passage, fighting in the First World War as a fighter pilot. It happened to be one of those slow nights at the Arts Centre. There were only three of us in the audience. One left halfway during the show. Dan, not missing a beat, played on as though it was to a packed house. After finishing his last line – 'that merely going on living takes courage' – I clapped for the audience who should have been there to watch this very fine performance. I turned to the other person and asked how he'd liked it. I wanted to share this rare theatre moment with him. He looked back at me sheepishly and said: 'I don't know. I'm the cleaner. I'm waiting for him to finish so that I can lock up and go.'

Dan and I have committed enough gaffes over the years to fill a joke book. And this one is too good not to repeat. After their critically acclaimed performance of Samuel Beckett's *Endgame* (1990) at the Fringe, Dan and Nigel Kingsley-Thomas were thrilled to be invited to perform it at a school. This was how he remembered it:

'We were staying with Peter and Joanne Gwynne. Up early, we stopped for an Egg McMuffin for breakfast and arrived at Island School about 8:00 a.m. to set up before the students came in. We offered an abridged version of *Endgame* for the combined upper years. It was very well received, probably because of its brevity. The post-performance speech went like this. Ms Boase, the drama teacher who'd invited us, announced to the class: "These are professional actors who've come all the way from London. They make their living by performing in plays. But this morning they offered to do this for us for free." Needless to say, both Nige and I nearly lost the Egg McMuffins.

103

LIFE ON THE FRINGE

A shocker and a life lesson for us. We were *boased*.'

Boased – This newly minted word became our way of saying we'd been gypped, and Dan would repeat it over and over again, and we'd laugh our heads off.

The 1984 Festival Fringe ran its course, the finale at the Fringe Club falling on 18 February, a Saturday night. Those few weeks went by like playing speed chess – there's no time to ponder your next move. We were supposed to pack up and leave the keys behind after the closing party – that was what we'd promised the SCSA. But it was a bit much to face up to that time of night. We'll come back tomorrow, I told myself without much conviction, when we'll have the whole day to pack.

Berny turned up when the party was still in full swing. A crowd had been gathering. This was our last night; everyone there wanted to dance on, before the upbeat music turned into a dirge. I waved to him. I wanted to at least buy him a drink for everything he had done for us.

He made it through the crowd and sidled up to me. He took out an envelope from the pocket of his tweed jacket. I was about to put it away when he said I should read it first.

On Government letterhead, addressed to the Chairman and copied to me, the letter was signed by Mr Patrick Williamson, who wrote that we could stay on, with the proviso to quit on one month's notice. I was ecstatic, over the moon. As long as I could stay on, my mind didn't properly register the part on notice to quit – 'who cares about what's happening next'.

I leaped on to the bar counter, signalled to the band to bring down the volume, and shouted loud enough for everyone to hear: 'I

A METEOR SHOWER

have an announcement. We don't have to leave. We're going to stay!'
The house went wild. We finished the last drop of the beer, and I
had no recollection of how the night ended.

Our Chairman didn't think it was a good idea for us to stay
on. 'I could smell it in there,' David warned. 'Dry rot. The upkeep
alone is going to cost us.'

He went on to tell me about the house in England he'd lived
in; all the trouble and headaches dry rot had brought. He could see
from the vacant look on my face that I wouldn't know what dry rot
was even if my nose was rubbed in it, so he arranged for his friend
William to talk some sense into me.

William was a retired chartered accountant. In his avuncular
way, he laid it out for me and explained why I should walk away to
save myself from wasting any money. With no disrespect to him,
I said, sotto voce, 'Money doesn't seem to be a problem; we don't
have much of it anyway.'

Of course, he and David were right. We weren't prepared for
this. Dry rot aside, our budget was very tight; it was for the mounting of the Fringe once every year. We had nothing extra to keep the
club open all year round. To do that, we'd have to pay for more staff
to run shows, hefty electricity bills, and maintenance. I had every
reason to follow their advice, but I had somewhat lost my mind,
just as Ophelia did for Hamlet, turning a deaf ear to the common-
sense talk of Polonius.

Maybe David had sensed that both Keith and Barrie were
willing to take a chance with me. After all, Barrie had just taken the
Urban Council on board and talked the then Chairman, the Hon.
Mr. Hilton Cheong Leen, into giving annual financial support to
the Fringe. This would pave the way for Dr Ronald D. B. Leung to
succeed as Chairman when David stepped down.

Ronald became the de facto Mayor of Hong Kong and was widely known for his tireless campaigns to modernise public latrines. He's as colourful a character as he's bold. We would have tales to tell about him, as he led the way to bring the Fringe to the next phase of development.

But I've got ahead of my story: the Festival Fringe would be subsumed under the newfangled Fringe Club to become its annual headline event.

There was a host of other clubs coming to the market, taking advantage of the lax regulation for club operation. One that had come along which made a lasting impression on me was I Club. Located at the Bank of America Building, formerly Hutchison House, a stroll from our office, it was the creation of Alfred and Juliana Siu, a young couple returning from New York, the epicentre of all things modern. Not only did they have the eye and taste, but they also had the spunk and dosh to make it happen. It was contemporary and original; every piece of furniture and painting on the wall seemed to have been carefully curated.

I Club made its glamorous debut shortly before the market crash. It was everything the Fringe Club was not. Designed by Joe D'Urso, who also did the trendsetting flagship store for Esprit in Los Angeles, it was complete with restaurants serving Cantonese and European cuisine, a cafe, a bar, a discotheque, a gym and spa, a library, and a space called Art Forum for exhibitions.

Robert Rauschenberg had just finished a tour in Anhui Province and produced a series of collages which he called assemblage. It was shown in the Art Forum as part of the Fringe programme. It should have created quite a stir, for the influence he had on a generation of contemporary artists in China. But it didn't. It went largely unnoticed. Rauschenberg's mixed-media works were ahead of their time. So was I Club. Those original Corbusier, Mackintosh, and Barcelona chairs installed as part of the furniture and Pop Art pieces by Andy Warhol and Roy Lichtenstein displayed on the walls didn't get as much as a second glance from the lunch crowds or those who came by night for some action in its discotheque.

Alfred and Juliana also hosted Andy Warhol's visit to Hong Kong. He came with Jeffry Deitch, the art agent who had also helped Alfred acquire his art collection. They were put up in the Mandarin Hotel nearby. Warhol had a ball with the glitzy side of Hong Kong. As a throwback to the Roaring Twenties, when the hotel doorman stood witness to the excesses of the times, Warhol had a photo taken with an obliging bellhop in uniform at the Mandarin's entrance. He looked more like a gauche tourist than pop icon. He offered to do silk-screen portraits for the society ladies and local celebrities, but no one took their chance of fifteen-minute immortality in an Andy Warhol art piece.

The second Fringe exhibition (1984) at the I Club was an echo of Rauschenberg's innovative works: a collection of traditional Chinese landscape paintings using the technique of fire-marking on bamboo. By this time, the economic recession had deepened, and the euphoria of transforming Central into a new Manhattan evaporated. Businesses wilted; I Club was on the list. Rumour had it that they were strapped for cash, and a white knight from Singapore would buy them out.

The Fringe Club, operating on a different plane, was to face its own existential challenges.

chapter 6

THE MORNING AFTER

'AND NOW WHAT?' So I said to myself. Empty beer mugs and cigarette butts were strewn all over the room from the party the night before.

This might have been what Mother felt, after she had eloped to join my father, enduring twelve seasick days, arriving with two bags of her life's belongings at the door of a shack in mosquito-infested Bukit Timah, on the outskirts of Singapore, not far from a sprawling cemetery, and waking up in a strange bed next to a man she barely knew.

After checking the conditions of the rest of the place, I was racked by buyer's remorse, made even worse by a head-splitting hangover. The three rooms on the first floor were in various stages of decay; the one below the flat roof showed a row of exposed beams eroded by seepage of rainwater. They looked like the rib cage of a whale carcass. The walls were mouldy and spalling. The other rooms were no better off. I balked at the thought of all the

LIFE ON THE FRINGE

backbreaking work ahead.

Not only that, but there's no way we could plan our programmes on the proviso of one month's notice top quit. So I called on Mr Patrick Williamson for help. Patrick had taken over from Barrie as the new Commissioner for Recreation and Culture, and was also an ex-officio member on our Board. He told me to join him for a breakfast meeting at the new Hong Kong Club. Gone was the elegant Italianate building; in its place now stands a modern commercial block that looks like an upended Napoleon cake.

'They took the old clubhouse down on the flimsiest pretext,' Patrick started with some small talk. 'At first, the club members voted against it. The developer then brought in a team of architects and surveyors to give their professional advice and assessment. They said if anything heavy fell on the roof, the whole building would collapse. In fact, it was a rather ridiculous assumption. But nobody questioned the wisdom of the experts. Nobody asked what heavy object that might be, and how come it would choose to fall on top of us.'

Patrick had the demeanour of a discerning professor. Having carefully considered our request, he agreed to extend our notice to quit from one to three months, thus allowing us more time for planning. He also said he'd try to line up some sponsors. And sure enough, we soon got funding to renovate the rooms from the HSBC Charitable Foundation, which was headed by Nina MacIntock, another Scots angel that appeared on the scene when help was sought. For the structural repairs, Nick came up with a treatment by injecting an epoxy mix into the spalling beams. It has held up to this day.

We needed to keep the club humming, with music and shows and anything to draw an audience. We opened up the rest of the

THE MORNING AFTER

rooms and offered them rent-free to arts groups. To cover costs, we took a 30 per cent split from gate receipts. We shared the risks: if an event didn't do that well at the box office, we'd take the loss with them. This way, we could always fill our theatre with shows and concerts. But it didn't quite pan out for the first few months because we didn't have a real theatre to offer. There was no proper sound or lighting equipment, only gaggles of mismatched folding chairs for seating, risers put together for a make-do stage. In fact, everything was make-do.

We started off by showing films, Monday through Friday, except Wednesday. The French Cultural Service provided movies from their official catalogue for free, and we borrowed a 35 mm movie projector from Salon Films. We screened what was available: mainly old, scratchy, black-and-white French movies. It wouldn't have worked even if we had had the ambience to match; even the musty odour in the room matched that of the art houses in the Quartier Latin you took refuge in on rainy days.

We needed to hire a projectionist but couldn't afford the wages. At the time, we had two interns working with us – Jacqueline and Elaine – both fresh grads from Hong Kong University, both keen and bright as buttons. But we could afford to hire only one. Elaine was prankish and fun to work with, whereas Jacqueline was handy with tools and knew how to splice a film. In the end, we picked Jacqueline over Elaine, who has gone on to a brilliant career to head the Leisure Culture and Sports Department in Government. Jacqueline is now a well-regarded potter residing in England.

On Wednesdays we did open mic. It was supposed to pack the house and build a following. Anyone could have a go on stage with their act. We thought that would attract emerging artists, who would bring their friends. To our dismay, the audience stayed

LIFE ON THE FRINGE

away. Apparently, some of the acts were taxing to sit through even for friends.

We added a night of theatre for variety. Theatre Workshop was conducted by Bill Poon and his partner, Carmen Ling. They pulled together a group of aspiring actors and scriptwriters, meeting once a week to improv and play theatre games and iron out scripts. It was full of possibilities, but then tragedy struck. Young, talented, and very much in love, Bill was diagnosed with terminal cancer. We lost him within months. His death shocked, saddened, and sobered us to life's fragilities.

We carried on with the film nights. Sometimes we'd spice it up by doing all-nighters of French Classics. In the morning, we served croissant-and-coffee breakfasts to complete the Gallic flavours. One of the gems that had caught our eye in the long list of unfamiliar titles was *Les Enfants du Paradis* (*The Children of Paradise*). This 190-minute classic, made under incredibly harsh conditions in Nazi-occupied Paris, is lauded as one of the best films ever made – Marlon Brando has called it the top film of all time. The male lead was played by Jean-Louis Barrault, who was also a mime artist. This must have stoked the imagination of some mimes-to-be hanging around the Fringe Club, such as Chan Hung Yu and Henry Chung, who formed Marble Mime; Sheila Self and George Beau of Impromime; and Philip Fok, who had just made his début in the Chater Garden Arts Fair.

Sometimes things do happen in mysterious ways. Barrault studied mime with Etienne Decroux, who also taught Marcel Marceau – best known for playing Bip, the mime character that got Philip Fok hooked at Hong Kong City Hall Theatre. And Philip, circuitously, got sent to London to study with Desmond Jones, who was taught by none other than Decroux himself.

Hong Kong Fable a Mime Performance Presented by the Fringe Club, directed by Desmond Jones, produced by Benny Chia, cameo appearance by Cheng Pik Yee, sponsored by Council For the Performing Arts & The British Council in September 1986 at Fringe Club Theatre. Booklet designed & printed by Progressive Design & Production Ltd.

Six Chapters of a Floating Life, premiered in 'A Celebration of Hong Kong Artist – City Hall Silver Jubilee' on 19th October 1987. The original production was commissioned by the Urban Council & sponsored by Esprit. It has since performed in the Forum, Macau; Price Theatre, Adelaide; National Theatre, Taipei; Carnivale, Sydney.

Lament of Sim Kim produced by Hong Kong Fringe Club for 1991 Chinese Theatrical Arts Festival, directed & choreographed by Kai Tai Chan, scripted by Benny Chia. Photo by Bobby Lee.

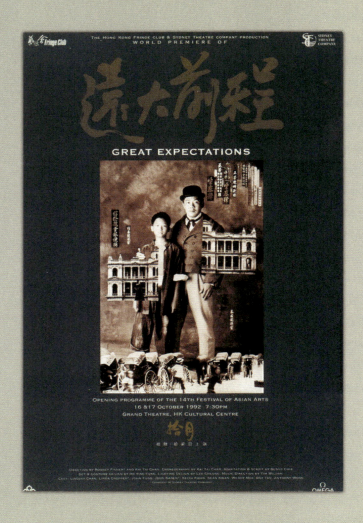

Great Expectations, produced by Hong Kong Fringe Club & Sydney Theatre Company in 1992 Festival of Asian Arts Opening Programme, directed by Rodney Fisher, script in Cantonese & English by Benny Chia. Photo by Osbert Lam. Concept by Kai Tai Chan. Design by Suen Sio Wah.

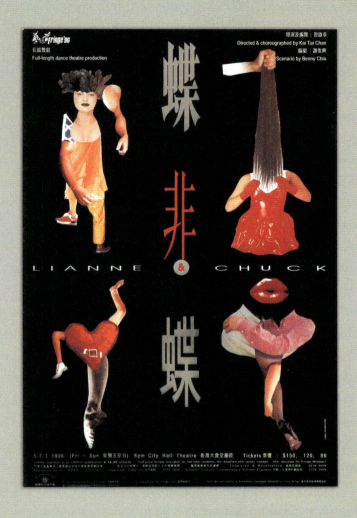

Lianne & Chuck, produced by Hong Kong Fringe Club in 1996 Hong Kong Fringe Festival programme, directed and choreographed by Kai Tai Chan, scripted by Benny Chia. Collage by Christopher Doyle.

At 'Death in Hong Kong' exhibition 1999.
Left to right: Yuen Kwok Chung, Wong Shun Kit,
Tao Wun, Wong Leung Shek, Benny Chia.

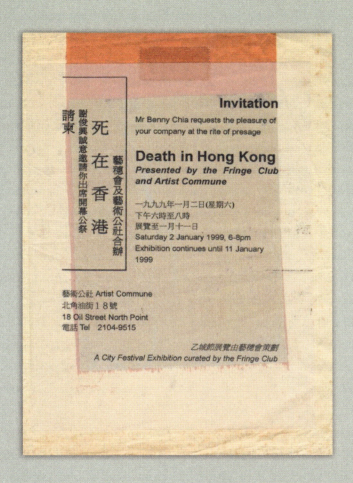

'Death in Hong Kong' curated by Benny Chia, a mixed-media exhibition of works by artists from the Artist Commune, part of the visual arts programme in the first edition of the City Festival in January 1999.

LIFE ON THE FRINGE

What do we do with a bare stage with no proper sound or lighting equipment? The inspired answer – mime. All we needed was some white make-up on the face and red lipstick, and there you go. David Glass could do a mime piece using only his hands, under one spotlight. He called it Movement Theatre. David had been sent by the British Council to perform in Outer Mongolia, forty years before, in an effort to disseminate British culture to the far-flung corners of the world. In his prime, he had the build of a ballet dancer with well-oiled couplings for body joints. He liked to swear, and his jokes would stop at nothing. The first time we invited David to do a show, he was with his beautiful and gracious wife, Peta Lily, who would become a teacher, show director, and mentor of the Fringe Mime Lab.

David's hands-only piece was a tour de force, a revelation. In fifteen minutes or so, he took us into primordial time when our planet was teaming with squiggly life forms that morphed into humans that eventually would 'fuck up the world', as David liked to say. We had borrowed a single spotlight from the Arts Centre, hung it directly above the stage, and plugged it into the nearest socket – no dimming effect, just on or off. His hands swam and glowed in the pillar of light, telling stories wordlessly. That's all it took to create magic.

David would become a Fringe regular, playing solo or teaming up with Peta or his ensemble. On a rare occasion, he offered a six-month residency in London for one of our young mimes, Jim Chim, who became a well-known comedian on stage and on television.

The following year, Camilla Hale returned with six top-pick street entertainers from a contest held at the Covent Garden Piazza.

All of them were skilled performers who could enthral kids and grownups alike with comedy, spoof magic, juggling, slack rope walking, escapology, and miming to Lionel Ritchie's best-known songs. We had them play and bottle (slang for taking the hat to the audience) all over town even though it was illegal to do so in Hong Kong. Camilla didn't want her buskers to be arrested; she suggested I call the police – as she'd do in London – to forewarn them. After plucking up enough courage, I telephoned the district commander, who took it rather well, telling me to send him a show schedule, where they perform etc. He'd tell his men to look the other way.

After her work was done, Camilla would often watch the shows or help out with pulling beers at the bar. She was always brimming with energy. One night, she attended a recital by Krishnamurti Sridhar. Her fate was sealed. The concert was held at Salle Victor Segalen in Admiralty; the audience was asked to sit on the floor. Sridhar played the sarod – a seventeen-string instrument similar to the better-known sitar – with a tabla player on tour with him. He had just won the Deutsche Grammophon's Grand Prix du Disc and exuded the calm and quiet assurance of a musician who has completely mastered his instrument. Time was on his side; he no longer had to pit himself against it.

There was something of a mystic about him. Sridhar told me he had left home at a young age to be apprenticed to his guru to learn to play the sarod. Every morning after breakfast, his guru would ask him to play all eighty-three ragas. He would put two cups in front of Sridhar – one with grains of rice, the other empty. One raga for one grain, until all the rice in the cup had been transferred from one cup to another; that's when he finished the day's practice.

LIFE ON THE FRINGE

His guru lived in a part of India where spiritual practice is a way of life. He told me over a leisurely cup of chai that his teacher had supernatural powers, that people there could perform incredible feats. I read about ascetics who could levitate, and I wanted to believe in miracles.

'I once saw with my own eyes,' Sridhar said. 'He extracted from nowhere a roll of silk cloth and some gold rings to give to his niece as wedding presents.'

I asked if he'd ever seen anyone levitate. 'If you believe it, it'll happen.'

My grandfather liked to read Chinese pulp fiction. After he died, my grandmother kept the books and left them on a shelf nobody ever touched. I used to take out an old classic by the name of *Arson in the Red Lotus Temple* and flip through the well-thumbed pages of grass paper that had turned grey from age. I was captivated by the illustrations inside: woodblock prints of swordsmen with supernatural powers that could fly in the sky or burrow into the ground. As a child with a febrile imagination, I wanted to believe in things thought to be impossible.

Sridhar told me about other equally fantastical things. I don't care if he was fibbing or telling the truth. It's not that fantastical to make something materialise out of thin air. The same way as his guru had done, turning thought into reality. That's what we do in arts – turn thoughts into realities, conjure up beautiful objects and life-changing experiences from nothing more substantial than a fleeting idea – just as his guru had done. He himself has performed one of life's most mystical feats by turning a chance encounter with Camilla into a lifelong relationship.

After returning the Fresnel spotlight to the Arts Centre, our lack of proper lighting equipment became more obvious. Two miracles followed on the heels of one another. Camilla, who had returned to London, wrote to ask if we wanted some old stage lanterns, all eighteen of them, free for the asking. The only catch was we had to pick them up from Gloucestershire, England. A tall task. Cat got a contact at Cathay Pacific Cargo from a former colleague. Not only did CX provide free freight but also door-to-door delivery. In a matter of weeks, the 'pig snouts' as they're called for their resemblance, arrived in several large wooden crates. We couldn't contain our excitement to see them laid out in neat rows on the bare stage of our humble theatre.

All we needed now was a lighting grid to hang them up.

We found an easy solution the next day. We went to a metal shop on Hollywood Road to buy metal hand railings by the yard, cut them down to size, paint them black, and batten them to the ceiling of the theatre. It was a roughshod substitute, but it worked just fine for us.

For control of the lights, we needed to install a lighting panel board which cost as much as a small sedan car to buy; we couldn't afford a bicycle, even if we emptied our pockets. There was a young guy who hung around the theatre, didn't talk much but was always ready to help with chores. I chatted him up and asked him his name. 'Chiu Ming,' he replied. I couldn't believe I heard him right, so I asked him once more. Yes, he's called Chiu Ming, which in Chinese means lighting. He also knew how those pig snout Fresnel lights worked. 'Am I dreaming?' I pinched and asked myself.

It turned out that Yip Chiu Ming (his full name) was an electrical engineer by day. At night, he enjoyed being around the theatre. It took him just six weeks and a bit to build, from scratch, a lighting console for us.

The road taken by Philip Fok to head the herd in mime was a long and arduous one. In 1988, *Asia Magazine* did a cover story on him and crowned him 'King of the Whiteface'. His journey had started with baby steps five years before.

Mime had suited our bare stage. We're poor, so what? Let's do it as *poor theatre* then, with a certain *je ne sais quoi* flair. No other arts outfit was doing it. It could be the niche for the newborn Fringe.

We had singled Philip out to be groomed with limited resources because he was keen from the word go. Besides, he had a compelling story to tell. He was raised poor. His father was a street vendor and couldn't afford to put his son through higher education. He wanted Philip to be apprenticed to an ivory carver, to learn a craft, and maybe to make a good living. Left to his own devices, he took up painting instead, which his father didn't think much of. Eventually he learned to drive and became a driver of government vehicles, and then was promoted to chauffeur. That's what he was doing when he turned up at the Fringe. Between driving his boss to his evening engagements, he found time to take a swing at mime skits.

We were planning for a fundraising event and had to come up with some acts to entertain our guests. I created a short piece called *Chrysalis* for Philip to tell his story, and invited Eric Poon, a talented composer and pianist, to improvise the music. We had Philip dressed up in grubby overalls car mechanics wear; at a turning point in the show, he struggled like a butterfly breaking out of its cocoon. Eventually, he shed his overalls – after some soul-searching gestures – to reveal the tight-fitting garment of a mime artist. It was meant to be a parable of the liberating power of art.

THE MORNING AFTER

So far, Philip had been self-taught. We knew he'd benefit from receiving some formal training. Mark and Chrissie of the street mime duo Nickelodeon, brought to the Fringe by Camilla, had studied with Desmond Jones. Desmond had learned from the great masters, Etienne Decroux and Jacques Lecoq. Philip couldn't be in better hands, they said. All he needed was a study grant, a plane ticket to get there, someone to pay for his living expenses during his stay, and another not-so-minor detail: he would have to take long leave from work.

Philip's boss at the time was the Director of Education, who was empathetic and accommodating. He granted Philip three months of no-pay leave for his overseas training, even if it wouldn't necessarily make him a better driver. The British Council promptly came up with the funding as soon as we asked, and British Airways let him fly free. London is a city that comes with a high price tag. He would have to find the means to pay for his living expenses there.

Another consideration was: Philip had just become a father. Going to London would mean that his young wife would have to tend to the baby by herself for three months and with little money. But his destiny was aligned to get him there. Around this time, he was showing four of his paintings in a group exhibition held in the lobby of the Bank of America building. A collector came along and bought three of them for a tidy sum of $8,000, the equivalent of what Philip earned in three months. Before this, he had never sold any of his works. To have a bit extra, Philip also sold his motor-cycle. He was all set to take off for the adventure of his life, away from Hong Kong and home.

Camilla set him up at a homestay, a few Tube stops from the Desmond Jones School of Mime in Shepherd's Bush, West

London. He hadn't expected London to be this cold and wet. He hadn't brought enough warm clothing to wear. Transport used up a good part of his daily expenses. He was always counting his pennies, and he was always hungry. He said he lived on instant noodles that he soaked in hot water from the thermos his landlady put in his room every morning, and seasoned with a big chunk of butter. He found he craved fat as never before. 'My body needs it,' he said.

He spent his free time in the library to keep warm. 'I look on the shelves for books about mime,' he said. 'I look at the photos mostly, and try to look up the meaning of the words, which are many, in the dictionary.' It couldn't have been easy with his limited English. 'In class, if I don't understand what Desmond is talking about, we use a kind of sign language – hand and face gestures – to communicate. He's always patient.'

Philip showed his teacher a lot of respect, like a good Chinese student. It also helped that they got along well. This might be his only shot, and he didn't want to miss out on anything. In those three months, he was like a sponge, soaking everything up. By the time he made his way back to Hong Kong, he must have felt not only a lot lighter in bodyweight but also like someone who has been touched by the vagaries of destiny.

An opportunity came for Philip's homecoming show. The Fringe was invited to participate in an outdoor carnival held at the Happy Valley Racecourse. We introduced a new indie band called Beyond. The lead singer, K. K., was a Fringe Club regular. He would sit in a corner and strum on his guitar, a mug of beer by his side. We didn't mind having him around. He caused no trouble, and the flamenco music he played was quite decent. Later, he and his band shot to fame with their torchbearer number, *Sea Wide Sky*.

THE MORNING AFTER

The then Governor of Hong Kong, Sir Edward Youde, was the guest of honour at the carnival. He and his entourage came to a stop in front of our stage. Philip improvised; he mimed the stem of a rose and, with a flourish, presented it to the Governor, who good-humouredly played along. The press photographers standing by snapped away furiously, and Philip made headlines and photo captions in all the papers the next day.

The next step up for Philip was to be featured in a mime performance. But there was none around. So we decided to produce one by ourselves. It'd be the first of such an attempt, I thought, a milestone event for Hong Kong. It had to be done right. We had to look for a theatre director with the experience and know-how to direct mime shows, but there wasn't anyone around who could fit the bill. It took us a while to hit on a name: Desmond Jones. He knew how; he'd done it before. What's more, for Philip, it would be like doing advanced training.

I put a trunk call through to Desmond. In the early 1980s – still the era of cable transmission – it was a big deal to call long distance. You had to make your way to Cable & Wireless located in Mercury House, Central. Book a time to call and wait in line for the connection. When the call came through, you would be told to proceed to a numbered booth. And then, nervous as hell, I shouted into the mouthpiece as though my voice had to cross the oceans and continents to reach Desmond, who had been waiting for my call.

The British Council stepped up to the plate once again. Maria Ho, the arts officer then, liked the idea and came up with the funding to bring Desmond over. He was to stay for five weeks to rehearse and direct the show. Instead of putting him up in a hotel, we set him up in a room next to the rehearsal studio – a single bed tucked in a corner, an old school writing desk and chair, and a water heater in the shower installed at his special request. Apart from this *luxury* item, Desmond lived and worked like a Franciscan monk resigned to hardship and deprivation with total devotion to his task.

Every morning after a breakfast of toast and tea, he'd start rehearsal at 9:00 a.m., followed by a short lunch break, to finish at 5:00 p.m. Pat Woo, a fresh graduate from the Chinese University of Hong Kong and an aspiring mime, acted as interpreter. The pixie-like Cheng Pik Yee, trained at the Jacques Lecoq School in Paris, joined the rehearsals and paired up with Philip for the second part of the show. For the script of *Hong Kong Fable* (1986), we roped in a young playwright called Raymond To, who had debuted with Chung Ying Theatre's production of *I am Hong Kong* (1985). To Kwok Wai would become Hong Kong's best-known playwright and screenwriter. Scores of box office and critical successes to his credit, *I Have a Date with Spring* (1994) topped the list. It enjoyed unparalleled success as a musical stage play, film, and television series.

It was a very intense time for Philip, his first taste of being in a professional performance: four weeks of rehearsals followed by nightly performances for one whole week. Again, it required him to take leave from work to do it.

The opening night was played to a packed house. It was a well-crafted piece of classical mime, simply staged. Philip rose to the occasion; he shone. He had a strong stage presence, and those months of physical training, honed by hunger and determination, paid off.

Some of those in the audience knew about Philip and his fairy-tale journey, the personal sacrifices he'd made – leaving his family, a new baby, and his job to take a chance with mime – for an artform he might already be too old for (he was thirty-eight). The least they could do was to cheer him on and overlook his flaws and lapses as a first-timer. Those who had given him a leg up along the way felt rightfully proud. Desmond spoke highly of him: 'Philip has three qualities rarely found all together in one mime performer: a sense of comedy, a sense of tragedy, and a sense of warmth and gentleness.' He was gracious enough to let Philip take full credit and the limelight for his hard work and perseverance. That evening, I felt that the Fringe Club had found its raison d'être.

Then a review came out in the South China Morning Post under a glaring headline: 'Milestone Is More a Millstone'. Not only did the writer give away the plot, but he trashed the show with all the spite he could muster. As uncharitable theatre critics go, in gratuitous cruelty, he certainly beat many to the post. He managed to do all that by using a pseudonym to hide his real identity as an out-of-work actor.

Philip shrugged it off; his limited English might have shielded him from the hurt the scathing review inflicted. Desmond took it in stoic silence. He didn't defend himself or fight back. There's really not much you could do to such a stinker except to let the box office speak for itself. *Hong Kong Fable* sold out five shows, followed by an invitation to perform at Dom Pedro Theatre in Macau. Philip and Desmond were not going to let any bad fairy spoil the party.

Besides the creative work in the arts, the daily routines such as who was to take out the garbage and keep the Fringe clean began to creep into our conversations. We couldn't afford to pay anyone,

LIFE ON THE FRINGE

so we made trade-offs with some young artists: they were offered the use of our space in exchange for their service.

Lorette van Heteren was an actor from Amsterdam who came to Hong Kong with an avant-garde performance group called KISS. She stayed behind after their departure. She wanted to live in Hong Kong and, meanwhile, learn to play the role of Monkey King in Peking Opera.

She was looking for accommodation. We took her in and let her stay in one of the vacant rooms on the first floor with an ensuite broom-closet-sized washroom. In return, she doubled as our night guard and cleaner. Tall, fair, strong, and slim, she was caring and kind and, oftentimes, excitable. If she were to run a neighbourhood store, she would give credit to anyone she thought might need it, even the dodgy ones.

There were always discarded newspapers and other detritus left behind after a busy night. She hoarded them. One day, she told us she wanted to do a show in the room that had been used for storing winter clothing and keeping them mildew-free in the hot and humid summer. The space had grey peeling walls and a gritty tiled floor; at night, the only light source came from the street lamps and the moon through the dusty French windows. She got hold of some low stools for seating and mustered a small audience to watch her show. She did her own version of *Birth of Venus*, using heaps of crumpled newspaper to create the effect of a polluted sea. Lorette, who played the Goddess Venus, emerged from it in an old nightgown. Raw and edgy, it conveyed the message of how contemporary society distorts traditional values and trashes the environment.

The closing moment was visceral and dramatic. Instead of a Venus borne by Botticellian sea spray and springtime flowers, she

Lorette van Heteren in 'Dream of Survival' as Venus,
a show lit entirely by street lamps through the windows (circa 1984)

Fringe rooftop with overgrown plants (1984)

Fringe rooftop artist studio, from 1984–89. Artists – mentored by sculptor Antonio Mak and painters Yank Wong and Josh Hon – were Yeung Tung Lung, Chan Ching Wah, Chak Chung Ho and several others. It was later converted into Fotogalerie and, subsequently, Colette's ArtBar.

Studio Theatre before renovation (circa 1984)

Studio Theatre years after renovation

Left to right: Benny Chia, Glory Wang of Atelier Pacific,
Robin Howes of Kenward Consulting, and Nic Banks of Atelier Pacific
on site (Underground Theatre), 2010

was drenched in wastewater poured down from an air vent on the roof by Paola Dindo, acting as a stagehand at the denouement of the play. It was a frosty winter night; the audience could feel the shock of cold water in their bones. Osbert Lam took some photos during rehearsals that he's kept to this day, recently exhibited in *Be40* that celebrated the fortieth anniversary of the Fringe.

This was how Lorette, our first cleaner, left a mark in what has now become the Jockey Club Studio Theatre. She went on to create the solo piece *A Report to an Academy*, adapted from Kafka's short story, playing an ape that has regressed to become a human, the forerunner to the role of the Monkey King that she would adopt as her life's work. 'Many people have felt I had been Chinese in my former lives,' she wrote from Shanghai years later.

We turned the derelict rooftop, once the living quarters for the local staff of Dairy Farm, into a workspace for young painters. At one time, some twenty-two artists were bunked up there in tiny cubicles. Nine or ten artists worked in the studios, mostly at night-time, after their day jobs, and three mature artists, Antonio Mak, Yank Wong, and Josh Hon, agreed to mentor them.

'We talked over a beer or two once in a while. The mentoring was very casual,' said one of the rooftop painters, Yeung Tong Lung. He was the one who worked hard at his paintings and practically lived there. 'When it was too late to go home, I used a door that had fallen off for a bed,' he recalled.

'The club started to get busy. Some nights, the band playing in the bar downstairs was so loud I had to stop work. I sat in the far end corner on the roof and smoked. There was a hostel for young delinquents across the road, and they watched me smoking on my own. I bantered with the bold ones. We became friendly. But one day we found some poop in one of the cubicles. After that, I was told not to have anything to do with them. It might not have been the kids, but they were blamed anyway.

The rooftop studio went on for about five years. By the end, most of the artists had either left or moved on to something else. Tong Lung – whose works are now in the collection of museums and private collectors – was the last one to leave. Eventually, we would turn the space into our office to make room for a black box theatre.

By that time, our de facto landlord, Government Property Agency, wanted to make a deal: they would draw up a lease, provided we render the building wind and watertight. That means fix the windows and doors and make the building habitable. We were given nine months to do it.

chapter 7

OPENING BELLS

'HOW ABOUT ANOTHER mime show?' Winsome Chow from Festival Office asked.

This conversation probably took place soon after our performance of *Hong Kong Fable* at Teatro Dom Pedro V in Largo de San Agostinho of Macao, November 1986.

This Grande Dame of a theatre, in Greek-temple-revival style with a chalk-white and sage-green pillared façade, was built in the mid-nineteenth century. In its heyday, it was where Macanese society congregated to celebrate Christmas and New Year and attend musical soirées and comic opera. Its fortune, tied to that of the Portuguese enclave on the South China coast, went into a long decline and eventually lost much of its former glory. It was converted, in turns, into a popular cinema and then an adult entertainment hotspot hosting the infamous *Crazy Paris Show*. By the time we brought our show there, albeit as a shadow of its former self, we remained impressed by its history and felt rightfully proud to have been invited to perform there. Macau was still a foreign country. So legitimately it was our first overseas tour, if only forty-one sea miles away.

Teatro Dom Pedro V was also the venue chosen by Senor Eduardo da Silva, a cultural visionary, to hold a symposium to discuss whether Macau should look into its diversified cultural identity and decide if it should establish its own Fringe. Winsome was one of the speakers. She might have caught Philip's performance in *Hong Kong Fable* there and liked it well enough. Maybe that's why she commissioned us to devise a show for the Silver Jubilee celebration of the Hong Kong City Hall.

The year was 1987. To be able to perform at City Hall meant a great deal to me. Not that long ago, I was a starry-eyed kid, trying to catch snatches of a show from the back of the theatre. And now, this.

I felt I was punching above my weight. Although I'd done this one show with some success, it's as we say in Cantonese only 'clay cannon material', which means it falls apart when put to test. It was no more than make-do theatre done on a makeshift stage, with hand-me-down lamps, operated by a homemade lighting console.

City Hall Theatre was in a different category. Winsome took Philip and me there for an inspection. It was equipped with everything you could think of in a theatre. The inside of the control room reminded me of the cockpit of a jumbo jet that's covered in switches and knobs. It entered my mind that knowing how to fly a kite doesn't mean you can fly a plane.

Later on, Winsome recalled that it wasn't such a hard decision to make. 'Back then, the local talent pool was small. It was either traditional music or dance, or Cantonese opera singing. Having a mime show in the programme would be quite refreshing, so why not? Anyway, it was just one show among many.'

We were given a Monday to open and play just for two nights. No one would've noticed anything even if we'd fallen flat on our face.

Strictly speaking, the Fringe's mission was to provide an open platform for emerging artists to showcase their works, not to produce shows. That requires a different set of skills. What's more, it takes a lot of resources to create a show that's any good. It didn't help that we were perennially strapped for cash.

The success of *Hong Kong Fable* was a fluke and not easy to duplicate. Also, I didn't find it quite so exciting to cookie-cut another one. The irony is, despite my stamina, my threshold for repetition is remarkably low.

Philip couldn't afford to quit his day job to become a full-time mime. He was by now the father of two young children and the sole breadwinner. It was hard enough for him to find time to keep in practice and stay fit. Meanwhile, his wife complained that he spent more time at the Fringe Club than at home; instead of slowing down, he started giving mime classes and one thing led to another. In order not to let his students disperse at the end of the course, he rounded up the keen ones and formed a group. We christened it the Fringe Mime Laboratory. Slimmed down to just Mime Lab, it celebrated its thirty-fifth anniversary in 2022 with a mime production and online video clips.

In March 1987, I got invited to the Adelaide Fringe. Once again, Peter offered to meet up with me. By that time, he had left the Fringe to join the operation of an aboriginal art museum. Meanwhile, all I could think of was our City Hall debut. So far, I only had a show title and story outline from the back cover of a book. This was all I could muster for advance publicity.

I found a paperback version of this Chinese classic in the Swindon bookshop in Tsim Sha Tsui, Kowloon. I was drawn to the book title and the picture on the cover depicting a couple enjoying themselves by a lotus pond in a Chinese garden – an idyllic scene from olden days. The book is called *Six Chapters of a Floating Life*. An apt title for a mime show of six sketches.

I hadn't read the book yet. After I did, I was all misty-eyed. It's a love story with a sad ending, based on the journal of Shen Fu, a down-and-out scholar in the Qing Dynasty. It's a candid account of his conjugal life, told with an honesty rare for the time. The scenes of domestic bliss set in a classical setting were exquisite and deeply moving. But I just couldn't see how they could be adapted for a mime show, complete with white face, striped sailor shirt, and moon walking.

Something in the Adelaide Fringe programme caught my eye. I'd been scanning the pages for leads to a mime group that might throw me a lifeline. I drew a blank. Instead, I spotted a Chinese name – Kaitai Chan, choreographer and director of One Extra Dance Company from Sydney. He was doing an adaptation of Shakespeare's *The Taming of the Shrew*. It didn't seem like something that a troupe from Sydney's Chinatown would do. I was curious.

The show was sold out, but Peter managed to squeeze me into a matinee performance. I sat in the back row, unsure of what to expect. What I was about to see took me by surprise. Whoever made this show must be a genius. Through the use of body movement, dance, and spoken word, he told with clarity and energy a romp of a story of a high-spirited woman who refuses to bend to the will of her man. He also had a way of using apt images and ingenious set designs to highlight the dramatic moments. I particularly liked how he added layers of subtext reflecting on the subjugation of women in contemporary society. I wanted to meet the director. He was what I'd been looking for.

I stayed behind until the audience had cleared out. A balding bespectacled Asian man of slight build with a wispy moustache came out from backstage. Wearing crumpled T-shirt and shorts, he took up a broom and began sweeping the floor. I went up to him and asked where I might find the show's director, Kaitai Chan. He stopped sweeping, looked at me and said, 'I'm Kaitai. What can I do for you?'

I muttered something in reply. I was expecting a studied version of Ryuichi Sakamoto, in linen jacket and horn-rimmed glasses. After regaining my composure, I told him I was overwhelmed by the performance and would like to invite him to come to Hong Kong to direct a show. He quickly warmed to the idea and invited me to see his other work, *My Father's House*.

'You must come see it,' he said. 'I'll introduce you to my company manager.'

I told him I was flying out the next day, but he said not to worry, he'd drive me to the airport afterwards. It turned out that I liked this one even better. It's a sad tale of the breakdown of a once-loving family living an ordinary life in an Australian suburb, told with the simplicity of a biblical parable, searing imagery, and telltale dance movements. It touched the nerves of those who'd experienced domestic unhappiness. I was so moved that I missed my plane for the first time in my life.

That night I ended up staying in a love motel, as all hotel rooms were booked. It got kind of noisy, so I went out looking for

LIFE ON THE FRINGE

something to do. I spotted an eye-catching poster of a show called *Boozum*, a rock opera by Peter and (his twin brother) Martin Wesley-Smith. I knew Peter from Hong Kong; he had performed his musical satire *Noonday Gun* during the early days of the Fringe.

Naturally I was keen to see it. It was playing on a campus way out of the city, so I took a taxi. Before reaching my destination, the driver told me to get out.

'No cars allowed beyond here,' he said. 'You gotta use your legs, mate,' pointing me in the direction of a slope. I couldn't understand why he couldn't drop me at the door, but it was getting late, and I didn't want to argue. I got out and took a brisk walk up. It was dark by now, and I could feel a car creeping up behind me, its low headlights shining at my feet. As I got to the top of the slope, the car door opened and then shut. I turned around and came face to face with Queen Elizabeth II and Prince Philip who, in passing, said hello to me.

I've been looking since for some meaning to this encounter and found nothing cosmically significant. Except that I had managed to get Kaitai to agree to come and direct a show for me.

I made it sound like a big deal, dropping the names of City Hall and Philip, Hong Kong's leading mime, many times. But I left many of his questions unanswered and didn't tell him I had only done one show in my life, with Desmond and Philip.

I learned what 'Kaitai' means; he's Straits Chinese, or someone whose family has originally come from China, generations ago, and has settled in places such as Penang, Malacca, across Malay (Malaysia) Peninsular where they still adhere to their traditions and practices. Kaitai's upbringing, according to him, was strict but didn't manage to keep him on the straight and narrow. Being the eldest son, he was expected to become, at the very least, a doctor or a lawyer, and certainly a respected member of society. Kaitai was sent to London to attain that. For his studies, he chose architecture, which he found more to his taste.

Away from the watchful eye of his family, he learned two things about himself: that he loves to dance and is blooming gay. In the evenings, instead of spending his time in the library to be a better student and a more dutiful son, he took classes at the London Contemporary Dance School near King's Cross.

'I found I could count and follow steps,' he recalled, 'and my body is very loose and supple. I could do all the moves I was taught to do.'

After getting his architect's qualifications, he got a job offer to practise in Sydney. 'I worked with a firm there for a year or more, but my heart wasn't in it. I'm what my father would call a dilettante. I spent my free time with this dance company downtown. I danced for them and made myself useful generally. One day, I was asked to choreograph something for them. I found I had a knack for it and soon became quite good. Then I decided to set up my own company and call it One Extra Dance Company, because Sydney already has too many of them. One more wouldn't hurt.'

It didn't take long for the audience to discover his choreographic talent and dance critics to toast him. Yet success didn't sit well with Kaitai, as I found out later.

He took a sabbatical from his company and flew to Hong Kong on a weekend in September. By that time, I already had the cast in place. He had expected an audition, but I told him we didn't have many mime actors to choose from, and Philip would be the top pick anyway. For the female lead, I told him I'd found someone perfect for the role. He said that's not the way he would conduct it but would live with it, just as he did when he was shown our spartan guestroom where we'd put up Desmond. Later he would tell Lindzay it was haunted.

I saw Lindzay Chan in a ballet performance at City Hall. Throughout the show, I had my eyes only on her. Eurasian, she has the best of both worlds: jet-black hair, Greek statuesque profile, and porcelain skin. I could see her playing Yu Lian, the wife and muse in *Six Chapters of a Floating Life*. With her Caucasian features, she might not have the physical likeness one would expect for this role, but she emanated a luminosity of grace and gentle kindness. That's how I imagined Yu Lian on stage.

Years later, I asked Lindzay why she had agreed to take the role. 'You were already a well- known ballerina. You didn't know me, and I don't think you knew who Philip and Kaitai were either. You got a cold call from me, and you said yes right away. Why?'

'I'd been with Hong Kong Ballet for ten years,' she said. 'I always like to try something new. To see if I can do it. Also, you know, it's always nice to be asked.'

Kaitai wasted no time. He got down to business as soon as we finished his welcome lunch. He fired the first salvos of questions:

'A mime show doesn't use dialogue. Is there still going to be a script? Can we use spoken words?

Do you see it as a period piece in Chinese costumes?

Or contemporary?'

I said there was no script, only a story outline. That wasn't comforting to hear, as we were to start rehearsals the following week. The truth is I'd never written a mime script. It was my concept, if you can call it that. I'd read the book a few times and knew it well. That was about all I had to offer.

'The plot is simple and easy enough to follow. Why don't we do it as a one-act play with six scenes?' I suggested. 'I can write a synopsis based on the original text.'

After I showed him my notes and some whimsical ideas, he started to interrogate me as though I had committed more than one crime.

'Why are you doing this show?' Those facile answers – because we were commissioned, or to promote mime – wouldn't do. 'There has to be something in the story that resonates with you. What do you want to say? What does it mean to you?'

Even though the word 'love' doesn't come up once in the book, the relationship between Shen Fu and Yu Lian makes a convincing case of it. Not only is it a thing of beauty, but it's also resistant to the coarseness of everyday life and stands the test of time. Compare this with the brevity and short shelf life of modern-day romance. I found in a quote attributed to Ring Lardner, an American writer, that the condition in which love can thrive is when a man and a woman catch sight of one another and fall in love immediately, while they're sitting on trains moving in opposite directions. Nowadays, we've become cynical and have lost faith in love that endures.

Kaitai used that for the opening scene: Lindzay's Yu Lian in a beautiful flowing Chinese gown is being conveyed across the stage on a swathe of white silk. She's gazing at the audience, accompanied by a voice-over commentary of the Ring Lardner train moment.

Once this contemporary reference was found and set the tone, the rest began to fall into place. We combed the text for the most memorable scenes and spoken lines. Kaitai was giving me a master class and conducting rehearsals at the same time.

In rehearsals, Lindzay fit right in. 'Kaitai taught me a lot,' she said. 'He gave me the tools that would be useful for other works.' Lindzay went on to win a best actress award for the movie *To Live* (1992).

But Philip had a tough time trying to meet the physical demands as a dancer. Trained in classical mime, he used a different body language that Kaitai had to adjust to. Kaitai was accustomed to working with his own professional dancers and to having his way. He demanded a lot from his cast and was not about to coddle Philip. He pushed him to his limits.

Actress Rita Wong, an addition to the cast – she was a nurse by profession and an aspiring dancer – played her several vignette parts beautifully. According to Philip, she was always cheerful on set even when everyone got tired and testy.

Instead of the implicit silence of mime, Kaitai filled it with music. He chose from 'Songs of the Auvergne', a song collection by French composer Joseph Cantaloupe, sung by Victoria de Los Angeles with Orchestre Des Concerts Lamoureux and excerpts from Law Wing Fai's composition. A soundtrack was made with the help of Richard Porteous of Radio Television Hong Kong (RTHK). It wasn't just to dance to – more than that, it painted a special mood for the piece. The music sung in an old French dialect sat well with the Qing dynasty romance.

Kaitai also did the set design. This was when Lena Lee came on board. She had just joined the Academy for Performing Arts. Before that she was the Stage Manager of Chung Ying Theatre Company. We'd connected through Veronica Needa, who later performed her solo debut at the Fringe and was well known for her Playback Theatre. Lena and Kaitai hit it off right away. They built a working relationship spanning a decade and four productions. She was more than a stage manager: she was there to realise Kaitai's concepts on stage, no matter how implausible they might seem.

To create the effects of a distant past, he framed the action with a rectangular white Marley mat, which can be hard to find as it usually comes in black, but Lena managed to source one second-hand. It made everything seem ethereal in the reflected lighting. The set was made up of a few simple props, primarily a plinth that was used as a low writing desk that converted into a bed and then into a rowing boat – like toys in the hands of imaginative children.

It opened to a full house at the City Hall Theatre on Monday, 19 October 1987. I sat in the audience instead of wringing my hands nervously backstage. I had also stayed away from the dress rehearsal, so I didn't know what to expect until the opening scene. I watched, got lost in it, and when it was over an hour later, I felt I had lived a lifetime of indescribable beauty. Coming to the end of the show – the heart-breaking scene of Shen Fu mourning the passing of Yu Lian, played to Samuel Barber's lachrymose 'Adagio for Strings' – the audience applauded, thunderously, or so I thought. I looked around the auditorium to savour the moment. I saw David Li, who'd stepped down as chair the previous year, sitting by himself, a couple of rows in front of me. I waved at him but he seemed lost in thought.

Later after we got home, Margaret told me how much she had enjoyed it. 'This is going to be a classic. Well done!' she exclaimed. 'By the way, I saw David in the audience. I think he was wiping tears from his eyes. He must have been so moved.'

I never found out if he'd cried over the tragic beauty of our show or because the Dow Jones Index had fallen over 1,000 points on that infamous Black Monday.

Three rave reviews came out, in the English *and* Chinese press. That they were written by the directors of three dance companies was particularly validating.

We took *Six Chapters* on tour, invited by the legendary composer and impresario Shu Po Yun, as one of the inaugural shows of the National Chiang Kai-shek Cultural Centre (later renamed National Theatre and Concert Hall, Taipei). The venue is the size of a grand theatre. The scenes played on the vast stage were like something you'd see from the wrong end of a telescope, or a stamp on an envelope. It sold out three consecutive nights. The opera glasses provided for the audience in the new theatre must've helped.

This was followed by the Macau Forum. The Portuguese show title alone, *Seis Capitulos de Uma Vida Flutuante*, was poetry to my ear. Then Adelaide, Sydney, and back to Hong Kong for another run at the new Ngau Chi Wan Civic Centre Theatre and eventually Shouson Theatre Arts Centre.

During the second summer of the pandemic, while writing this, I gave Lindzay a call. She was in quarantine in London: 'What do you remember from that time in Adelaide?' I asked.

'Such a long time ago!' she said. 'I remember how free I felt. It was such a wonderful experience. Kaitai taught me such a lot. I also remember watching *Mahabharata* [Peter Brook's all-nighter production] in the old quarry outside the city. You brought along a large suitcase stuffed with blankets and cushions. At dawn, it got freezing cold; we couldn't have survived without them.'

Three years later I invited Kaitai back to direct another show, which also premiered at City Hall. *The Lament of Sim Kim* (1989), a grim tale about infanticide that I made up, is set in a dirt-poor village where the men go abroad to look for work. The village folk, in order to preserve their male offspring, drown baby girls. This time, I was more prepared, with the dialogues, scene descriptions and whatnot. This part of our story with Kaitai would have to wait.

148

chapter 8

UP AND RUNNING

THE ROOFTOP STUDIO went on for about five years, by which time most of the artists had either left or moved on to something else. It was around the time that our de facto landlord, Government Property Agency (GPA), proposed to draw up a lease with us.

It was at this junction that Lorette introduced me to an Australian couple who were catering from home. 'Their cooking is very delicious,' she said. 'You must try it.'

In their late twenties, Michelle Garnaut and Greg Malouf had arrived from Melbourne to try their luck in Hong Kong. Michelle had had a stint at Christian Romberg's La Crêperie as a short-order cook. She told me that, a few times, while mopping up the place, she got electric shocks because the sockets were fixed much too close to the floor. Fed up, she quit, and that's why she and Greg had started their home catering business.

They invited me and other guests to their flat. They sat us down on the floor around a low table and served us a snack-sized tasting dinner on mismatched plates and cutlery. It was, as Lorette said, delicious. They were pitching to set up a restaurant at the Fringe Club.

Everything was hinged on getting our lease signed. We still had some way to go in raising the money necessary to replace the missing windows and doors. We could only talk tentatively about their ideas, but we showed them the space anyway. They were very excited when they finally saw it and said they'd come up with some design sketches and a business plan.

Weeks later Michelle returned, ashen faced. Greg had had a heart attack and had to be flown back home for medical care. She wrote from Melbourne to say she had to be there to look after Greg. His doctor told him that if he wanted to live another day, he shouldn't work in a restaurant again. It was quite a shock. He was only twenty-eight, the picture of health. What a disappointment for them to have to drop their plan, their dream.

It might have been the end of the story, but four months later, we heard from Michelle again. She was in Hong Kong. She had come back to restart the project by herself. This time, she was prepared: she'd got herself a financial backer in tow with the design architect Hugh Zimmern and mural artist Paola Dindo to draw Grecian figures on the walls that have survived two world wars.

Michelle named the restaurant M at the Fringe and picked the part of the building that had been used as the Dairy Farm taipan's living quarters and, later on, our office. It's a lovely space with high ceilings framed by the original mouldings, wrap-around tall windows, and a fireplace that still breathes.

We now had to move our office to the former staff's quarters on the rooftop to make room for her. The only way to the roof was to climb up the fire escape on the outside of the building.

We had to install a proper staircase on the inside. To do that, we had to cut an opening in the concrete floor – a major operation. Again, we turned to Nick Ratcliffe for help. He supervised the work and roped in two of his work buddies: the architect Scott Findlay and the quantity surveyor Brian Dingwall. Two Scots, two angels in disguise.

We managed to raise $780,000 – the price of a flat in Taikoo Shing at the time – to meet the costs for the structural works and fenestration, a new word for me, which basically means restoring the windows and fixing the doors. This marked the beginning of multiple phases of renovations, fifteen in all, spanning over thirty-eight years, converting the old building and giving it a new purpose.

All of the renovations were done not only with the consent of the authorities but also the custodian spirits of the place. Sometimes, while working late at night, I could feel them traipsing around the place. I wanted to think that they were giving me nods of approval.

M at the Fringe had become a talking point. On the opening night, the guests took readily to its eclectic decor, the stunning mural drawings on Tuscan terracotta walls by Paola Dindo, and the Mediterranean-style dishes on the menu. The most admired piece of furniture was the three-legged cello-back chairs with seductive curves. The guests, warmed by the wine and food, relaxed into boisterous exchanges of conversations. Looking around the room, my eyes were transfixed on a guest who, leaning back, slipped and fell in slow motion to the floor. He picked himself and the elegant chair up, both unharmed. Nobody paid much attention to this until it was repeated at another table. This time it happened to a lady whose companion caught her just in time, but her chair tipped over and made a loud crashing noise. It made for one of those Man Ray Dada moments. Soon afterwards, the chairs were removed and sent back to the factory to be fixed: two additional legs were added for extra support. For many years, these five-legged chairs, inelegant as they looked, stood firm and served the customers well.

Getting her start and having nineteen years of steady support from the Fringe, Michelle went on to develop her business in China, setting up M on the Bund and Capital M. Meanwhile, the restaurant and the other food and beverages outlets that we operated ourselves generated streams of steady income. This allowed us to run our facilities under our own steam without having to rely solely on public funding as non-profit arts organisations tend to do.

Since there were no other places like ours, we soon became popular with artists who wanted to try out new material or make their debuts. During the Fringe Festival and at other times, we gave them free rein to create. Our motto was: we don't necessarily agree with what you say, but we defend your right to say it. The only time we ever cancelled a show was when a performance artist, as part of his act, stuffed a live fish into a blender and turned it on in front of the audience. No cruelty to animals or human beings, physically or mentally, was our only bottom line.

It was plain sailing for us all the way until it struck a reef, ironically, after we hit a $24 million jackpot. Our relationship with Michelle turned sour quickly, like milk on a hot day. What really happened? I mustn't get ahead of my story.

'Friends of mine told me I must have been Chinese in my past lives,' Lorette wrote in a letter to me. She wanted to come back for a visit and to introduce her son, Yoshi, to us. I didn't know she was dying from a rare form of cancer. Lorette passed away in Amsterdam, some time afterwards. If I'd known it was the last time we'd see each other, we would've spent more time together, instead of being side-tracked by work and other trivia and frittering away our last chance together. It's one of life's if-I-had-known regrets that keeps coming back to haunt me.

Backtrack to 1988. We kept our end of the bargain to 'render the building wind and watertight'. In the following year, GPA drew up a tenancy agreement to lease to us the Dairy Farm Cold Storage Warehouse at 2 Lower Albert Road, South Block, Central. It had been five years of squatting and flying by the seats of our pants. All the while, we kept several irons in the fire.

On my second visit to Adelaide, Peter showed me his favourite parts of the city and introduced me to his friend Andy, a clairvoyant. I told her I wanted to start an entertainment magazine, like *Time Out* in London, or *Pariscope*. I thought every big city should have one. It'd certainly fill a gap in Hong Kong. But I knew nothing about publishing.

Andy lived in a bright and airy flat near the beach. She dealt me a hand of tarot cards and gave me a reading. Looking into the future, she told me she saw clouds rising from a valley. I liked that image and took it as an auspicious sign. I let the idea brew in my head, not acting on it until a year later. By that time, I had come up with the name for the entertainment guide – *Night & Day* – lifted from a song by Cole Porter. I also set up a company called Rumutang 如沐堂, whose meaning was borrowed from the Chinese saying, 'like bathing in the spring wind 如沐春風'. It turned out that my clairvoyant friend wasn't far off the mark. Water is a Chinese symbol for money and, in this particular case, a fair amount of it would go down the drain, as water tends to do in a bathroom.

LIFE ON THE FRINGE

A bilingual guide would serve both a Chinese and an English readership. We all wanted to know what's on, I thought. By reaching more people, it'd create a wider circulation, thus more income. Common sense logic. I took a trip to London to meet with one of the founders of *Time Out – Arts & Entertainment Guide*. He readily gave me some pointers and reminisced how, after a long day at work, he'd make his rounds in the West End handing out the guide, free of charge, to the theatre audience. 'Give it a go,' he said and wished me luck.

After returning to Hong Kong, I hunkered down to produce a dummy copy that took me a few months. This was used as a calling card to find investors and advertisers. Meanwhile, I got Eric Wear, a Rhodes Scholar, conceptual artist, and art historian, to be my English editor, and Lo Shu To, editor of a highly regarded Chinese literary journal. Helen Cheung, an arts writer, was hired as the full-time all-rounder. She compiled the event calendar, wrote filler articles, and, most importantly, chased the deadlines. The rest of us, with day jobs, would come after work. It was pretty intense, but we were all fired up. We wanted to stake a claim on this uncharted territory: to be first to publish an event-listing magazine in Hong Kong. There had already been a TV guide around for some time, but that didn't deter us.

Dummy copies were printed and sent out to gauge readers' responses. I showed it to some potential investors. I found three equal-share backers, each sinking $60,000 into it. I committed double that amount in order to have the controlling shares. The seed money in hand, *Night & Day* was all ready to roll. Nearly everyone I talked to thought this a sure win. All except John Sherwin, a young administrative officer I'd met. He was blunt, 'Bilingual publications don't work.' We did a layout with two front

154

covers, so that you could open it from either way. 'So unwieldy,' John said, flipping and turning it over to prove his point. I maintained it was a brilliant idea. In any case, it was just one person's opinion; everyone else told us this would work for Hong Kong readers, so we went ahead.

I didn't realise that this would mean more than double the amount of work in writing, editing, and pagination. I figured that bilingual readers like me wouldn't want to read the same article twice. Yet, the two different language sections required their own writing and editorial teams, and because of this, instead of publishing weekly, we could only manage it bi-weekly. We lost momentum as well as the reader's attention span.

Someone experienced with the magazine business told me he was surprised that we hadn't lined up the advertisers before launching. That's very risky, he warned, almost like skydiving without a parachute. I argued that this wasn't just any commercial magazine. This one had a social mission. I couldn't see why anyone in the world did not want to support it, especially those with a stake in the arts. *Night & Day* would draw more audiences to their doors. Who wouldn't want that?

We lined up theatre critics, social commentators, trend spotters, and food writers to contribute to the different sections. We held lofty principles: no advertorials, no pandering, no personal vendettas. We wanted to be honest, firm, and fair with our opinions. When someone sent us an article that made harsh but valid criticisms on the operation of the theatres managed by the then Urban Council, we went ahead and printed it. We weren't aware of the repercussions. The gorilla in the room, the Urban Council cultural section, pretty much ran the shows in town. The magazine needed their blessings as much as their paid ads on our pages.

One morning, I made a courtesy call on the big kahuna in her office, with a copy of the *Night & Day*, hot off the press, in hand. She sat in a swivel chair in her large corner office, her back to the windows that overlooked the harbour. She waved me to sit down on the low sofa, and I set the copy on the uncluttered desk in front of her. She gave it a desultory flip-through; while listening to my sales pitch, she took out a nail clipper. It went 'click, click, click,' while I struggled with my presentation.

My calls on other advertisers met with no better results though not the same treatment. Any new launch, if it doesn't catch on right away, will have to make a much bigger effort later to get to where it wants to go. I didn't want it to stall. The magazine was sold at the newsstands, so I went around trying to talk the vendors into displaying them on their top shelves. Usually, I'd find them way down on the bottom shelves. This is what's usually done with new print that hasn't yet picked up on sales. Sometimes I'd pretend to be a customer and repeat the name *Night & Day Entertainment Guide* enough times to get them to think a lot of people were looking for it. I sweated it out, pounding the pavement like this on summer days. With no marketing budget to speak of, I thought this was the rite of passage every rookie entrepreneur had to go through – handing out copies in the streets and getting rejected countless times. We thought of giving it away instead of selling it for $8 a copy. But we were proud and fell for the so-called endowment bias, giving it a higher value than what it's really worth. We also thought if you got something for free, you wouldn't think twice about throwing it into the dumpster.

We pushed on valiantly for thirty-two weeks to produce sixteen issues, until there was nothing left in the food truck to keep the troops going. In all, this venture endured for a year and a half, including the prep work. Not only did it cost me, but it knocked me down a few pegs in terms of my belief in my own ability. What I learned from this expensive lesson wasn't clear. I just knew it was time for me to have a reset.

Dimon Liu, a lecturer of architecture, introduced me to Richard Lanier from New York. Richard ran the Rockefeller Fellowship from an office on Madison Avenue and invited me to visit the United States. 'If you accept, you'll be our last Fellow,' he said with a smile. 'And our first grantee.' The fellowship would be renamed Asian Cultural Council, as it is known today.

I arrived on a late flight on a Saturday. My first night in New York ran hot and cold. I checked into a hotel room in SoHo that had exposed hot water pipes on one side of my bed and the air conditioner on the other, both on simultaneously. Police and ambulance sirens took turns puncturing the night, reminding me that some human lives somewhere were in danger. The graffiti I saw on every blank space in and on the outside of subway cars told me this was no place for a flaneur after dark, unless I had a death wish.

Sunday, my free day. Venturing uptown, everything looked very different from the way it did the night before. I did a tourist round of the sights. Hollywood movie scenes complete with soundtracks – showing the side of New York where people fall in love, live a beautiful life, and die a beautiful death – were superimposed on what I was seeing of the city. Leaving Central Park and heading between Lexington and Park, I found myself in front of the Waldorf Astoria, its name in gilt-edge Roman letters inscribed above the grand entrance. It's what I remembered from the movie *The Eddie Duchin Story*, where the eponymous pianist and bandleader – played by the dark and handsome Tyrone Power – woos the dreamily beautiful Kim Novak with his syrupy rendition of a Chopin nocturne. I also remembered crying in the dark cinema, as a twelve-year-old would, seeing their ill-fated romance frustrated by the tragic circumstances of life. This was etched in my memory as the quintessential lush life in Manhattan.

Uncertain that I should show my face there in my crumpled shirt and unpolished shoes, I slipped in through the door held open by a uniformed doorman – whose eyes I tried to avoid – into the Art Deco lobby.

Everywhere I turned was lit up in gold and even the marble glowed; I thought of the epigram in the opening chapter of *The Great Gatsby*:

> *Then wear the gold hat, if that will move her;*
> *If you can bounce high, bounce for her too,*
> *Till she cry, 'Lover, gold-hatted,*
> *high-bouncing lover, I must have you!'*

I chose a table on the mezzanine overlooking the lobby and ordered a Manhattan cocktail. A jazz trio appeared and started playing something by Cole Porter who, in his perennial black tie with a white gardenia in the buttonhole, had entertained guests in the hotel's penthouse suite. Tasting the bittersweet tawny cocktail, I made a silent toast to F. Scott Fitzgerald, another doomed romantic, who wrote about his maudlin moment in New York:

> *...riding in a taxi one afternoon between very tall*
> *buildings under a mauve and rosy sky; I began*

*to bawl because I had everything I wanted and
knew I would never be happy again.*

Leaving the Waldorf Astoria and my overblown feelings behind, I went back to walking the city on its broad sidewalks. Some lights had already come on, profiling the majestic facades of the buildings on both sides of the avenue. I passed St. Patrick's Cathedral. With its gothic spires and lofty stained glass windows, it rose from among the crouching mass of commercial buildings like a miracle to the city pilgrims. It drew me away from the hedonism in the air. Inside, vast and empty of worshippers, only traces of the incense from an earlier mass lingered. There was a choir in rehearsal, the King's College Choir from Cambridge. They were rehearsing Alegri's 'Miserere' and sending their high notes to the upper reaches of the arches. Sitting by myself in the pew, I didn't just hear the holy music, but I could feel it as though there was really a soul in me. I remained in this state of grace until the choir rehearsal was well over. Suddenly I was hit by a sharp pang of hunger as my jet lag kicked in. I reached for the guidebook in my shoulder bag to look for a good place to eat.

I took the subway to Little Italy, next door to Chinatown. On the train, I sat next to two women. One was telling the other things you'd only hear in a confessional: how she was trying to disentangle herself from an unholy relationship. Where I come from, I realised, we seldom air our feelings openly, much less make public disclosure of our intimate life. The pairings of the sacred and the profane, prudishness and exhibitionism, private and public – this mental picture of New York, full of bold contrasts, was like my hotel room blowing hot and cold on my first night.

LIFE ON THE FRINGE

I ended that day with a pasta dish. I chose a restaurant that looked like the one in *The Godfather*. The friendly waiter approved of my choice of spaghetti with meatballs, saying it was what the Mafia bosses who come to the restaurant order every time. He also asked if my name was Bruce.

Come Monday morning, I went looking for Mr. Richard Lanier's office on Madison Avenue. I was given a warm welcome. Richard took me to the pantry, offered to make me a cup of tea, and introduced me to everyone, who already knew my name and where I came from. He and his associate, Mr. Ralph Samuelson, a Japanophile and shakuhachi player, took me through my proposed itinerary and suggested people I should meet. They had arranged an apartment in Chelsea for my stay.

I started to make my round of visits. From Lincoln Centre to BAM, Public Theatre, Dance Workshop, and La MaMa Theatre. From the Metropolitan and Guggenheim Museums to Bell Tower, Kitchen, and cutting-edge holes-in-the-wall art spaces that New York had chock-a-block. For my evening diversions, I checked out Paul Taylor's latest masterpiece the dance world had waited eagerly for; *Les Misérables* had just opened on Broadway with Colm Wilkinson as Jean Valjean; and this New Music phenomenon by the name of Philip Glass was performing in a SoHo loft. Nothing I asked for seemed too much to my host. All the doors of New York were open for me.

Richard invited me to his home for dinner. I felt flattered. It was a big deal to me. He made it seem like something he'd do every day. The evening with Richard and his family was like a page from a book of Norman Rockwell illustrations. Simple and wholesome: both the meal and everything about him, his model children and hospitable wife. After dinner, over a cup of Chinese tea – he took special care to make it for his Asian guest – he said to me: 'Make sure you'll have everything you need for your stay in New York. Don't feel pinched, because the grant is on the lean side. So, we'd like to offer you something extra – a book allowance. It's called that, but you can use it to buy anything you like. You don't have to account for it.'

On my last day, after returning to New York from a brief visit to Boston to check out I. M. Pei's White Cube at MIT, among other sites, I went to say my goodbyes. It had been a long time since I had been away from home for this long. I had become accustomed to things – taking American breakfasts of bagels, pastrami, blueberry pancakes, and nonstop coffee at the corner deli; finding my way on the subway; jogging around the lake in Central Park. I felt I could come here to live anytime, maybe in a loft somewhere, overlooking the Hudson. I felt I hadn't been looked after so well that I had to be torn in half to leave. I asked Richard if I had to submit a report to account for my fellowship grant. 'Only if you'd like to,' he replied. 'But it's not a requirement. We'd like to hear what you think and what this has done for you.'

I didn't write up a report and, to this day, this outstanding item still weighs on my mind. Sometimes, it's hard not to remember generosity and kindness given to you without expecting anything in return.

chapter 9

ROMPING AWAY

BY THE TIME I got back to Hong Kong, David had stepped down and we had a new Chairman. It was none other than the amazing Dr Ronald Ding Bong Leung – a medical doctor, a serving councillor with the now defunct Urban Council (that looked after public amenities, arts, and entertainment), as well as head of his family-owned bank. David (later Sir David) couldn't have found someone with a more impressive curriculum vitae and social clout to step into his shoes. What he probably didn't know was, behind all those impressive credentials, Ronald harboured a childlike love for fun and play, and lots of energy to spare. Ronald took to the Fringe like a steak to a sizzling pan.

Our first encounter was at the headquarters of Kwong On Bank, founded by his money-wise father. It was located on Queen's Road Central, bordering Sheung Wan, the business quarter that had seen little change since pre-war days; it was crowded with the same shops selling Chinese herbal medicine and dried seafood. He told me to meet him there after lunch for our first pre-board meeting briefing session.

LIFE ON THE FRINGE

It was baking hot that day. I made my way through the dense lunchtime crowd to the bank, slow cooked under the suit and tie I put on especially for the meeting with my new chairman. I pushed through the revolving door, relished the air conditioning inside, announced myself at the reception, and was taken through a corridor to a back room by a staffer in uniform who knocked on what looked like a hefty burglar-proof door. Ronald answered it himself, dressed in his socks, a white singlet, boxer shorts and suspenders. His shirt, tie, trousers, and jacket were put neatly aside on a vintage clothes horse. The room was cavernous and dim, probably unchanged from when the bank first opened its doors for business half a century ago.

There was a mustard-coloured settee flanked by two large and well-worn upholstered chairs. He told me to pick a seat. He himself returned to recline on an old Chinese hardwood divan, saying, 'I just took a nap. Didn't want to crease my clothes, so I took them off.' Then he added reassuringly, 'It's okay; I'm a doctor.'

Ronald is of medium build, tanned, bespectacled, comfortable in his own skin, and unafraid to speak his mind. He wouldn't have stood out from his lot if he hadn't that playful sparkle in his eye. We were a good fit, for the Fringe is supposed to be fun and playful. During his ten-year reign as Chair, we rarely locked horns. Maybe once or twice. Otherwise, we had a ball.

One of the things that an arts board does is fundraise for the organisation that it serves. In the beginning, we did it like everyone else: hire a banquet hall in a hotel to put on a fundraising dinner, sell tables and raffle tickets, and auction off some art pieces and oddities. You often find that most of the money raised has gone to pay for the food, decorations, and entertainment. Also, the fundraising committee, if there is one, can be high maintenance.

For all the trouble, it makes you wonder.

For the paying guests, attending these charity gigs can be a bit of a chore. It's all done for good causes, of course. So, you'll hold your tongue when you're served some corrosive wine and bland, lukewarm food. At every turn you're offered things you don't really want but are expected to buy for the cause. The person sitting beside you through the proceedings of the evening may be as bored as you are and has lost the will to converse – and you both wish you were someplace else. A day or so later, after getting over your stiff back from sitting too long, you say to yourself, never again. I'll just write a cheque next time.

We didn't want any of that inflicted on our guests; we wanted to make it as fun and as painless as possible for people to part with their money. We came up with some zany ideas, befitting the Fringe, and Ronald gave them a good run for their money. We must have chalked up ten of those, at the rate of one per year, while he served as Chair.

In the beginning, it was a rather tame event, just like the others; and the dress code was the vanilla smart casual, and everything done with propriety. Partying was not something I knew a lot about. I was brought up with the notion that celebrating one's birthday was by adding an extra dish to the dinner table. Cutting birthday cake, blowing out the candles, and singing 'Happy Birthday to You' was all unknown to me in my childhood.

I told Cat that to make our fundraising swing, we had to look for people who loved to party and had the party genes in them. Of course, if we had the money, we could hire the help; there were always event organisers out there. Yet, while you can buy the know-how, you can't buy love: the love you put into what you do, whether cooking sweet-and-sour pork, painting the Sistine Chapel,

LIFE ON THE FRINGE

or hosting a memorable night out.

There's a young actress who attended our theatre workshop. Colette Koo had well- proportioned features, almond-shaped-eyes, and looked a tad androgynous to make a convincing Peter Pan in a Christmas pantomime. Colette told me that her father was a doctor specialising in treating male sexual dysfunction and that she never wanted a desk job. She had worked as a production assistant for a film director but preferred to be in front of the camera; and sure enough, she soon went off to London to study drama.

We reconnected when I saw her in *Lysistrata* at the Young Vic Theatre in London. She lived in a ground floor flat in Bayswater which doubled as a props room. I was impressed that she could sew and make things and had a good eye for fabric. After she returned to Hong Kong and we were looking for a party planner, I asked if she'd be interested. She jumped at the offer. She also introduced me to Greg Durham of House of Siren in SoHo, a ground floor shop in an old low-rise block near Hollywood Road. Next door was a Buddhist nunnery, and passing by, you could smell burning incense and hear nuns chanting for the departed.

Doe-eyed, fair-skinned, painted nails, never seen without make-up, Greg could do a quick change from drama queen to boy next door on a whim. He made his neighbours' shaved heads and flowing robes seem normal. He went about calling everyone darling and punctuating his heightened sentences with limp-wrist and hands-on-waist gestures. He was a real darling himself. His shop carried enough stock of feather boas, hats and capes, strings of plastic pearls, and burlesque queens on platform heels to deck out a fleet.

Between Greg and Colette, our annual fundraisers at times tipped the balance between proper and risqué. They became more

166

like fancy-dress parties. We came up with themes and dress codes to match. Some of the fundraising items put on auction were quite imaginative: Kaiseki dinner prepared and served at your home by a celebrity, Ronald appearing as a dancing Michael Jackson upon your order, or flying a jumbo jet.

For several years, Hans Lodders of Agfa Film was a sponsor. He and his wife were arts patrons and they loved to party. Hans had a side business, and when I told him we were looking for a fun theme for our fundraising party, he volunteered to provide gifts for auction and to take home. He gave us an address in Kwun Tong and told us to go and choose anything on display there. 'Anything you want,' he insisted.

Hans didn't have time to explain things before going on his urgent business trip, so we hired a goods van and asked Colette and Greg to come along. We expected slide projectors, photography equipment, film rolls, and that sort of thing, in line with his business. We made our way to a large factory showroom where people were busy unpacking cartons. On the display shelves and tables were sex toys of all varieties, shapes, and sizes. I didn't know Hans had such a distinctive sideline. We had a field day taking our pick. When we informed Ronald what the fundraising theme might be, he blithely replied, 'I'll dress up as a condom.'

It didn't take long for Ronald to rise from the ranks to become Chairman of the Urban Council, the de facto mayor of Hong Kong. We were all so happy for him. As the saying goes: 'A rising tide lifts all boats'. Together, we took the Fringe on a romp.

By that time, the Fringe Festival had made its way into the Hong Kong cultural calendar. It caught the attention of audiences who were more adventurous. With Fringe acts, you didn't quite know what to expect. We kept our doors wide open. Any group

Wong Ka Kui 黃家駒, singer-songwriter of the band Beyond, rehearsing at Rotunda, Exchange Square for a Festival Fringe fundraiser, November 1985

Left to right: Catherine Lau, Elaine Wong and Colette Koo surrounded by the Hunting Party (Australia) in costumes and on stilts at Fringe fundraising party

Past Fringe board members at fundraising dinner.
Left to right: Ronald Leung, David Li, E. Barrie Wiggham

Left to right: Pan Shih, Benny Chia, and New York–based harpist Daphne Hellman at Festival Fringe 1996

Left to right: Osbert Lam, Catherine Lau, Christopher Doyle at the Montblanc exhibition – Black, Round and Erotic – in 1999

New York singer-rocker-accordionist Phoebe Legere
performing at the Festival Fringe (circa 1995)

Roaring 20's Jazz Age Party, Fringe Dairy, 2018

Proustian afternoon tea at Fringe Dairy (circa 2020)

ROMPING AWAY

of any standard could pitch for a show. There are bound to be some duds among the lot, and to keep audiences keen enough to take some chances, we did two things. First, we put the seasoned players side by side with the newbies and promoted them equally. This way, we gave the punters the chance to pick their own winners, to choose what shows to see. The benefits for the players were that they could raise their standards; as in sports, you tend to perform better competing against better contenders. The effect of rubbing shoulders with the pros is for the newbies to aspire to be pros themselves someday.

Another incentive for the audience was that we made sure that there were enough attractions in the draw. The Edinburgh Fringe, Festival d'Avignon Off, and Adelaide Fringe by sheer scale were bound to have a good percentage of shows worth seeing. We, by contrast, had to cultivate our small patch with husbandry and care. To make sure I could have a choice crop to pick from, I headed for Edinburgh in August, when the Fringe took over the entire city.

One thing I've noticed is that Fringe Festivals tend to thrive better in cities with a smaller population – where everything is within walking distance, and everyone involved stands to gain something. The terroirs of big cities don't seem to favour their growth. London and New York have tried but could only manage to cast wimpy ripples in their big ponds. Yet over in the Scottish capital, it makes a big splash every summer. I made my first visit in 1985 and would return for fifteen consecutive years.

Those first four weeks when the Edinburgh Fringe was on were intense. I watched how it managed to move the arts from the sidelines of everyday life to centre stage, even into daily conversation. Like it or not, during this time, there was no escape from it. Every pub, shop window, empty wall space on street corners was plastered with posters of Fringe events. Shows found their ways into every nook and cranny – school halls, garages, and even people's living rooms were used as makeshift venues. Hotels and popular restaurants filled up so quickly they had to turn customers away at the door. Households with spare rooms tidied them up to rent to performers and visitors who flocked to the city in droves. Townsfolk who knew how to make a sandwich and a cup of tea would become vendors of pre-show quick bites. Those who didn't have a chance to tread the boards and glory in the spotlight also caught what they could of the theatre bug by helping out backstage or front of house. Everyone could get something out of it while the Fringe was on, even the couple who rented out their apartment to us on the Royal Mile - they couldn't stand the street noise and the spike of crowds in their city - told us they could use the extra income to buy themselves a nice trip to, well, Hong Kong.

But it wasn't always like this. My first impression of Edinburgh was coloured by a scattering of stories and images gleaned from books and old movies. Stepping out of the Waverley train station, the first thing that caught my eye was the castle. Sitting atop the dark cliffside of the hill, it lorded over the landscape sprawling at its feet. At night, when it's lit up, it rekindles the scenes of murder and scheming by the likes of the Macbeths and Bloody Mary, Queen of Scots. You could imagine how they had dispatched them in those echoey chambers and torch-lit corridors that they allegedly haunt to this day.

This plus what I could glean from *Treasure Island*, by Robert Louis Stevenson, the lauded storyteller and favourite son of Edinburgh. As a child, I had watched the 1934 movie adaptation in the courtyard of a Canossian convent one Sunday after evening mass. The nuns on Caine Road put it on at Christmas to entertain the children in our poor neighbourhood who couldn't afford any other celebration. The makeshift screen hung from a stone wall, fluttering when the wind came through the cracks. I could feel the blustering Scottish winter in my bones as I watched, slack-jawed, how Jim, the young and brave protagonist, played by Jackie Cooper, the prodigy screen actor of my age, went for pulse-raising adventures in the treacherous treasure hunt.

It wasn't all dark and sinister, though, now that I was in Edinburgh. Staring into the night sky, above the sea of chimney stacks on storybook Georgian buildings, I saw in my mind's eye Peter Pan and Tinkerbell flying with Wendy and her brothers in tow, linking hands, across the shining moon, heading for Neverland.

On my first day, I remember walking around in the Old Town looking for a place to have a bite and rest my feet. No blanket of fog rolled in from the coast. It was one of those long northern summer days, stretching into night with no end in sight. Not much was happening in the streets, and all the places seemed to have barricaded themselves behind big thick wooden doors for secret pleasures. I pushed open one to enter. It smelled of beer, fags, and chips. There was a wall of tall Scots in front of the bar counter having a pint and speaking in a loud Scottish brogue. I sheepishly sat down in an empty booth by the entrance. I had my first shepherd's pie, washed down with lukewarm ale.

I looked around the pub and took the measure of the things bobbing up in my head. The Edinburghers came across as people you'd have a hard time prying two words from, dour and Calvinist. But somehow, they let in the zany Fringe, once a year, to raise hell in its tracks, as a kind of self-administered antidote to alleviate their dourness. Over the years, as this slowly took effect like a personality-changing drug, and the city began to lighten up.

LIFE ON THE FRINGE

Activities started to spill over into the streets: buskers rounding up innocent bystanders, actors in costumes handing out leaflets of their shows, cafes going continental and outdoorsy. Edinburgh finally, as they say, had 'come out'.

I couldn't have made it this far west without the backing of the British Council, and Estella Tong, their doe-eyed, diminutive, soft-spoken Arts Officer who – seldom without a Camel cigarette (unfiltered and a favourite brand for long-haul night time truck drivers) between her dainty fingers – threw her weight, all eighty pounds of it, behind our plan to bring home, at any cost, the best acts we saw.

'We only had a small arts budget,' Estella recalled years later over *a dim sum lunch* at Nove@theFringe. 'Every year, we'd allocate a good part of it to support the Fringe. I went to Edinburgh on my summer leave. It was a busman's holiday. I'd make it to five, six Fringe shows a day. To separate the wheat from the chaff could be hard work. But fun and exciting, too.'

We would meet up after shows in a pub where artists and show-spotters hang out, and we were bound to hear about who was hot that week and the must-see shows. For Estella, any show fatigue could be done away with by a few pints. David Glass and Peta Lily would also come to that pub and would watch in awe and wonder as she chain-smoked her Camels while downing a bucketful of lager, all the while talking shop. 'Where does all that go,' David would ask, 'in that matchstick body?' So many years of working miracles on a shoestring budget meant Estella's radar for a good show was always spot on. So was her faith in what we did.

Before I took off for Edinburgh for the first time, Keith Statham and everyone else in the know said I must check out the Assembly Rooms – the prominent Fringe venue converted from a grand historical building in the town centre – and talk to William Burdett-Coutts. I called on Mr Burdett-Coutts and we met over a late breakfast. He introduced himself as Bill. He was (and still is) a tall and handsome man, with the good looks of a young Rex Harrison with lidded eyes that don't suffer fools and the slow-witted easily, both of which I must've appeared to be on that morning. Over the years, I'd watched many shows at the Assembly Rooms that I wanted to take home: Slava's *Snow Show*; *Kitchen*, the Korean Broadway hit of percussion and comedy; Steven Berkoff's solo performance of Edgar Allan Poe's *The Tell-Tale Heart*. They were mid-to-large-scale productions and would be snapped up by Festival directors and theatre agents. The Assembly Rooms was the Potemkin Steps for the Fringe acts to scramble over to the mainstream.

My consolation prize was getting Berkoff to have *yum cha* at the Luk Yu Teahouse on Stanley Street, when he was invited to perform at the Hong Kong Arts Festival. He turned out to be mild mannered, not at all fierce in-your-face as he appears on stage and in film. He was curious and interested in the tea and dim sum served and deflected my invitation to perform at the Fringe by introducing a very good actress, Linda Marlowe, who performed five of his short plays: *Decadence, Greek, East, Agamemnon*, and *From My Point of View*. There's no such thing as free *yum cha*, you know.

For a better catch, I shifted my attention to the smaller venues – such as the old Traverse in Grassmarket, Pleasance, and Richard Demarco Gallery. Traverse Theatre was named for the way its stage was placed: in the middle like an alley, the audience sitting on two sides. My guess is that it was designed this way not only because of space restrictions but by someone with a quirky idea. Having sat through a long performance, I had a stiff back and a sore backside, blaming the banquette seating that was more suited for monks to do their penance on. I brought this up with the lady in charge of the venue. 'We like to keep our audience from dozing off during our shows,' she said dourly. Later, the Traverse took over from this lyric opera project on Cambridge Street that hadn't completed construction and turned it into a swish theatre of glass and chrome. By then, alas, it had lost its signature traverse stage, along with its doze-proof seating.

The Pleasance was across the bridge, down and then up a knoll. Going into its cobblestoned courtyard – drizzling, chilly, windy, exposed – you'd feel that this was where the fragile Scottish summers had come short. It looked deserted, until you got inside. You'd find the pokey theatres and smoky bars packed with men and women in their raincoats and parkas, suspected of conspiring for Scottish independence.

The Richard Demarco Gallery showed art exhibitions and put on performances like no other. Richard, the man behind it whom the locals call Ricky, was always courting controversy by pushing limits. He supported Jimmy Boyle, a notorious gangster and condemned murderer turned sculptor, and got himself into trouble with the Scottish Arts Council, and in newspaper headlines, as an intrepid arts presenter.

He was always doing something to rile the straightlaced main festival by not following rules, while turning his back on the easy street of shallow, crowd-pleasing shows proliferating on the Fringe. Unlike others, he was not motivated by commercial success but by the excitement of the search for the new and extraordinary in the arts. He followed no other drumbeat but his own. For ideas, he looked to the far corners of Europe instead of to posh London and came up with Joseph Beuys, Marina Abramovic, Tadeusz Kantor,

ROMPING AWAY

Yvette Boszik, and others with names not easy to pronounce.

'I took the coach from town to a ferry pier with other ticket holders,' Cat recalled of the Macbeth that Richard presented on Inchcolm Island in the Firth of Forth. 'It began to rain and get dark. We got onto a ferry and were given blankets to keep warm. The three witches in costumes were on the ferry and started to play the opening scene to us. When we arrived at the island, we were led into a dark castle [the Inchcolm Abbey] by actors carrying torches. We're all wearing the same grey blankets that made us feel part of the cast. The scenes were played along the dark corridor, in the cells and the mess hall. I can still see and smell it to this day.'

Cat called on Richard in his office the next day. He greeted her formally, asked her to sit and wait, and then disappeared into his office in the next room to dictate a letter to her. He wrote to inform her that he would like to visit the Fringe in Hong Kong. 'I still don't understand why he didn't tell me to my face,' Cat recalled. 'I was sitting there all the time.'

Before 1997, Hong Kong was on many people's bucket lists. Travellers wanted to catch the final acts in one of the last British colonial outposts. When Richard finally came, he went everywhere by himself, giving his opinions on everything he saw. He thought Hong Kong looked in part like Venice. He showed me photographs he'd taken along the waterfront in Kennedy Town. He didn't believe any of the post-1997 doomsday talk. 'Just as Venice has done in the past,' he pontificated, 'mind you – many times – it resisted the absolute monarchists from turning the city into their chattel state. Hong Kong will prevail, eventually.'

Over the years, we had brought to our theatres some of the shows that Richard had presented at the Edinburgh Fringe. Many have been seared in my memory. I first saw Yvette Boszik perform in his gallery. She danced inside a sealed Perspex balloon until the oxygen ran out. She was dreamily beautiful, and her self-asphyxiation act kept the audience gasping on the edges of their seats for a whole hour. We flew her and her company from Budapest to perform *The Soiree*, a dance theatre adaptation of Jean-Paul Sartre's *No Exit*, which posits that being cooped up in a room with other people that you can't get away from is hell. Three actors dressed up for a costume ball told the story in dance and acrobatic slapstick, to Jean-Philippe Heritier's music. Yvette, like the temptress from *Les Liaisons Dangereuses*, was seductive, voluptuous, and mesmerising. 'In dance terms, it is masterly. As theatre, it holds the audience riveted,' Zelda Cawthorne wrote in the *South China Morning Post*.

Zofia Kalinska's *If I Am Medea* that played in Demarco's basement under a single five-watt light bulb dangling from the ceiling gave a different taste of East European theatre. It pushed poor theatre to its limits that we had no difficulty reaching. Kalinska was the lead actress of Tadeusz Kantor's Criot 2 Theatre. It was the darkest *Medea* I've ever seen, both in trawling the murky depths of the human soul and a very dim theatre.

Many of these shows literally wouldn't have been able to get off the ground if it hadn't been for the help we got from the British Airways (BA) as sponsor. Choi Fong, who was our main contact there, was herself interested in the arts. Cat also liked to mention that she'd used to be a BA flight attendant and a former colleague as she ironed out flight itineraries and schedules with Choi.

Offering free flights can be a big incentive for the performers to say yes. The other one was lodgings. We couldn't afford hotels; that's for sure. I was still reeling from the debacle of putting up Performance Exchange in a presidential suite. Even if we could pay, we didn't want them to fly in, do the shows, and then fly out the next day, as other festival presenters tend to do to save on hotels. Since we weren't paying them performance fees – we worked on a box-office split of seventy/thirty in the performers' favour – we wanted to offer something money can't buy. We'd spend time with them, get to know them, let them meet the locals, and do some sightseeing. That's what we enjoy doing anyway.

'I sent out letters to 500 members,' Cat recalled. 'All handwritten, asking if they would like to put up an artist in their spare bed or on their couch. Nobody thought this would work. "This is Hong Kong," they said. "No one has any room to spare. Even if they do, they don't want strangers in their tiny apartments."'

That turned out to be not true. We got a better-than-average response from our appeal letters. No artists who came here to do a show ever spent the night without a roof over their heads; members who, living near or far, welcomed them into their homes, often without question.

Peter Wong, a local journalist, offered his only bedroom in his cramped apartment in Sai Ying Pun. Sara Kendall left us the keys to her apartment on Garden Road filled with art objects. Gabriela and Peter Kennedy put up some strange ones. We knew it isn't to everyone's taste to let strangers into their homes. You have to have faith in humankind, a generous spirit, and game for a bit of adventure. During those chancy encounters, some had become friends, and some had fallen in love; we know of one wedding.

Our favourite story is bringing the fabulous Phoebe Legere, singer-rocker-accordionist from New York, into Professor Shih's house in Sandy Bay, Pok Fu Lam. There was no one around, only her pet dog. We had a set of the professor's keys but no clear instruction as to where her guest would stay. We looked around and found a room with the door open. That's it, we thought. We went inside, put her bags down and helped settle her in. The dog, a mature male pug, waddled in and looked at us woefully as only a pug can do, and without uttering a sound, jumped on to the bed, and stayed put. I shushed at him, but he turned his head away and refused to budge.

'He wants me,' Phoebe sighed. 'They all do.' We ceded the bed to Pug, retired to the living room, and waited for our host to return. In fact, Professor Shih had prepared another room for her guest. We knew we shouldn't have barged in on Pug's own room like that. No wonder he never cosied up to Phoebe like other men would do during her stay.

It was Daphne Hellman who brought Phoebe from the Lower East Side of Manhattan, with her bassist, Lyn Christie, to perform as an ensemble and on her own. There must be a fifty-year age gap between the two. Daphne played the jazz harp at the Village Gate with her trio, Hellman's Angels, for thirty years on a roll, a record run for jazz gigs. Phoebe played the electric guitar and the piano, and sang rock, country western, French chansons, and her own compositions. She had a four-octave vocal range and formidable instrumental skills that she liked to show off on stage, along with her mane of blond hair and proud curves.

Daphne stayed married to her third husband, Hsio Wen Shih, architect, writer, and the brother of Professor Shih, but kept her second married name, Hellman, because it made a good pun for her jazz trio.

On Daphne's first visit, we put her up in an apartment in Glenealy, a short walk from us. On the way, she asked to stop by a supermarket to pick up two sacks of oranges and a carton of Salem cigarettes. 'I'm fully loaded now,' she smiled contentedly. 'Got everything I needed.' She ate like a bird or lighter.

That's my first memory of Daphne, who performed at the Fringe, every year between 1989 and 2000. I remember reading about her in Peggy Guggenheim's memoir *Out of This Century*, describing her as beautiful – an adjective rarely used for other women in her book. She'd turned the heads of Max Ernst and Marcel Duchamp and other men in her day. Pushing 80 now, she looked stunning in a different way. She showed off the ravages of time on the chiselled bone structure of her face with dramatic make-up, while sporting a rag lady's look.

She didn't like to talk about the past, except about her friend Norman Mailer and her mother, heiress of the Seaboard National Bank, who'd raised her young daughter with a French governess, hoping to mould her into a society lady like those in a Henry James novel.

She never had a bad word for anybody. After downing a few drinks, she might just say, 'My mother had mucho money,' without going into detail. But it's clear that she didn't want the life of a socialite that her mother had wanted for her, conversing in French, playing the harp, becoming a trophy wife, mingling only with the rich and people of the same type. Instead, she lived a life without being dictated by money or the snobbish social registry of her class.

'She loved to do what she knew you weren't supposed to do,' her bassist, Lyn, once told *The New York Times* in an interview (2002).

Daphne knew how to roller skate and later took up skateboarding. Sometimes, she said, she'd skateboard to pick up a packet of cigarettes from the neighbourhood store. One year, while she was here to perform, she had a traffic accident: she was knocked down by a taxi while crossing the road. She was taken to Queen

Mary Hospital, where the doctor on duty at the ER told her she was lucky: nothing was broken this time. She was discharged, and Daphne went back to her apartment in Wan Chai to rest. In the middle of the night, her host called us: she was in terrible pain. We sent for an ambulance to take her to Hong Kong Central Hospital, around the corner from us. She was X-rayed again, more thoroughly this time, and they found she had broken six ribs. She had to be hospitalised right away. We asked her afterwards if she wanted to file a complaint against the taxi driver to make an insurance claim. 'No, it's my fault,' she said firmly. 'I forgot this isn't New York. I looked the other way when I crossed the road.'

The hospital insisted that she did bed rest for at least a month. Ten days later she booked herself a plane ticket home. She said she had to get home to feed the birds. She was not to be dissuaded. We tried. She endured the pain, lying down on the floor under the seats all the way on the long flight back home.

I paid her a visit in New York. We met at the Village Gate where she performed with Lyn and one other player. Then she invited me home for supper. She lived in a three-storey brownstone townhouse on 61st Street. She opened the door and showed me into a living room with ageing Venetian mirrors on the wall and crystal chandeliers dangling from the ceiling. There were French windows overlooking an overgrown garden, and inside the room were parakeets, cockatoos, and some crawling animals. She called the airborne ones 'birdies'. Some were perching on the chandeliers, making noises and flapping their wings; it felt like being in an aviary. Daphne had a lodger called Mr Spoons, who performed using spoons as percussion instruments. She said he was playing on the street and had no place to stay, 'So I took him in,' she said.

ROMPING AWAY

She told me to make myself at home. I was careful not to sit on birdies' droppings that had landed on the sofa. She rummaged for food in the kitchen and called out, 'Come and get it.' She held open the fridge for me. It was almost empty, except for bits of cheese on some plates. She took them out and announced, 'Still good. Never mind the mouldies.' She put them on a piece of bread she'd pulled out from a cupboard drawer or somewhere and offered it to me, saying, 'What doesn't kill you will make you stronger.'

Later that evening, she insisted I take the subway back instead of taking a cab. 'Don't waste good money. The New York Subway is quick and easy.' She showed me how to get to the nearest station. I didn't know where I was going, so I got on the first train that came along. It quickly transported me outside of New York City, into the dark ominous night, where I was certain that I'd soon be mugged or shot dead by a crackhead. That didn't happen, so I took the train back to where I'd started and took a cab home.

Daphne's third and last marriage ended abruptly. One day, her husband, Hsio-Wen Shih, literally walked out of their marriage and their home on 61st Street, never to return and never to be heard from again. Daphne and her sisters-in-law, Hsio-Pan and Hsio-Yen, remained friends.

'We didn't know what happened to Wen,' Pan said. 'He never got in touch. We don't know where he is. Daphne half expected him to come back one day. She's even set up a trust fund for him, in case he shows up one day and she's not there.' One night, in a moment of indiscretion induced by too much alcohol, Pan told us, 'We suspected that he left because he walked in on her, in *flagrante delicto*.'

Both Pan and Yen went to Wellesley, a private women's liberal arts university in Massachusetts, and the alma mater of the Soong

LIFE ON THE FRINGE

Sisters, three of the most powerful women once upon a time in China. Pan and Yen's father had been China's Ambassador to Brazil, and Yen – Professor Shih – would become Dean of the School of Fine Arts, the University of Hong Kong. A scholar with a razor-sharp mind, she had no time for slackers. Pan loved listening to jazz, watching shows, and hanging out. Though a voracious reader of books and appreciator of the arts, she was what her disciplinarian father would call a dilettante. Pan had married the owner of a hardware store in Shau Ki Wan. 'Because he asked me to,' she said. They had a son. When Pan found out they had little in common and that he read nothing but tabloids and girlie magazines, she divorced him. He also liked betting on horses, so she went and worked for the Jockey Club. 'All I do every day is to scan the local newspapers and translate any write-ups about betting for the non-Chinese bosses. I start work early and finish by noon, so I have the rest of the day to myself.'

Like Daphne, Pan liked to slum it at the Fringe. She also did everything she could to help. She liked to go through our programme guide and pick out the gremlins and spelling mistakes, which were plenty. She volunteered to copy-edit for us. She had no interest in money whatsoever. She told us that once she'd retired from work, she'd blow her pension on flying first class around the world and study art for a year in France. She did just that: she went off to Toulouse. 'I had the best collection of crayons in class,' she admitted with pride. 'My classmates liked to nick them from me. I bought them drinks, and meals they couldn't afford.' In that year, she'd had the time of her life, with no one to answer to, and not a worry in the world.

Around that time, Ronald also planned on taking a long break during summer recess. He had never travelled in Europe except for brief work trips; he wanted me to work out an itinerary for him.

'You're the expert,' he said to me. 'I'll leave it to you.' Though I was hardly an expert, I was more than happy to oblige. I drew up a deluxe tour for him, starting from the Ritz on Place Vendôme, Paris, where they purportedly warm up your monogrammed bath towels in cold winter.

Through to those vineyards with musical names in Burgundy – Gevrey-Chambertin, Vosne Romanee, Chambolle-Musigny, Montrachet – by way of La Maison Troisgros where he'd dine and meet with the legendary chef Paul Bocuse. Then swing by the Riviera to spend a few nights at Le Negresco on Promenade des Anglais in Nice and finish at the Danieli in Venice. It was a tour I'd very much like to take myself, that is if I'd just sold a bank with the sales proceeds in hand. That was precisely what Ronald had done, after going public in the stock market with his bank.

When I booked him into some of these places, I introduced him as the de facto Mayor of Hong Kong. With his infectious bonhomie, he made friends along the way. He showed us the photos he'd taken, and he looked truly happy, as good fortune was shining on him. In Venice, he went to Murano and took a fancy to blowing glass sculptures. 'I was treated like a prince,' he said. He invited the artists to Hong Kong and held an exhibition at City Hall for them.

He wanted a painting to be hung in his chairman's office at City Hall. His mind was set on something 'lucky and cheerful'; he asked me for my 'expert' advice. He'd already picked a large oil painting in red and orange that he showed me. It reminded me of a blazing sunset, and I had a presentiment of something coming to an end. But, in that moment, when everything was going his way, there was no way to know that, in a few years, the Urban Council would be dismantled, he would be remembered as the last Chairman, and the most colourful of them all.

The year 1997, marking the handover of Hong Kong to China, was tapping its fingers nervously on everyone's mind; no one knew what to expect, and the uncertainty became unbearable. It appeared as a tiny speck in the distance. You heard the engine sound swooshing down, as it got nearer it started to growl, louder and louder, and then thunder and run you over.

chapter 10

LOOK TO WINDWARD

I WAS IN CANBERRA, the capital of Australia, when the Creative Nation policy paper was handed out to us in the audience, sitting in the auditorium. That morning was memorable for its clear open sky, wide avenues empty of cars, and the brief encounter with a nation about to open its mind. I was among those who'd come all the way to attend the Performing Arts Market, a biennial event organised by the Arts Council to promote Australian culture to festival directors, cultural reps, and impresarios. We were chatting or idling in the auditorium without much enthusiasm for the speeches and the programme updates due to start.

At first, nobody had any idea of what that handout was about. It looked like another book of printed matter to be chucked into our already bulging bags of publicity bumfs. I flipped through it and settled on the foreword by Prime Minister Paul Keating. Next to it was a photo of someone who'd mistaken a scowl for a smile. I recognised the man from a parliamentary debate I'd watched on TV to induce sleep the night before, in my hotel room. His exuberant performance had made me sit up and watch. Not only did he have a way with hurling colourful insults at the Opposition, but he'd pulled no punches, staging a parliamentary slugfest worthy of late-night television watching. That's how I'd come to know him.

That day, Keating announced that his government would add AUD252 million to fund the arts. This piece of news gave the doubters in the auditorium pause. The audience was a mixed crowd from overseas and other parts of Australia; most of us were there to shop for shows and were not sure what all this fuss was about. Apparently, this had been kept under wraps and was a big deal. I heard someone sitting behind me wisecrack: 'This time he's putting money – not his foot – in his big mouth.' The prime minister was not very popular. He was known to prescribe bitter pills for the country's economic ills, not bothering to sugarcoat them or make himself more likeable. This discussion, however, belonged someplace else.

The Creative Nation document starts off by acknowledging the roles of indigenous and migrant cultures' roles in the forging of a national identity for Australia. This was new, coming from the Government, for the first time, in no uncertain terms. For a change, this wasn't the usual drivel about propping up some high-maintenance arts for the elites in society. Art is for everyone, and cultural engagement is the nation's concern. Not only that, but the document went further, saying that 'culture' is something 'which gives us a sense of ourselves.' This took the wind out of the sails of the kind of jokes about finding more living culture in yoghurt than in Australia.

Make no mistake: what he's saying wouldn't cut any cloth or change people's negative perceptions about the arts and those who 'waste' time indulging in them, if he hadn't found a way into it through their purses. Coming from an accounting background, Keating resorted to backing up his proposal with numbers. He went on. 'This cultural policy is also an economic policy. Culture creates wealth. Broadly defined, our cultural industries generate 13 billion dollars a year'; now we hear you, you could almost see them nodding their heads and saying.

'Culture employs. Around 336,000 Australians are employed in culture-related industries.' This was the first time the word 'industry' was used to describe something considered to be vocational, like religion. (No one has ever called religion an industry. God forbid. Even though there are many similarities.) Four years later, the 1998 Mapping Document published by the Arts Council in the UK nicked the term 'creative industries', which has since become the talisman against threats to cut arts funding by the Government.

'The level of our creativity substantially determines our ability to adapt to new economic imperatives. It is a valuable export in itself and an essential accompaniment to the export of other commodities.' This might sound a bit abstract to some people, so he added, in plain language, 'It attracts tourists and students. It is essential to our economic success.' Keating was unapologetic in using arts to spearhead trade and make it more palatable. It's now kosher. Nobody would object to 'investing' in arts and culture if it paid dividends. For me, it was the moment when I felt like buying some of their produce to see how far this would take me.

I hadn't always felt this way about this part of the world called 'Down Under' by some. Each time I landed there, I got a funny feeling; I got bushed, as they'd say. It's not normal, I know, but I couldn't help imagining that I was hanging upside down like a fruit bat, being in the southern hemisphere, and that everything inside me, my blood and guts, were turned over. Staring at the water in the toilet bowl flushing down clockwise only made it worse. There were other things, too. The choice of food was limited, English food mostly. Any other kind was exotic and not wholesome. White bread and white sugar were halal. So was the skin colour.

But change began to happen, albeit slowly. I first noticed it, sitting in a tent, watching Circus Oz, in Rymill Park, Adelaide. It was part of the bicentennial programme to celebrate Captain Arthur Philip taking his British fleet into Sydney Harbour to colonise this remote continent 200 years ago. It was not the usual circus act with clowns, jugglers, and performing animals. The arena was almost bare, except for a strung-up safety net. Looking up, under the big-top tent, you could see the set – the interior of an early settler's home with a bed, writing desk, pantry, and even an outhouse – laid out, upside down. The trapeze artist-actors played the scenes like a bunch of astronauts hanging from the ceiling of a spaceship.

It was riveting to watch at risk of courting a chiropractic injury of the neck. I read a slogan near the arena drawn boldly across a banner: White Australia has a Black History. In the show, there were scenes of Aborigines massacred by armed white settlers, and other atrocities. I was both shocked and amazed by the show, and years later, I invited Circus Oz director Michael Finch for a residency with us. The social conscience of the arts came up in our conversations. Deep wounds eventually heal, but the scar and pain won't be forgotten. At the time, it was inconceivable the Government would make a formal apology and start the reconciliation process. That this eventually took place takes some cojones to do for any wrongdoers.

We did a rerun of *Six Chapters* in Adelaide that year. After that, I talked to Kaitai about doing another show together. I had written a short story based on a recurrent nightmare that's disturbing and theatrical. It's about a peasant, looking for her lost child, and finds her lifeless body in the field. Devastated, she reports it to the local magistrate, in the middle of the night. The scene turns macabre when the magistrate, a mystery figure, becomes the suspect of sacrificial infanticide. With a shading of this, we develop it into *Lament of Sim Kim*: a show for the new Chinese Theatrical Arts Festival (1991), launched by Winsome and her team at the Festival Office. Danny Suen from the Fringe Mime Lab, and Opium Wu, APA dance graduate, played the leads. Casey Sebille designed the sets. Kaitai Chan, Director and Choreographer, and Lena Lee, Technical Director. It tackles the themes of female infanticide, gender inequality, dehumanising poverty – pretty heavy stuff – redeemed by the eventual triumph of the human spirit. Set in an impoverished seaside village where the men have left to look for work, leaving their women behind. To save themselves from male extinction, and the burden of feeding another mouth, the women routinely drown baby daughters. Sim Kim, the protagonist and mother, refuses to follow this barbaric practice. The story is woven around how she rises above her tragic karma.

I asked Lena recently about all the shows we'd done together. She recalled this one with pride. 'We constructed a seashore on stage, real enough for Danny to drown himself in the sea. And we dug a well into the floor of the stage, filled it with water, then lit it up from the bottom. We also used a naked flame and a live chicken as props. It's probably the only time the City Hall Theatre bent the rules like this for any show.' It was well received despite the harrowing subject matter. We did a sold-out run. After we finished the last show, we struck the sets and brought the props back to the Fringe Club to store. We had drinks and celebrated with the cast. Someone found a cage so that the chicken could join us. We thought it had played its role admirably: no unscripted chook-chasing scenes. But we had no idea of what to do with it now that the show was over. When someone suggested chicken soup, Stage Manager Owen Lee said dismissively, 'We do not eat our actors.' The next day, he put it to pasture at a farm in the New Territories. I hope it didn't eventually end up in a pot.

Kaitai wanted to do an adaptation of Charles Dickens' *Great Expectations* - changing the setting from Kent, England, to Fan Ling, Hong Kong - to reflect on the menaces and social injustices of colonisation. Brought up in British Colonial Malaya, he'd had first-hand experience.

Miss Havisham was transplanted from an English manor to a run-down country house in Fan Ling, in the New Territories. Abandoned by her heartless fiancé, she lives out her life as a bitter and eccentric recluse. She adopted Estella, a beautiful Eurasian girl from the village, and uses her to avenge the plight of a woman spurned. Estelle is trained and brainwashed by Miss Havisham to ensnare and mentally torture men who have fallen for her thorny beauty and aloofness. Pip, a local Hakka boy and her playmate, is enthralled. She gives him a terrible time, belittling him at every turn for being who he is. She makes him feel inferior for the way he speaks, behaves, and thinks. Miss Havisham has brought her up to feel white racially and therefore superior even though she isn't pure-bred herself. Pip's benefactor, ironically, turns out to be a Chinese convict and not Miss Havisham, the half-crazed English memsahib.

'Two Wongs don't make one White,' Kaitai repeated this to

me. 'This is the kind of racist pun whiteys thought up. They think it's alright to say things like this, as long as it's for larks. If you dare to take offence, they'll say you're a bad sport.' These puns, he thought, could be as insidious as a backhanded compliment – You speak such good English. Where are you from? – even though you're every bit as Aussie as they are. Coming from the White-dominated Sydney arts scene, Kaitai took these things rather to heart. I guess this is because he's always at the receiving end. What irked him most was that he felt he had to do battle to get funding for his company, each and every time, instead of being awarded for recognised merit. 'When there's any disagreement, they'll close ranks. Being Asian, you're not considered one of their own. Just because you talk and behave differently, they don't think you can be trusted. You can see that from the way they look at you.'

Sydney, in the 1970s, with its newly opened Opera House, designed by Danish architect Jørn Utzon (after a long internecine feud between him and the Minister of Public Works), unfurling its glorious stack of sails on the harbourfront, was poised to win the race for its position as the cultural capital of Australia. No other city came close. Certainly not Canberra, sparsely populated, landlocked, with an artificial lake. Melbourne took a shot at creating a cultural landmark to rival that of Sydney: it erected a dwarfish tower over the roof of its Arts Centre by the Yarra River and missed by more than a whisker.

Creative talents were drawn to Sydney. The number of artists multiplied. It got to a point that anyone with a sister had a dancer in the family. In Kaitai's case, he became one because he could, and the opportunity was there. It was during this wildly hopeful period that he had started his own company with its self-depreciated name, One Extra Dance Company. He had no idea how good he really was. By then, in the 1980s and early 1990s, the big players – the opera, ballet, symphony orchestra, theatre, and dance companies – had made their way to the edge of the harbour like hordes of large and thirsty beasts around a watering hole. They staked their claims – before being overrun by shops, cafes, and fast-food joints – and created a cultural presence that might have inspired the conceptual planning of West Kowloon Cultural District (WKCD).

Back to dream time, when Richard Wherett was looking for a permanent base for Sydney Theatre Company (STC), which he'd founded, he'd set his eyes on the disused Walsh Bay Wharf, a street-long, dark-timber cargo wharf at Dawes Point. He wanted to convert it into a clutch of studio theatres, rehearsal rooms, and offices, on water. How he managed to convince the City Council to give him access to the wharf and the funding to do what he proposed, is beyond my knowledge, and the scope of this story.

I was taken on tour on my first visit to the wharf. By then, Wherett had passed the baton to Wayne Harrison. I was met by his associate, Brett Sheehy, who showed me around. I could feel and hear the waves lapping rhythmically on both sides. A view of Sydney Harbour through the windows of the rooms; I was full of envy. Wouldn't it be wonderful, I thought, if Ocean Terminal – next to the Kowloon Star Ferry pier where the cruise ships used to berth – was turned into something like this? Would it not transform the Pearl of the Orient into a cultural destination and do away with the label of cultural desert once and for all? But that's not going to happen. Shopping malls have somehow become our places of worship and money making, our religion.

Fast-forward to now, on this hazy winter afternoon, I'm on the Star Ferry, crossing the harbour to the Kowloon side. To my left, I could see the WKCD out there by the waterfront. The charcoal grey Xiqu Centre on the near side by Canton Road, where retail shops are lined up. The angular Palace Museum in earth tones is put at the far end. And M+ Museum stands between the two – its giant TV screen, the size of a soccer field, switched off – like a huge, exposed aircon filter.

Part of the site is still under construction. These three signature buildings – instead of drawing attention to themselves – seem to have got lost in the dense, chaotic, and dramatic urban landscape of Yau Ma Tei and Tai Kok Tsui. Right behind them is a rampart of massive luxury flats and commercial blocks. And, towering above them, the International Commerce Centre (ICC) – all 108 storeys of glass-and-steel modern architecture – the tallest skyscraper in Hong Kong that turns into a giant light box that runs commercial messages at night. From where I'm sitting on the ferry, they appeared mismatched like a painting drawn by artists of different styles, or the bodywork of a car styled by wildly different designers.

This isn't what I imagined it to be. While serving on the Museum Advisory Group and other WKCD committees over the years, I'd gathered from my learned fellow members that we'd settle for nothing less than the Sydney Opera House or the Southbank in London (hence hiring the very capable Mr Michael Lynch, former CEO of both organisations). We set our sights on an unmissable, eye-catching, and memorable landmark, if only to replace the obsolescent fishing junk icon we've been using to represent Hong Kong since time immemorial.

Many 'what ifs' have come to mind. What if we hadn't shot down Norman Foster's concept design? He was the first prize winner over 161 entries, selected by an international expert panel in the 2001 open competition. What he proposed to do was to build a flowing, gleaming, curvaceous glass canopy roof to cover 55% of the site, in tandem with a half-moon-shaped lagoon for boats to glide in and out of the Victoria Harbour. We didn't go ahead with it because there were some voices of objection from the general public and informed groups. We hadn't done a head count. It was probably fewer than those raised over the building of the Eiffel Tower or Pompidou Centre. What we knew was that some of us taxpayers were irked by the idea of footing the hefty bills for maintenance, such as cleaning all that glass and air conditioning. Hong Kong gets really hot and dusty most of the year. What's the point? Just to look good? So impractical.

In fact, it's rather more complicated than that. And for a multitude of perfectly good and sound reasons that nobody now gives a hoot about, we missed the boat of having something potentially spectacular to look at on our waterfront.

Lord Foster is not someone who gives up easily. Ten years later, in 2011, he returned with another winner, the conceptual master plan of 'City Park'. And again he was chosen over two other competing candidates: Rocco Yim's 'Cultural Connect' and Rem Koolhaas's 'New Dimension'.

The two finalists from abroad were flown in to present their proposed designs in the new WKCD Authority office. Rocco probably just drove there. I remember Norman Foster was first. He opened by saying that every great city should have a park. 'London has Hyde Park,' he said, 'and New York, Central Park.' He went on to show images of how WKCD could be made into one that's as iconic as the other two.

His concept wasn't hard to grasp. Everyone loves a park. It's a good way to draw people. Once there, they may want to check out the museums and theatres they may not have come for specially. He proposed putting the motor traffic of loading trucks, tourist buses, all the public and private transport below ground, to free up the entire park for pedestrians. He also proposed designing all the museums, grand theatres, arena, and other open spaces for the purpose of consistency in style and looks and putting a distinctive imprint on his works. With the best intention, some board members suggested that, instead of letting Foster design all the buildings, we should let other architects have a go and add some variety.

Sometimes you can't help but wonder whether asking the right question will get you the right answer. From where I was sitting on the ferry, it looked like a missed opportunity to me, the kind that makes you want to hit yourself thinking about it. We should stick to the choices we made, shouldn't we? There's a chance they might turn out absolutely brilliant. Who knows?

We were joined by Wayne Harrison for a coffee. It was the first time I came this close and personal with a honcho in an Australian outfit. He was friendly and forthcoming in fielding the rookie questions I threw at him. In our subsequent dealings, he was every bit as fair dinkum as Aussies could be.

Wayne came to visit Hong Kong soon after leaving STC, where he was at the helm for nine years. Tall and in good shape, he showed the assuredness and calm of someone in control. He said he wanted to get away from the Sydney scene and see more of the world. Years later, we caught up again. He had moved to London and mentioned a circus cabaret he was writing, or had written, called Absinthe, for Spiegelworld, to be played at Caesar's Palace, Las Vegas. I think he also directed it, and the show is still running at the time of writing.

I had just written a one-woman show called *To Love & War: The Mickey Hahn Story* (2003), and I asked him to be my dramaturg, to which he readily agreed. He expertly ironed out all the bumps and creases in my script. He even suggested seasoned actress Greta Scacchi for the part. Unfortunately, it was bad timing for Ms Scacchi and didn't work out even though I'd had the backing of Hong Kong Arts Festival to produce it and the Adelaide Festival Centre showing interest in staging it.

On another timeline, we proposed *Great Expectations* to the 1992 Festival of Asian Arts (FAA), which was Urban Council's major event of the year. Kaitai suggested the Fringe co-produce this show with STC, as a bilingual production in English and Cantonese. 'That's how most people communicate here,' he pointed out, 'mixing the two languages for their own convenience and territorialness.' He also wanted to play it big this time. STC was building a reputation as Australia's leading theatre company; with Wayne's support for the project, he could tap into STC's considerable resources and, more importantly, its pool of English-speaking players. Wayne bought his idea, and so did the FAA. It was the first collaboration of its kind. The Fringe had had some success with its previous stage productions. When the FAA told us we would be the show to kick off the Festival – at none other than the Grand Theatre of the new Hong Kong Cultural Centre – we almost burst with pride. And I said to myself, 'Nothing could top this.'

In the first place, why would Kaitai pick Rodney Fisher to be his co-director? To this day, I can't figure it out. I knew nothing about Mr Fisher, but Kaitai told me he would be good for the show – very experienced, had worked with STC a lot, knew many of the actors– he's just what we need to make it kosher, or something like that.

Rodney and I met for the first time at the Fringe conference room. He had arrived the day before from Sydney, bringing two STC actors: Linda Cropper (Miss Havisham) and John Gaden (multiple English-speaking roles). Everyone was very cordial. Everything was hunky-dory. A reading of my script was scheduled for the next morning. I had written the dialogue, alternating the language to fit the characters, and Kaitai said he'd translate for Rodney and the English-speaking cast.

To kick off, Kaitai talked about why he was adapting this Charles Dickens story, the colonial context, cross-cultural references, and so forth. He also wanted the actors to take their eyes off the script, stop being talking heads, and use their bodies, just as he asked his dancers to do. But that's not how Rodney wanted to do it. He didn't want to put himself in a place where he hadn't been; dance theatre wasn't something he knew or wanted to know. He's the type who didn't care to be seen out of step on a dance floor.

Rodney was of medium height and all lean meat. In a high-pitched voice, he told us that he only needed four hours of sleep and ate like a Franciscan monk. To keep himself going, he took royal jelly, a health supplement made from bee secretion, what a queen bee feeds on to keep herself breeding. Rodney had an intense, hawk-like look about him. From the first week of rehearsal, he showed that he wasn't one to share his marbles or dance the dance with anyone. He wanted it all, and he wanted the show done his way.

LIFE ON THE FRINGE

He told me we needed to talk, just the two of us. He came all prepared. He showed me a version of the script that he'd done, neatly typed out – unlike mine which had crossed-out lines and Chinese characters written all over it – and made his first attempt to sideline his co-director, the one who'd got him on board. 'He asked personal questions,' he started. 'What's he trying to do? I don't understand.' He continued. 'They're not relevant. That's not how it's done. Everyone in rehearsal was made uncomfortable when he tried to do that.'

There are ways to make actors feel small and inconsequential, especially in the early days of rehearsal, when you don't quite know which way to go and whether you're up to it or not this time. To make those who are already insecure even more insecure, you just sow some seeds of doubt, about them and their abilities. I didn't know why he did that and thought it was just whingeing to let off steam, and they were both seasoned professionals; they could work it out between themselves.

The thing I had to do, no matter what, was to get the show on. Even at this late stage, I only had two-thirds of the local cast in place. Lindzay Chan agreed to play Estella; it was the second time we had worked together, after *Six Chapters* five years previously. The part of Pip, the main character, had taken me all the way to London, Singapore, and then boomeranged to Hong Kong to find an actor versatile enough to play it in two languages.

Sean Kwan had graduated from the Hong Kong Academy for Performing Arts in acting two years prior. Not only did he look the part, but he could play, convincingly, the whole age range of the character, from that of a gauche country boy to a man of the world. I also had photographer John Fung, whose acting skills were honed in playing male lead in B-movies, as Pip's good-natured brother-in-law, Joe. Magwitch could just be a cameo appearance in rags with the heavy make-up of a stock role, but we cast Anthony Wong Chau San, arguably the best actor of our generation. He was doing a movie shoot at the time, on a tight schedule, so he was quite happy with a cameo role. He wasn't going to wing it though, I found out. He was going to play it like the opening bars of a symphony. 'There was a lot of loud discussion during rehearsal,' Sean would recall. 'They all voiced their opinions. I just looked on. I felt like a kid among adults. I put my head down and ploughed on.'

We got Kevin Ho to design the sets. Kevin always had grand visions for his work. He wanted it to last as long as those ancient gates preserved in museums after the city they had guarded was long gone. Kaitai, by contrast, liked his designs to be fluid, minimalist, leaving room for imagination. As he had trained and worked in architecture, he wasn't shy about coming up with design ideas and liked to go into a process with the designer that could be quite daunting. I'd been through this process with him with my scripts: you had to be prepared to put your ideas on the line in front of others, and it could make you feel vulnerable and defensive. Rodney wanted none of that. He'd rather leave the sets to the designer, so that he could concentrate on the blocking and speaking the lines with the actors. He'd defer to Kevin and not question his work too much.

Kaitai didn't work like that; he didn't like to copy himself and took the sure way. And he got voted out: two against one. Like any group dynamics, there're always neutrals and a silent majority. When he suggested how to play something, Rodney would brush it aside, or rush it so that it'd look half-baked and unsound. He'd counter-offer with some well-tried options. This way he chipped away any credibility Kaitai might have as co-director, slowly edging him out and putting him on the reserve bench. One evening after rehearsal, I found Kaitai slumped face down on the table of our meeting room. I asked him what the matter was. 'I want to kill myself,' he sighed. He felt the show had slipped away from him and become a run-of-the-mill theatre adaptation of the book. There was nothing left of his original concept – that colonialism, in its worst form, plays mind games to disempower and emasculate those put under its yoke.

On the opening night, the audience seemed to like it well enough as a polished piece of theatre with good production value appropriate for a festival opening show. But Kaitai and I knew it was a missed opportunity to transform it into something striking and deeply felt, and we never really discussed this afterwards. An arts centre in Kuala Lumpur wanted to book the show, but because the set was too bulky for touring and too costly to transport, it was called off.

Our link with STC flatlined after that. Several years later, it was resuscitated by Katherine Thomson, who came as a playwright-in-residence. Hong Kong had recorded one of its wettest seasons (1996). The sky, overcast and heavy with rain, was pressing down; on the ground, we were flooded with gloom and doom news on the city's future. Katherine herself was getting over a tough patch in her life. It felt like all the pressure was converging on this nexus where all things were somehow connected. Suddenly something gave: a retaining wall in Kennedy Town collapsed, causing a fatal mudslide. It felt like an omen for the city. All these events segued into Katherine's writing that she had come here to do. Fragments of Hong Kong, as it's called, was made into an award-winning radio play for the BBC. The following year, STC sent Sancia Robinson to do *What's the Matter with Mary Jean?* It was based on Sancia's own hellish descent into a life of anorexia and bulimia and how she's survived to tell the tale.

Kaitai had a quick bounce-back. City Contemporary Dance Company, a leading dance company in Hong Kong, commissioned him to choreograph and direct a dance theatre piece called *Made In Hong Kong*. He was back in his element, working with dancers on a subject that mattered to him. After it premiered in Hong Kong, he toured it in Australia for a month. 'We had lots of fun,' Sean, who was in the show, recalled. Some of the audience wondered and worried about what would happen to Hong Kong after the handover. 'We're asked a lot about that,' he said.

I was invited to lunch by Jocelyn Chey, Consul General of Australia, to meet with the Chair of Asialink, a cross-cultural organisation, initially with a mission to change people's perception of Australia as Eurocentric, by engaging with its Asian neighbours. I was expecting polite conversation with a diplomatic type in a formal suit and a meeting that wouldn't go beyond polite social exchanges. Mr Carrillo Gantner turned out to be a different breed: a theatre maven, a straight shooter, and someone who's comfortable in his own skin. He came from a family of means that had a long history of sponsoring the arts and had served as cultural attaché in Beijing where he met, Ziyin, now his wife.

'I was travelling around Asia,' he said in an interview. 'There's a lot of bad press about our immigration policies. We were being described as racist and colonial, when I had always thought we were rather a charming, enlightened, multicultural society. I don't think most Australians had any idea that anyone was out there in Asia, let alone taking any notice of what was happening in their own country.'

Jocelyn knew a lot about Hong Kong and would have been called a 'China Hand' in the old days. She studied at the University of Hong Kong, married her Chinese neighbour, returned to Australia to bring up her child, joined the diplomatic service, and returned to Hong Kong to be appointed Consul General. At the time, Hong Kong had been dubbed a transit lounge kind of city, where people come and go, but not stay and put down roots. She asked me about my family and whether we were leaving or staying. I told her I had no idea since so much was at stake – my kids' schooling, my job, Margaret's job, family and friends.

At a friend's farewell party, one of her parting gifts was Machiavelli's The Prince, a leather-bound book bought from a rare bookstore in Chancery Lane. The host passed it around for all to admire. When it came to my turn, I made a quick flip-through and caught the following paragraph on a page. I read it out aloud for comments around the table: 'Whoever takes a city used to living in liberty according to its own customs and does not ruin it risks being ruined by it . . . No matter what one does, if you don't disband the citizenry and immediately eradicate the customs and traditions, they come back to haunt you . . . You can't leave them alone and you can't allow the memory of the old liberty. The safest way to deal with them is ruin them and then live there.'

'Sounds a bit extreme,' someone responded. 'That's Machiavelli talking,' another added. 'Don't think it'll ever come to that.'

Still, Jocelyn suggested I should give serious thought to going Down Under. 'Just in case, as an insurance.' I kept putting it off. It seemed such a chore just to fill in all those forms for a passport. I let them sit for a long time at the bottom of the pile on my desk. I didn't think anything would happen soon. The other thing was I wasn't ready to move away, not just yet; there's more for me to do here than to sit out my time over there.

At that lunch, Carrillo told me all about Asialink. It was set up to give those working in the arts in Australia a chance to spend time in an Asian country and learn about their customs and cultures. They offered a residency programme for selected candidates to attach to an arts organisation and to build up their own networks of contacts. He wanted the Fringe to be on the list of those host organisations. 'Come to Melbourne,' he said. 'We'll show you how it works.' He gave me a long steady gaze through his presbyopic glasses and smiled. Before long, he made it possible for me to pay a visit.

Melbourne didn't win me over right away. I arrived after spending a few glorious days in Sydney, soaking up the sun and breathtaking beauty of the emerald, blue coves and sweeps of sandy beaches on the oceanfront. It was after five in the afternoon when I checked into my hotel near Flinders Station; everything was shutting down and people were hurrying home. Those were the days before Fed Square, a cultural space (and minefield for high heels and weak ankles) in the city centre, was built. It was rainy, blustery, and cold, and it wasn't even winter yet. I needed some hot food to warm my forlorn heart. I couldn't understand why anyone would choose it over Sydney, if they had a choice. The place looked dismal and inhospitable to me.

I was to meet everyone Carrillo wanted me to meet at the Malthouse, a brewery converted into a corral of intimate theatres with an art gallery, cafe and bar, also known as The Playbox Theatre. The original banner with its 'Making the Improbable Inevitable' slogan, a bit flyblown perhaps, could still be seen on the back wall in the foyer. Carrillo was one of its founders and an artistic director who wanted to give local playwrights a chance to be heard and seen: to overcome the 'home-grown-ginger 本地薑唔辣' syndrome – anything foreign and exotic is better than anything local and, therefore, plain Jane – which isn't that unique, I found out, as we're all likely to be susceptible to it, no matter who or where we are.

It was quite a gathering that day at the Malthouse. There was a drinks reception going on, and Carrillo was giving a speech to a standing crowd. He'd gone on for quite a bit, and the guests started to look anxious to get back to their drinks and conversations. I saw Jill Smith, who'd just been introduced to me as the General Manager, arms crossed standing at the back. She's a tall woman with deep-set dark blue eyes and sculpted features. She caught my eye and gave me a commiserative shake of her head that seemed to be saying, 'Bear with us. He's like that, but he's alright.' Then Carrillo turned to a round-shouldered, ursine, and affable-looking man next to him and said, 'Now Aubrey will tell us more about what's coming next season.' Aubrey Mellor during his tenure as Artistic Director had presented works by local playwrights who would otherwise be overlooked.

Later on, Carrillo showed me the three theatres there like treasured toys to the new kid. One of them is named Beckett. 'After Samuel Beckett?' I asked. 'No, it's named after him,' he replied, pointing to John Beckett, the designer of the theatre who was in tow. 'Everyone thinks it's named after the other Beckett.' He guffawed, while John took this standing joke stoically. I wondered what kind of deal Playbox had offered him for the naming. The other theatre called the Merlyn is named after Carrillo's maternal grandma; he must've tapped his own contacts and whatnot to pull this off. I know what it takes to make something like this happen. I really liked the feel of the place – the people seemed very committed and looked out for each other. A good outfit, one I could trade horses with. Years later, I invited John to Hong Kong to design our studio theatre, but it didn't work out. Too bad; it could've been really cool to have a theatre called Beckett.

The Playbox Theatre brought *Sanctuary* to Hong Kong, David Williamson's new two-hander, a hard-hitting two-act play about a retired journalist made captive by a young radical idealist who's prone to violence; he holds the older man accountable for betraying his professional integrity for money and fame. It was their calling-card show – polished and well-acted – and they made ingenious use of our pocket-size stage and the few pieces of equipment available. It's as good as any professional theatre show. William Gluth, who played Bob, the journalist in question, has come to be known to us as Will, the partner of Jill and a certified oenophile. Will and Jill have returned many times, in different roles, including that of fond denizens of Wan Chai, where we put them up. In all, we did six productions with Playbox between 1996 and 2002: *Vincent, Stolen, I Don't Wanna Play House, Confidentially Yours, Sanctuary,* and *Second Spring.*

Stolen stands out among them. It's an Ilbigerri Aboriginal & Torres Strait Islander Theatre and Playbox co-production about this skeleton in the cupboard of White Australia Policy. Between 1910 and 1970, Aboriginal and mixed-race children were forcibly taken away from their parents and put in White foster homes by State agencies and Church missions, to be raised in the White and therefore culturally and socially superior ways. It was meant for their own good and done with the best intentions. Over the years, tens of thousands of families were torn apart, inflicting terrible

The rooftop, City Festival 2000

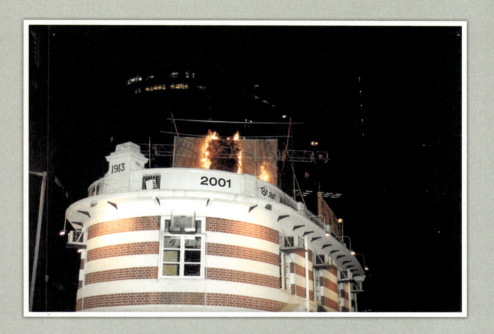

The Gargoyles performed by erth (Sydney, Australia) on the Fringe rooftop in City Festival 2001

Melbourne International Comedy Festival, Melbourne, 2014
Left to right: Harley Breen, Ronny Chieng, Joel Creasey, Anne Edmonds, Luke McGregor

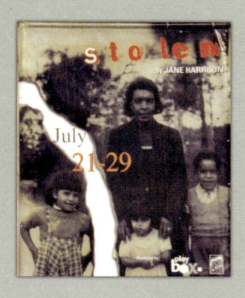

STOLEN, a play from Australia co-presented by Playbox Theatre Company, Ilbijerri Aboriginal and Torres Strait Islander Theatre Coop, toured the Fringe Club in 2000

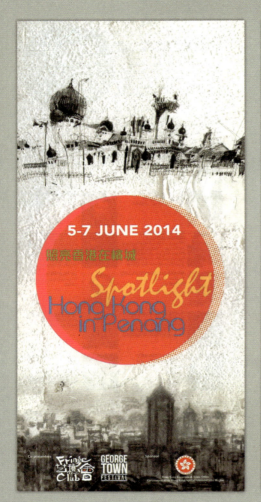

Spotlight Hong Kong in Penang, 2014 and in Singapore, 2015

Eugene Pao on guitar, Jeremy Monteirio on keyboard performing at Barber Shop, Spotlight Hong Kong in Singapore, 2015
Photo by Jeremiah Choy

pain and scarring them emotionally for life – both the parents and the stolen children.

Stolen was gut-wrenchingly authentic. The script, based on the lives of five individuals who lived through this ordeal, is by Jane Harrison, a descendant of the Muruwari people. It was played by indigenous actors from the so-called Stolen Generation, and the director, Rachel Zoa Maza, who experienced racism first-hand in her upbringing – her indigenous father, an actor and social activist, had married a Dutch immigrant, and the whole family endured discrimination.

This is subject matter that needs to be put in context to be properly understood, and I suggested we hold some background talks. Most Hongkongers had no idea of how this had come about and how deeply it had affected those involved. 'In what way is it relevant to us?' I wondered. And how will our friends at the Australian Consulate take it? Would they rather have nothing to do with it? They've been supporting us all these years, and it would be a real pity if they pulled out. To their credit, instead of sending us to the gulag, they said they didn't have any problem sponsoring the programme.

Taking such matters into the open, no matter how shameful or wrong, makes healing and reconciliation possible, whereas suppressing the truth does not make us strong, only fearful. Tammy Anderson followed this show with her own story as a biracial indigenous child who was shunted around to live in sixteen homes in fifteen years, enduring racism and abuse. Her one-woman show, *I Don't Wanna Play House*, has become the longest-running show in Australia.

'*Second Spring – A Letter to My Daughter*' deals with another kind of guilt and fragility. It's based on what photojournalist

Michael Coyne wrote to his daughter on a night in wartime Rwanda, when he was unsure if he'd see her for another day again. The monologue was co-written and performed by William Gluth. This coincided with Michael's book project called Disappearing Villages. We arranged for him to stay in a village in Kaiping, Guangdong, to photo-document a traditional wedding and how the villagers live their lives there. He gave an illustrated talk about this and other experiences afterwards on the Fringe Club roof.

Between 1997 and 2014, we hosted Asialink residencies for Geraldine Tyson, Simone Lourey, Anna Marsden, Santha Press, Christina Soong, Steve Mayhew, Keiko Aoki, Jane Fuller, Rebecca Allen, and Joon Yee Kwok. These people were arts managers, show producers, or promoters with a few years of working experience under their belts. We scheduled them to come during the festival period so that they could make themselves useful and apply their knowledge and skills in a different environment at the same time. They spent on average of three to six months with us, enough time to get to know something about Hong Kong and find their way around. It didn't take us long to make them feel at home. We used English whenever they were around and shared the common language in the arts. As often as possible, we sat down for meals together. Food is a wonderful connector: around the dinner table, there's no stranger. We didn't just serve local food – they all loved *yum cha* and *dim sum* – but we also tried to cook up something from their staple diets. That's a treat and a change from being served rice all the time.

I've learned how to cook pasta from Mike Moran, a Scotsman of Italian descent, whom I'd met in a food paradise known as Valvona & Corolla in Edinburgh. Mike devised and performed an enchanting version of *Captain Corelli's Mandolin* that we invited

LIFE ON THE FRINGE

him to stage in our theatre. When he wasn't playing the ebullient Captain, he taught me how to use parsley to spice up a dish of spaghetti aglio e olio. 'Cook it no longer than a minute, or it'll lose its sweetness,' he told me. I was eager to show off what I'd learned, so I cooked a tasty pasta dinner for Santha, the Asialink grantee from Melbourne. I knew as much that Westerners eat bread and pasta, just as we do rice. When I proudly put my pasta dish in front of her, with parsley and all, she clearly looked embarrassed. Taking me aside, she told me she only ate rice: she couldn't consume bread and pasta without allergic reactions. After that, we never felt uncomfortable eating rice with her around. She'd become one of us, a culinary compatriot adept with a rice bowl and chopsticks in hand.

Simone Lourey, who was the marketing manager of Playbox, stayed the longest time, and met her future husband, Will, in Hong Kong. We were introduced to her parents, Margaret and Chris, when they came to visit. For Simone's wedding, I wrote a monologue as prenuptial entertainment for the guests. It was read by Deidre Rubinstein, who had performed earlier in Confidentially Yours in our theatre. Later, when Simone was relocated to Singapore, we connected her with the amazing Ivan Heng of Wild Rice Theatre Company. They hit it off, and she became his board member and helped with fundraising. In her case, Asialink couldn't have worked better in making friends and finding future partners.

Carrillo also introduced the young Susan Provan to me. She'd just been appointed director of the burgeoning Melbourne Comedy Festival and was running the show from her office in Fitzroy, Melbourne. Nowadays, she works all over the world, wherever there are comedy shows. Carrillo, who has sat on more arts boards than the sitting Buddha, was her chair. I started to tap Susan for the inside track on the comedy shows for our programme. In 2011, they rolled out the Melbourne International Comedy Festival (MICF) Roadshow, which packages the top picks and then puts them on tour, and we became their port of call. Hongkongers might remember having watched Ronny Chieng trying to teach his mother how to delete something on Facebook, long-distance, with hilarious results. Ronny has played here twice and has gone on to make the big time on Netflix, *The Daily Show with Trevor Noah*, and a cameo role in the hit movie, *Shang Chi and the Legend of the Ten Rings*.

The clock was ticking louder: just a year and twenty-one days to go until the Handover. We embarked on our fourth and probably last collaboration with Kaitai. He told me he was going to quit the Sydney dance scene after twenty-five years or so. He said he'd had enough of it. He said he wanted to experience *real life*. With the support of the Urban Council, we proceeded with the stage production of *Lianne & Chuck*, after the Cantonese opera version of *The Regrettable Romance of Leung & Chuk*, better known as *The Butterfly Lovers*. We transposed the hetero into a same-sex relationship. The main characters were played by Wong Yu and Qiao Yang, both female soloist dancers, courtesy of City Contemporary Dance Company. An excerpt from the programme:

> *They are good friends until love comes between them. Chuck is withholding a secret about his sexual identity from Lianne that will forever change their lives. Set against the backdrop of a Hong Kong teetering in uncertain times, the*

LIFE ON THE FRINGE

> *Chinese classic Liang Zhu [梁山伯與祝英 台 Butterfly Lovers] is given a fresh and controversial treatment to mirror a bittersweet contemporary romance story. Full of searingly beautiful images, it looks unflinchingly at forbidden desires, sexual duplicities, cross-and same-gender relationships.*

This was familiar terrain for Kaitai to delve into. He must have felt relieved not to have been asked to make another mime show. In fact, when Philip Fok migrated with his family to Sydney in 1992, he packed mime, as we knew it, and took it with him.

Kaitai got his pick of dancers and cast for the show. Wong Yu and Qiao Yang were compatible – both looking androgynous and lanky – and had good chemistry as a duo. He choreographed some of the most beautiful duets we've seen on the City Hall Theatre stage. About halfway through the production, his partner, who was struggling with a drinking problem at that time, came and joined him. It didn't help that we put them up in an apartment in the Wan Chai heartland of bars. But Kaitai wasn't to be distracted: he knew he was on a good run. The Chinese title 蝶非蝶, made a play with Taoist philosopher Chuang Tzu [莊子]'s conundrum: a butterfly isn't a butterfly, and a flower isn't a flower, which is meant to say all things in life are illusory and not really what they seem. I asked Christopher Doyle to create a set of collages for the show, one of which, the key image, captured the intricacies of a cross-gender relationship. Chris is well-known by his Chinese name 杜可風, and for the movies he's made with film director Wong Kar Wai, notably *Chungking Express*. A pioneer of handheld cinematography that induces intimacy as well as motion sickness in the viewer, he's seldom seen without a beer bottle in hand but seldom seen under the influence.

Lianne & Chuck drew the curtain on our collaborations with Kaitai, spanning over a decade. During our times together, we discovered that Kaitai could not only cook up a storm in the rehearsal room but also in the kitchen. Cat swooned over his chicken wings stuffed with sticky rice, and I'd swear by his spicy phanaeng curry. To return our hospitality, Kaitai treated us to a feast that took him two days to prepare. He spared no trouble getting the freshest ingredients from the wet market on Graham Street.

The wonderful meal put us in a mellow mood, and we sat around after dinner, shooting the breeze. He told us about his retirement plan. To rinse off traces of the dance world, he'd become a taxi driver, to roam the city and meet *real* people of all sorts, not just arty types. Then he'd go to an impoverished corner in the world, maybe in rural Pakistan, to experience poverty and human sufferings. Before doing that, he'd invite members of the Australian Arts Council Funding Committee to his company's final performance. After the show, he'd serve them hot curry. Then, to make his point and show his pent-up frustrations over all these years pleading for adequate funding for his company, he'd slit his wrists in front of them. We laughed together about this idea.

Sometime later, I went to visit him in Sydney. We met in a cafe in King's Cross. Over coffee, he told me he was now doing night shifts driving a taxi and saving up money for his trip to Pakistan. He'd located a village in the mountains where he'd teach children English and the women to use the sewing machine to get some cottage industry going. 'Did you slit your wrists in the end?'

LIFE ON THE FRINGE

I remember asking him in our conversation. 'I did,' he said. 'But it didn't quite work out. My fault. I hadn't rehearsed it. The stage knife was too blunt. It couldn't draw any blood, no matter how hard I tried.'

As Kaitai was preparing for his humanitarian journey, a path had been beaten to our door. On our last count, we had chalked up almost 150 Australian acts appearing on our stage or exhibiting at our gallery. To name a few: *Crying In Public Places, Sydney Front, The Umbilical Brothers, Paul Capsis, Hung Le & Ningali, William Yang, Fiona O'Loughlin, Moira Finucane, Sean Choolburra, Harlex Vargas Dance Theatre, Viable Options, Glass Jar Theatre, Lindsey Pollak, Company In Space, Adam Hills, Jeannie Lewis, Rick Lau, Tommy Dean, Max Sharam, Black Hole Adult Puppet Theatre, Erth, Vashti Hughes, John Michael Swinbank & Richard John, Batacuda, Narelle Marie-Louise, Catherine Woo, Martin King, Guan Wei, Judy Watson.* The list goes on.

chapter 11

SPIN IT AGAIN

THERE WAS A FEELING that all things were coming to a close. Nobody knew what the new millennium would bring. What we knew, with scientific certitude, was that the whole world would fall apart on the dot of Y2K. In this climate, the arts thrived.

The British Hong Kong Government began to loosen its tight grip and give people the right to vote and, *inter alia*, front-row seats for arts and culture. What had been a one-horse town – where the City Hall was the only place to go for concerts and such – was turning into a boom town. A string of cultural complexes began to shoot up, one after another, like a seed bed chasing the last spring rain.

First to emerge was the Cultural Centre – the large window-less tiled structure not unlike the jawbone of a mythical beast hulking on the edge of the Tsim Sha Tsui waterfront – complete with a concert hall, grand theatre, black box, and a clutch of eateries. It was followed close on its heel by the Museum of Art, a stone's throw away, clad in identical tiles used for public buildings designed for conformity. Then a rush of medium-sized town halls and compact civic centres. The latter ones got built mandatorily in districts that had reached certain demographic requirements. For instance, you'd get a civic centre built in your district if there were no fewer than 700,000 residents there. For a town hall to be built, your district had to have a population of at least 1.2 million.

The obvious question was: What do we do with all these arts venues? We'd need to have artists and audiences to keep the theatres from going dark. To nurture them, we'd have to have a resource-allocation and supply system in place. The Hong Kong Academy for Performing Arts opened at breakneck speed and made a dash for the finish line. It took just five years – from inception, finding the money, holding an architectural design competition, and the actual construction, to recruiting the faculty and enrolling students, the whole works – to open its doors to the first batch of intakes.

The next big leap was to set up an arts council to fund the arts to replace the existing Council for Performing Arts (CFPA) that was primarily for the support of performing arts, while largely neglecting other art forms, such as spectrums of visual and literary arts. Tseng Sun Man, then Chair of the Arts Administrators Association (known as 3A by those in the profession), formed a drafting committee to write and submit a proposal: 'An Arts Strategy for Hong Kong (August 1992) to the Government'.

To give the proposal a sense of urgency, it was subtitled Final Report – hoping that the Government would act on it. It was the first major report produced by a group of professional arts managers. I was involved with 3A from its nascency. At the time, when all of us were busy with our work, Sun Man and I alternated as Chair, a glorified title for team leader. In the early years, the membership was made up mostly of managers of independent arts groups that were in minority, for the majority of arts managers worked for the Government. If not for the active participation of some of the chief managers such as Tony Ma (Urban Services Department) and Agnes Tang (Regional Services Department), 3A would not have been representative of the profession in any real sense. Both Tony and Agnes were on the Drafting Committee. I was unable to help, as I was in the thick of producing *Great Expectations* (1992). The main bulk of the work fell on the shoulders of Sun Man and Martin Schulman, a visiting Fulbright professor from Binghamton University in New York State.

Marty happened to be the man of the hour. He showed up at the door of 3A's executive office, the Arts Resource & Information Centre (ARIC) at the Arts Centre, a godsend volunteer to facilitate the drafting of the report. Before he joined academia, he'd been called up to fight in the Vietnam War, learning the ways of the world the hard way. Unlike someone from a purely academic background, he seldom indulged in the theoretical to deal with a problem; he preferred to look for practical solutions. He and Sun Man launched a series of lectures on arts management, taught by those who were actually on the job. If we wanted to put the finger on a starting point, this might have been the Big Bang of arts management classes in Hong Kong. Sun Man, now Professor Tseng, has published two definitive books on the subject and is the undisputed 'Father of Arts Management'. He has also set a grand slam career record of running major arts organisations in Hong Kong.

As for Professor Schulman, during his year-long stay in Hong Kong, he had not only got himself a new hip in Queen Mary Hospital, but also found himself a new partner in Grace Cheung, who had sure-handedly put ARIC into orbit.

As arts managers, we'd like to see the future Arts Council informed and guided by those who are experienced, in the know; and its operation staffed by professionals, following best practices, instead of running as an appendage of a government department like CFPA. Arts boards in that period were made up of people considered to be pillars of society, such as lawyers, accountants, and bankers; bankers in particular were for some unfathomable reason thought to be more reliable and trustworthy than other folks and, therefore, were put high on the list. These board members tended to put social obligations before artistic merits. This, at times, would affect the quality of their decisions. Also, it was not a requisite for those civil servants put in charge of the arts to appreciate or show interest in arts and culture. It was not considered a drawback in carrying out their duties. Quite the contrary, it was deemed helpful for them to make objective and unbiased decisions. This, as a cynical pundit put it, is 'no different from giving the run of a hen house to a bunch of raccoons.'

Following the submission of the Final Report, we heard through the grapevine that the Government was finally going to take action in forming a new arts council (published in 'The Arts Policy Review Report', March 1993). We had great hopes that it would not only raise the profile of the arts but also create a society where arts and culture would be nothing less than quintessential. 3A was keen to be first to offer its professional opinions and well-informed views. We spent the following four months, from June to September 1993, on another paper, specifically about the establishment of an arts development board, called 'The Next Step for the Arts'. This report involved quite a bit of research – funded by the British Council and Business for the Arts – into examining how arts councils had done their work in the US, Australia, Japan,

New Zealand, and the UK. We were looking for role models. The members of this study group included Daniel Chung, Tony Ma, Agnes Tang, Estella Tong, Tseng Sun Man, with me as Chair, and Anthony Wraight as Coordinator.

Anthony had just resigned from the Hong Kong Ballet, having served as General Manager for four years. All that time he'd been an active member of the 3A Board. He was quite a bit older and the most experienced among us. We were working on a tight schedule and trying to be as thorough in our research as possible. Tony put in a lot of time and got quite intense about it. I remember the day we signed off the final draft of the report, when I asked him what he would do, and what we ought to do, if the Government didn't listen to what we had to say.

'Take it to the streets,' he replied. 'We'll fight them there.' I thought he was joking. But the steely glint in his eyes told me that he wasn't. I hadn't seen this side of him before. He'd always been mild and gentlemanly; I couldn't imagine him shouting slogans and raising his fist in a mass protest.

Soon after Tony arrived in Hong Kong with his partner, Sally, they invited Margaret and me to tea at their home on Lamma Island. They lived in a bungalow, the only one by a cove that's hard to reach. Idyllic from a distance, close up the shallows were covered in plastic waste. Unusual choice, I thought, for they could choose to live on gentrified Mid-Levels or Southside with their expat housing allowance. We were served scones and cream tea. Very English and a pleasant way to while away a Sunday afternoon. I asked what their plans were in Hong Kong. Sally volunteered that they planned to have a baby. 'After that, we'll move to Bermuda. Tony has bought a plot there. We'll build our dream home.'

One day, out of the blue, Tony was on the front-page news. It reported, retrospectively, that he had been charged for passing classified military information to a foreign government and had been sentenced to three years in prison – this was in the 1960s during the Cold War, when he was a junior RAF Flying Officer. He'd taken a flight from London to East Berlin to defect to the Soviet Union; afterwards he was settled in Moscow by the authorities and then Warsaw, where he studied photography. Three years later, he walked into the US Embassy seeking help; eventually they flew him back home. Soon enough he published a serialised memoir in a major daily on his time as a special guest of the Soviets. This drew the attention and the ire of the Foreign Office, leading to his subsequent arrest and charge for espionage. In his defence, he told the court he was disillusioned with capitalist society and its predatory ways of life; that's why he'd defected. And having lived in the Communist world, he'd become equally disillusioned with their kind of social wrongs and blatant lies.

All that had happened at a time when Cambridge University was practically running a recruitment office on campus for Soviet double agents: notably Kim Philby, Guy Burgess, and Don Maclean. Tony had been found guilty and was given a relatively light sentence for being young and naive. He was twenty-two years old at that time.

We didn't have to take to the streets. The Provisional Hong Kong Arts Development Council was created in the autumn of 1994. I joined the board as a founding member, and other members were the same type – artists, academics, and arts professionals. We believed that we were on an all-important mission: to build a viable future for the arts in Hong Kong. There was much to discuss – how to build it from scratch and get it off the ground quickly – and we felt that time was running out. We had to put things in place before it was too late.

We held frequent and manically long meetings several evenings a week. We came directly from work and seldom finished before eleven or twelve midnight. There were, among others, artist-curator Oscar Ho, poet Leung Ping-kwan, orchestra conductor Yip Wing-sie, art professor David Clarke, theatre director Danny Young, and educator Lo King-man. This might be the first time that a group of people who cared deeply about the arts got to sit down around a table, not just to talk but actually have a chance to accomplish something of importance.

These were heady times. Gushing with ideas, everyone had lots to say and argue about. Often the discussions went into the night, well past dinnertime. Initially we were content to subsist on biscuits and candy provided – sugar fixes to ward off drowsiness – but we ended up needing something more substantial. So, the dedicated staffers brought us a choice of sandwiches and flasks of coffee to last the distance. During the day, meeting papers flew off our fax machines like there was no tomorrow. Cat threatened to charge HKADC for using up so much fax paper.

Meanwhile, there was a construction frenzy going on. Every time you looked, miles and miles of new highways and bridges appeared like mirages in the desert. The new airport at Chek Lap Kok was estimated to take up to twenty years to build, but construction workers put in double and triple shifts, and it was completed in record time.

The preparatory work to turn the provisional arts council into a full-fledged statutory body with its own management team and operation guidelines was also steaming ahead. The Government appointed Sir Joseph Hotung as the Council's founding Chair.

LIFE ON THE FRINGE

'Call me Joe,' he said, when we met for the first time. Although he came from one of Hong Kong's best-known families, his was not a name you read about much in the Tatler or the social pages. Unlike his more flamboyant brother, Eric Hotung, Joe kept a low profile, keeping to himself, moving as discreetly as silk slippers on carpet within an elite group of art collectors and philanthropists, while dividing his time between Hong Kong, London, and New York. Tall, bespectacled, courteous, with a slight stoop, thinning hair, and Eurasian features, he brought with him Mr David Eldon to essentially serve as his Chief Financial Officer. Together, they brought the transactions of the Council to a corporate level.

In a way, David seemed to be the odd one out among the arty lot. He worked with precise figures in high finance (then CEO, later Chair of HSBC) and was more used to carefully executed boardroom manoeuvres than our off-the-cuff, speak-from-the-heart way of communicating. He was tactful. He'd often watch bemusedly as we traded impassioned words and entered into heated debates, and seldom volunteered opinions unless they concerned accounting matters. Outside of the conference room, he's personable and has a way of putting people at ease. At the time, we never suspected him of being a closet musician with an affinity for Scottish and Irish songs.

Throughout Joe's two-year tenure as founding Chair, I don't remember him ever being late or absent. He was conscientious and conservative, more a Cecil Burghley than Francis Drake of Elizabethan times, though. In hindsight, at that nascent stage for the Council, we probably should have been more adventurous and daring in our way of planning and thinking. Instead, we played the defensive and maintained the status quo. Whereas our predecessor, the CFPA, had focused on handing out grants, we could have made a few bold strategic moves to change people's perceptions and make arts really matter in Hong Kong society.

'Don't give up your day job' is the advice gratuitously given to someone who wants to have a go as a full-time artist and hopes to make enough to live on. What those well-intentioned people mean is that it's not going to be easy, and you'd better have something to fall back on. Many artists take this advice and instead of diving right in, they try the shallow crossings first. They try to set up their own studio, the first step if you want to commit and dedicate your life to the arts. Many artists in Hong Kong soon find that a studio is not only hard to come by, but it can be quite unaffordable. Over the years, this situation hasn't got any better, but worse. Hey, what do you know? This is Hong Kong. Space is a valuable commodity.

Lack of space, lack of grace. Anyone living and working in a tight space can make sense of this. It's not uncommon to find two or three artists huddling together in a bedroom-sized shared studio. Do we know what long-term effects this might have on their artistic development? One thing for sure: you won't find them producing XL works like those of Zeng Fangzhi or Anselm Keifer that astound viewers in museums by sheer size, volume, and power.

In a garden – if the Arts Development Council was the gardener – to make a plant grow and flourish, the way to do it is by working from the roots with fertile soil, not just by sprinkling water on the leaves from time to time to prevent it dying from drought. At the same time, a statutory body that dispenses public funds has to be accountable. So, the Council had to come up with a system that could be readily explained and justified by numbers – for you can't argue with numbers. To track and measure the performance

LIFE ON THE FRINGE

of a business, you can use a dashboard of KPIs, tools designed to provide the metrics for businesses to quantify and measure their success. It's much harder to use the same technical tools to qualify the value of the grants and determine whether they really help artists to become better at what they do. Using KPIs to gauge artistic merit is somewhat like using a user's operating manual to explain the intricacies of a creative process or human relationships.

The Government tended to play down the role of arts and culture in society, as it might not be in their self-interest for the people that they governed to foster a cultural identity. You don't want the plebs to think and ask questions, for they might become unruly. Putting arts in the same basket as sports and recreation was a safe bet. Label them as amenities that have little intrinsic value other than to provide mass entertainment or leisure activities. There are more worthwhile causes for the essential well-being of our society other than arts and culture. This way of thinking prevailed and cascaded down from parents to their children and teachers to students.

It didn't help, where public funding was concerned, that anything considered commercial or with profit-making potential, was discouraged. One of the requirements for grant applicants was to be registered as non-profit entities. Other clauses in the agreement included: profits made from shows had to be returned, and artworks were not to be sold where the exhibition was held. What this meant was that arts projects funded by the Council shouldn't aim to be a financial success. The noble intention was for artists to do what they do solely for the metaphorical enrichment of their lives but not to line their own pockets. They're supposed to lead a poor but blameless life, not to be tainted by such things as financial reward. In a city celebrated for its enterprise, opportunism, and money-making, this seemed self-contradictory and a tad squeamish to me.

Artists need to be seen and heard. They thrive in the spotlight. The council, however, didn't want to play favourites. Neither did it want to single anyone out to be the poster child. To promote one artist over another was against the fairness principle. It didn't want itself to be open to criticism – tricky enough having to deal with inflated egos and peer rivalries. The Annual Arts Development Awards introduced in later years tried to make amends but, despite its earnest efforts, it's more of a glorified graduation ceremony than a red-carpet event.

The Ministry of Culture, Sports and Tourism of Korea seems to have navigated these treacherous waters well enough. In two decades, it has used pop culture to give the country an image makeover, from one perceived as rigid, hick and misogynist, into one that's smart, tech-savvy, and gender-equal. It applied the gloss and broad appeal of K-Pop, TV sit-coms, and film exports to draw domestic and international audiences, while making a substantial contribution to the GDP.

The existential question, 'Do you keep giving people fish, or teaching them how to fish themselves?', hadn't been put on the Council's meeting agenda. Neither was the other quintessential question of how we can cultivate an environment where artists can live and work and thrive on their own without being managed as human capital. We couldn't have found the right answers even if we had talked ourselves blue. Joe, as Council Chair, wasn't interested in hypotheses, and discussions were kept to matters of a practical nature. Then without warning, Oil Street happened. The answers to these questions couldn't have been easier and more cost-effective.

chapter 12

LOOKING AWAY

IT WAS WONG SHUN KIT who told me there was a space for rent in Oil Street next to a government supplies warehouse in North Point that had just been vacated. The asking rent was unbelievably affordable.

We call him WSK; his artistic journey is full of twists and turns. The first time I met him was in 1984, soon after he'd arrived from Shanghai with his young and vivacious wife. He was introduced to the Fringe Club by Philip Fok. A painter, WSK was looking for a place to exhibit his work. I asked him what he wanted to show, and he said it was a series oil paintings inspired by photos he'd seen in a travel magazine showing some ancient rock carvings found on a half-deserted island in Hong Kong. No one knows who made them or for what specific purpose. They looked prehistoric and hieroglyphic. He hadn't actually seen them, but he wanted to. I found out they were on Tung Lung Chau, a small island off the coast of Sai Kung, and could only be reached by private boat.

LIFE ON THE FRINGE

I was intrigued. That weekend, Margaret borrowed her company's yacht, and together we spent an afternoon on a hunt for these mysterious ancient markings on the rocks around the island.

WSK's first solo exhibition, *Inspired by Ancient Rock Carvings*, went on show a year later in 1986, during the Fringe Festival. That's how it all began. Later he started an artist group called Artist Commune, with an impish nod to the communes in Maoist China. A dozen or more like-minded artists joined; they leased a corner space in a car park of an industrial building in Sai Ying Pun to work and meet. After a while, it became too much of a financial burden. He said he and the Artist Commune were prepared to move, if they could find somewhere cheaper to rent.

I got a call from him on a late spring afternoon. He told me he'd found a place and wanted to check it out with me. He sounded excited. We met in front of a low-rise in Oil Street, where rooms of various sizes were available at give-away rates because the stock and property markets had hit bottom. It was a plain, grim, grey concrete block. There was an iron grille gate, chain locked, in front of a loading bay that was covered in black grease marks. Nothing to get excited about. He wanted to show me the inside. We walked around the block looking for the watchman, or someone to let us in. No one was there, so we tried to force open the gate to slip in through the stretched chain.

An elderly man in a grey tracksuit walked past. He stopped. Watching us warily, he wanted to say something to us, but we didn't give him a chance. We walked up a ramp and disappeared into a dark hall for a quick tour around the place. It had enough space to fit in an exhibition gallery, backroom, office, and storage. The walls were bare and probably still had the original coat of paint on, way back when; oozing from its cracks was the residual

LOOKING AWAY

odour of chrysanthemum and burned incense.

'It's a lot more spacious than our car park corner,' WKS said, 'and the rent much cheaper.' I asked what it'd been used for. 'Funerals,' he said. 'For those who couldn't afford a proper one. They unloaded the coffins outside, and then brought them in here for a quick send-off. People think it's haunted. Don't even want to come near it. That's why it's available and cheap.'

Artist Commune set up their quarters in the old funeral home, but not before WSK had got someone to feng-shui the place. He came, sized up the place, took out his feng-shui detecting compass, pointed it at different directions, declared that it was alright and actually not inauspicious for artists to work there. He believed artists also work in the spiritual realm and are naturally immune to sapping yin energy emanating from ghosts that would cause harm to ordinary people. 'But I can't say the same for those working inside the depot,' the feng-shui master added. 'Someone had jumped off the roof there. The angry ghost is still wandering around at night. That's a really potent one: no one can be immune from its bad mojo.'

To brighten the place, they put up a pair of wooden plaques at the entrance with the name Artist Commune painted in gold on vermillion for everyone to see. Ghosts, if there were any, would soon find themselves being nudged out of their lonely haunts, for architects, artists, crafts people, designers, and performers, young and adventurous, were making their way to Oil Street in droves. Their tools of trade tucked under arms, they filled their heads with ideas of what they could do in all those deep and wide spaces, some of which had ceilings over four, five metres high.

Not wasting any time, artists took up the available rooms and converted them into studios, galleries, and workshops.

LIFE ON THE FRINGE

Without being constantly monitored, told what and what not to do, they brought the place to life. There was never a carefully worked-out plan to turn it into the Oil Street Artist Village it was about to become. All it took was something like clearing a plot of land in a rainforest and letting the plants and other life forms take over and thrive.

On their own or together, the tenants tirelessly came up with all sorts of activities and 'happenings' to draw people there. This began to grab the media and the public's attention. It's turning into a cultural phenomenon, so uncharacteristically Hong Kong. Soon enough, Oil Street was turning into a cultural destination that big cities wanted to replicate. It later took the West Kowloon Cultural District and Tai Kwan much more effort and capital investment to emulate it.

Meanwhile, Artist Commune had converted the funeral home into an arts space and achieved instant notoriety. When it opened to visitors, it drew mixed crowds of exhibition-goers, macabre thrill-seekers, and a mysterious roving artist.

The room in the back that nobody liked to go near at night was made into a lounge with a battered bar counter, rickety bar stools and chairs; after that, nobody wanted to leave. Two regulars of the place come to mind: Tony Leung, who played in the movie adaptation of Marguerite Duras' *The Lover*, and a young artist whose name no one could remember. Tony loved coming here because he could behave like a dork off-screen and no one took any notice.

The young artist was a species apart. Nobody knew who she was or where she'd come from. She turned up one night and, before you knew it, she'd become very much at home with the place and everyone there. She dressed nicely when most of us were in baggy tops and droopy pants; she was also beautiful in an unsettling way, with a pallid complexion that seemed to glow in the dark. We felt kind of proud to have someone classy like that slumming with us, so we didn't ask too many questions.

One day, a suitcase turned up in the office. There were also some very nice women's shoes laid out in a neat row beside it. When asked, she owned up that she'd left them there, for she had no place to put them, and she was in need of a place to stay until she found somewhere else to go. No one quite knew how to handle this. She had become a resident by default, but we didn't know what's going on with her and her family, if she had any. Somehow, we knew this couldn't go on, not like this.

She had been painting and talking about showing her work. We cut her a deal. She could hang them in an exhibition here, but after that, she would have to take all her shoes and belongings – they could be seen all over the place by then – and move out.

At this juncture, it's unclear why I decided to curate *Death in Hong Kong*, a mixed-media exhibition of works by artists from the Commune and her works alongside. This was part of the visual arts programme in the first edition of the City Festival I launched in January 1999.

We held a vernissage, and the smells of resin and turpentine from the fresh oil paintings covered up any odours left over from the building's eerie past. I had the invitations printed on beautiful handmade grass paper squares with yellow, crimson, and gold patterns on them that are used for burnt offerings to the recent dead. Some of the invited guests who got an invitation in the mail on New Year's Day were much offended by it. As part of the opening ceremony, the participating artists performed a mock exorcist ritual, dressed in faux Taoist robes made from garish yellow plastic sheets. They drew incantation symbols on them in red ink to ward off evil spirits, and each carried a willow branch that they used to sweep away imaginary ghosts as they locked steps in a slow funeral march while chanting some gibberish loudly. It was quite a show and a way of thumbing their noses at the fears and taboos associated with death and dying. We couldn't have found a more appropriate venue and time to do this. The artworks on display were said to be 'out of this world', wrote a reviewer who couldn't resist a pun.

The paintings by our unofficial resident artist were done in a minimalist style without titles or captions. She had hung them when no one was around. One night, sitting around, chatting and having drinks, we noticed her absence. She'd vanished with all her belongings and artworks. Just like that, and we still don't know anything more about her.

The City Festival replaced the Fringe Festival that had been running for sixteen years. Closing the chapter on colonial rule, Hong Kong entered into a new era. I could sense that there was a loss of interest in the narrative of a city in danger of being stripped of its freedoms and on the verge of disappearing.

Those months of non-stop rain after the handover, followed by the Asian financial markets going bust, gave us pause. The Fringe had had a very good run. We were made to feel good and important by the departing Government. Would our lives be any different under the new one now?

Before the final curtain, we had been routinely invited to tea with the Governors' wives and to banquet dinners with visiting dignitaries by the Governors themselves. They themselves would turn up at exhibition openings and shows. There was an artist-in-residence who, at one time, bunked up in Government House on Upper Albert Road – a most convenient location for her – just up the road from us. That was Yvonne Hawker, a British painter who loved painting scenes from our wet markets.

Our restaurant was in the neighbourhood of the 'First Family', and they came and ate in our restaurant a lot. A dessert called the Governor's Trifle was put on the menu. I was awarded a Badge of Honour, not for gratifying the Governor's sweet tooth, I'm almost certain, but for 'services rendered to the community'.

It's not exactly a knighthood, but it made me feel like I was bestowed one. I was at home on that day when the honours notification was delivered. It wasn't sent by mail but by a footman in gloves and uniform who came on a motorcycle with a sidecar that carried the insignia of the crown and flying the British flag. This created enough commotion to attract the attention of my curious neighbours. I didn't just get a medal pinned on me but was also given a lot of face henceforth by the habitually grouchy watchman of my block. Some years later, after the change of masters in Government House, I was awarded another honour for my work in the arts. This time there was no such fanfare. The era of pomp and circumstance had been replaced by dry pragmatism.

Close on the heels of the Handover came a sobering meeting in the new office of the British Council, beautifully constructed on a site in the old Victoria Barracks. It was where the Council hosted a champagne and orange juice breakfast in honour of Prince Charles (now King Charles III), who'd come especially on his big yacht to give Hong Kong back to China.

The British Council had been our sponsor since day one, a staunch supporter in our corner all these years. I was given a tour of the new office space on that special day by an arts officer. It looked modern and sleek, unlike the time when the Council couldn't have cared less how it looked to others, for it was as sure of itself as the unkempt mane in a pride of lions.

Then we sat down to talk. I was offered coffee from a smart kiosk in the reception, instead of the usual teabag tea in a mug. Taking in the change of atmosphere, I was also offered apologies that weren't expected. I was told there was going to be a major policy change. They had been instructed by Head Office to reallocate their resources to other branches. 'I'm afraid Hong Kong will no longer be our focus and priority,' the arts officer explained. I asked where. He said the Middle East.

I was expecting change but nothing this drastic. It felt like the breakup of a long and enduring relationship. No matter how amicable the parting was, it still felt hurt and torn. Snatches of a famous poem by Rupert Brooke had come to mind. Irrelevant though it might've seemed, I found it befitting the mood of the moment:

> 'Her sights and sounds;
> Dreams happy as her day;
> And laughter, learnt of friends; and gentleness,
> In hearts at peace, under an English heaven.'

Not really. Yes, I know. But I'm always sentimental when it comes to saying goodbye and seeing things coming to an end.

chapter 13

TURNING AROUND

WE COULDN'T HELP but notice a marked drop in the number of shows at the Fringe following the 1997 Handover. Especially among the overseas groups: they seemed to have lost the see-Hong-Kong-or-die compulsion. We were wary that it might be the start of a downward trend that turns an Adonis into a middle-aged yob. After all, sixteen years seemed a long enough shelf life. Time to change and reset.

The transformation of Hong Kong – from a colonial remnant into an open city that is part of China – was underway. The fifty-year guarantee of no change was given and enshrined in the Basic Law. What really calmed our jitters about losing the pleasures and freedoms we had been enjoying was, funnily enough, two pithy slogans in Cantonese, 'Horse Still Race 馬照跑', 'Dance Still Dance 舞照跳', which were supposed to have come from Chairman Deng Xiaoping to reassure us that life in Hong Kong would remain as bourgeois as before. This gave us the idea of a new festival, one that celebrates urban culture.

I took it to a few people whose opinions I respect to see if there was something going for it. Over lunch with Douglas Gautier – Director of the Hong Kong Arts Festival at the time – I said we were trying to come up with a name for it. Nothing fancy, pithy and catchy. 'City Festival' got the votes. I too thought this was what it should be called: simple, easy to remember, capturing the zeitgeist of the times. Orlean Lai, a new recruit, came up with an inspired Chinese translation, 乙城節. Benny Lau of Creative Café designed the new logo, and Vantjia; our creative designer of many years created the key images.

City Festival would give us a new voice and a chance to look into how cities are special and different. What makes them tick the way they do, and how they measure up to Hong Kong. A chance to see the world, pick up some fresh ideas, meet people we otherwise wouldn't. We thought it a splendid idea. Each year, we'd select a city to be the Spotlight City and use its unique cultural ingredients to cook up a storm.

We weren't ready to throw the Fringe to the junkyard. There was still gas in the tank. Its engine was still chugging along fine. This gave us the idea of creating a hybrid festival, part curated and part Fringe, with the Spotlight City as signature programme. We'd worked out a two-way exchange system. The incoming lane would bring in artists from the chosen cities. In reciprocation, the outgoing lane would take Hong Kong artists to cities where they could showcase their works and do some networking.

The timing was spot on. Dr Patrick Ho, Secretary for Home Affairs, was keen to get it going. He had been signing Memoranda of Understanding right and left with neighbouring cities, ostensibly for cultural exchange and building relationships, but the offshoots were to create opportunities for business and trade. A programme such as Spotlight Hong Kong would serve the purpose very well.

By chance, we were doing an off-grid cultural exchange ourselves in Seoul with the Seoul Fringe 2004. Cat brought singer Amabel from Hong Kong to perform with a Korean jazz band called Lazy Monday while Patrick was there on an official visit. We invited him and his aide, Mr Fong Ngai, to attend. The gig was at Evans, an intimate, down-to-earth jazz club; nothing glitzy about it. They came, enjoyed listening to the music and talking with the artists. The evening demonstrated how the whole thing would work, even without the obligatory ribbon cutting and speeches. The drummer, Jimmy Suh, had a Hong Kong connection: his father was teaching at the Chinese University of Hong Kong, so he came to visit often. He'd caught Amabel singing at the Fringe, and when they met, they hit it off; that's how she was introduced to his band.

How did Seoul – broadly speaking Korea as a whole - come into the picture? Before I went there, I knew nothing about the capital city, the country, or the people. My only impression of Korea was garnered from eating at the Korean barbecue restaurant in Patterson Street, Causeway Bay. The service staff spoke Korean among themselves but seldom to their customers; they were efficient, brusque, almost sullen. The menu never changed, the food dependably tasty and spicy. I'd deduced that Koreans were somewhat like that. Which was the sum total of my knowledge though I was aware that the country was divided into North and South, and that they were essentially enemies of each other. Seoul had never been high on my must-see list.

As they say, things happen. Cities have a way of presenting

themselves, as though they have minds of their own. I've come across this rather baffling experience time and again, in trying to make a carefully considered selection of the right one. I couldn't help feeling that, in the end, they chose me instead. This might sound haphazard, even mystical, the way life can be. I can't really explain it, just as when this phone call came through on my landline.

It was before the mobile phone had become an extension of our hands. It was an overseas call. The caller didn't speak a language any of us could comprehend. He seemed to be asking for someone with an approximation of my name. Then a female voice that spoke English haltingly took over. She said that was Mr Lee calling and he had a message for me: he wanted to invite me to come to Korea to attend the Seoul Fringe Festival. She went on to say Mr Lee had never met me but had heard good things about me from someone performing in the Avignon Off Festival.

I wouldn't normally say yes right away to a call from a stranger with whom I couldn't even conduct a conversation. But, to my surprise, I did. It might have had something to do with the state I was in. My brother Joe was dying of cancer of the bladder. Like our mother, he didn't want to receive chemo and other aggressive treatments but to live out the remainder of his days, resigned to his fate. I told the doctor of his wish, and he was very much against it. I told him that I knew my brother wouldn't be talked out of it once his mind was made up. I was in a quandary: I respected Joe's decision about his own life, and death, but I also agreed with his doctor's medical opinion that he mustn't refuse treatment. The stress manifested itself in a form of vertigo: I lost my balance and could hardly see straight. I just wanted to get away from it all.

TURNING AROUND

Just like that, I took a flight to Seoul. In the arrival hall, I stood there alone with my suitcase, wondering what I'd do if Mr Lee didn't appear. I wouldn't know who to call or where to find him. Am I not totally naive, I thought, putting trust in a total stranger?

Mr Lee turned up with an interpreter, an English major from Yonsei University, one of the many volunteers of the fledgling Seoul Fringe launched the year before. His hair, dyed pink, looked out of sync with the rest of him. He was wearing a plain white shirt and khaki pants. Of slim build with a slim face smoke-tanned by nonstop smoking, he broke into a big friendly smile and shook my hands warmly with both hands. I liked him already, before we were able to say anything we could understand to each other. Only then did I know him by his full name: Lee Gyu Seog. He would open up for me a vista to the friendly and art-loving side of the country.

He invited me back a year later. On the night the Korean soccer team won its match to secure a place in the World Cup Final against Spain, I ran out into the streets along with the excited crowd. Together we were cheering, chanting, and beating on drums. It was an 'Ich bin ein Berliner' moment that bonded me with Seoul and the friends I'd made there, all the way until now. Between December 2001 and July 2021, two decades, we coordinated seventy-seven exchanges between Hong Kong and Korean artists.

After Seoul, we brought Spotlight Hong Kong to Singapore, Ho Chi Minh City, Penang, Guangzhou, Kaiping, Shanghai, Taipei, Penang, and Singapore again.

We repeated Spotlight Hong Kong twice in Singapore, not just because I was born there, in Bukit Timah, when it was still

LIFE ON THE FRINGE

a kampong, untouched by developers, and was emotionally attached because of the stories my mother told me. Waking up to the calls of the Tamil kopi street vendors. Taking rickshaw rides to 'eat wind' to cool down in the tropical night before bedtime. Being haunted by the ghosts of the two young lovers found dead together in the pineapple field. The wreathing scent of magnolia in the moonlight. It was also the people: Kuo Pao Kun, Robert Iau, Benson Puah, Toh Hock Ghim, Amy Ho, Ivan Heng, Krishen Jit, Sinclair, Ginnie, Phan Mingyen, and my don – Colin Goh. On the family side, Lydia and Hawk – my dear sister and brother-in-law – and their two lovely daughters, Hannah and Sarah, my brother Tony, free-spirited niece, Monica, and all the other members of my extended family there.

Kuo Pao Kun, Singapore's best-known dramatist, brought two of his plays to our theatre – *The Coffin Is Too Big for the Hole* and *No Parking on Odd Days* – both satires of the government's intractable bureaucracies. Before he took to the stage, his critical views of the Singapore government had got him into trouble and landed him in jail. He said he always liked coming to Hong Kong just to breathe the air and enjoy the freedoms denied him at home. Pao Kun was a serious man, and he'd ask probing questions about the conversion works and operational needs of our ice depot. He was gathering information for a similar project involving a disused power substation on Armenian Street in Singapore. A few years later, in 1990, he set up The Substation, a contemporary arts space that's still thriving.

Robert Iau and Benson Puah, both executive directors of the Esplanade at different times, helped steer the facility on its tortuous journey to become the cultural landmark of Singapore. Nicknamed 'The Big Durian' for its likeness to the fruit's spiky rind, the Esplanade had once sat precariously on the edge of Marina Bay, facing the unlikely prospect of sliding back into the sea: the reclaimed land it had been built on had been found to be less than solid. In a lapse of imagination, it had almost become a convention centre for hosting business conferences and trade fairs. What a humdrum life it would have been for the Big Durian.

I'd met with Robert a number of times in Hong Kong. He was concerned about the length of time it had taken to build the Esplanade. Many new recruits sent abroad to train had dropped out, and efforts to prepare them had gone to waste. 'You could save us some Sing dollars,' he said, half in jest. 'You've already been trained overseas. Why don't you come back and join us?'

I won't forget how Benson had once got on a plane to fly to Hong Kong just in time to join our seminar as our guest speaker. He gave an inspirational talk, then hopped on the next flight on the same day back to work. As if that's not enough, in addition to being the CEO of Esplanade, he ran the Arts Council concurrently, putting an underachiever like me to shame.

Ivan Heng and I met for the first time at the Edinburgh Fringe, where he was performing in a show he'd also directed. I've never met an actor who could make his audience feel so cherished, even on their way out of the theatre. After taking his bows, he'd make a dash to the front-of-house, still in costume and make-up, and give everyone his big smile and the warmest thank you.

Ivan did a Hong Kong premiere of *Emily on Emerald Hill* (1984) directed by the legendary Krishen Jit. A one-woman show, Ivan appeared as a once-glamorous socialite now in her twilight years, looking back on her life and Singapore's bygone era. He played the role, transgendered, from Emily as maiden, to matron, to crone, as only he can. A good portion of the Singaporean population in Hong Kong turned out to see him.

It was a demanding performance and he gave it his all. Once offstage, he'd change back to his shorts and flip flops and be himself again. He and Krishen – with his crop of frizzy silver hair – would sit outside the theatre, one with a pint of beer in hand and the other, a large whiskey, or was it just a Coke? They were like the proud village chief with his congenial headman, shooting the breeze after a long day's work. Ivan now runs the Wild Rice Theatre Company, in his own theatre.

We couldn't run these Spotlight City programmes without the help of our partners. Looking for the right one is no different from what you do in life: you choose one that is compatible, reliable, and can charge up your battery when it's running low. In our case, we also needed their local knowledge and contacts. When Colin and Mingyen turned up one day at our door, it was destiny knocking. They had just converted the old Parliament House into an art house. It's the kind of project that you could only daydream about. Flanked by two museums, a short stroll from the bustling fares of Clarke Quay, this historical landmark has a majestic, neoclassical facade behind which more machinations and plots had been hatched in its corridors than in Hamlet.

It's also the kind of place that could cast a spell, reel you in, make you think of no one else, and then use up your love and tender care for fuel. Not unlike driving a high-performance car, you have to pump it with lots of content to get it going, which could be costly. You don't want it to become a money pit. So Mingyen and Colin were looking for sustainable ways to run the programming side of their operation.

They could've heard from Robert or from Amy that we might have found a way to do it. They wanted to know how it's done. I was flattered that they actually bothered to come all the way to Hong Kong to meet me. I could see that Colin and Mingyen function together like a super brain whose right and left hemispheres work to full capacity. Mere mortals are happy just to have one side of it performing well. Colin could crunch numbers for morning exercises, churning out business plans at the rate of the change of traffic lights. Meanwhile, Mingyen dashed through a set of ideas with the same dexterity as Lang Lang playing scales, oftentimes having a hard time keeping up with himself. I found out that, apart from working like clockwork together, they share paranormal sensibilities. I feel privileged that they confided in me some of the untold secrets of the old Parliament House. Those stories would never leave those walls and become any more real by telling. I bear the burden of keeping them to myself, but to any curious soul who ventures into the space, they reveal themselves as readily as the mystery of infinity does between two confronting mirrors.

It was the beginning of a beautiful friendship that we've kept up all these years. We presented Spotlight Singapore in Hong Kong with the Art House in 2006, and the following year, they reciprocated with Spotlight Hong Kong in Singapore. They liked this idea of using arts and culture as a calling card to other cities so much so that they adopted the name: they brought Spotlight Singapore to a list of cities, including Moscow. On that occasion, they brought with them a contingent of artists and some 200 or so trade representatives, from banking to hospital management, that were interested in doing business with Russia. Two former prime ministers, Lee Kuan Yew and Goh Chok Tong, went along. His Excellency Ambassador Michael Tay organised a big bash, inviting everyone to meet everyone, and as an invited guest, I was able to witness how this can be orchestrated: using arts to connect and break the ice at an upscale state event.

Later we had a chance to invite Michael Tay to speak at a seminar called 'Asia on the Edge', held at the Fringe. By this time, he had retired from diplomatic service. I found out that we shared two passions: wine and music. Few men in his position could have risen to the hepatic challenges of socialising in Russia as he had done. No other ambassador had made use of music to the extent that he'd done to build diplomatic relationships. He had commissioned Russian composer Vladimir Martynov to compose a symphony: *Singapore*, later renamed *Utopia* and recorded by the London Philharmonic Orchestra, celebrated the birth of the nation. Needless to say, this had caused some controversy: the price to pay for taking the less trodden path and doing something no one had attempted. Through Tay and several other diplomats, I learned that culture-minded ambassadors or consuls general – ones that not only tended their business dossiers – could show you how to cross the roadblocks into their countries. Especially if they happen to be friendly and helpful, which they often are.

The Honourable Mr Toh Hok Ghim, the Consul General of Singapore, took a real interest in bringing the two cities closer through our Spotlight City programmes. With his help, we managed to put the call through to MICA, Ministry of Information, Communication and the Arts. Once the main sluice was opened, others followed and all else flowed. That included the National Arts Council and the Hong Kong Economic and Trade Office in Singapore, and other target organisations. Hok Ghim is a foodie, and at his dinner table, I tasted the best roast goose cooked the Cantonese way. He also revealed to me one of the best-kept national secrets of Singapore: the cure for gout, caused by too much uric acid in the body. 'Soda water. Drink a can one hour after you've eaten. It works miracles for those gouty, sedentary middle-aged men doing national service training who know how painful it can get, marching in army boots all day.'

Dr Helmut Bock, Consul General of Austria, is another congenial dinner host. He's endowed with effortless charm and a sense of humour unusual among learned Northern Europeans. 'Call me Helmut,' he said on our first meeting, at dinner, 'Took me eight years serving my time in the library just to be called Dr Bock.' For dessert, he served Sachertorte – the famous Viennese chocolate cake that packs enough sugar to melt the coronary of your heart. One guest with a worried look on her face asked, 'Is this not very sweet?' He replied with a reassuring smile: 'It is very sweet indeed but zero calories.'

Dr Bock was keen on the idea of doing Spotlight Vienna in Hong Kong and did all he could to help. Without him showing the way, I wouldn't know where to begin. Vienna, once the political epicentre and cultural nexus of Europe, has a long and complex history. Even though its imperial past had been consigned to the vault, the protocols – handed down from the heydays of the Austro-Hungarian court where courtiers took their time to gild the lily – for official visitors were still very much alive.

First, I was to call on the Foreign Ministry to present myself and make known the purpose of my visit to a gamut of junior to senior officials. Then I was to make a courtesy call to the Mayor and the Governor's Office. I was met by his Deputy Director, Dr Margareta Grieszler, who had spent years in China and could speak fluent Putonghua. She looked not only remarkably young

LIFE ON THE FRINGE

for her office and title but was also extraordinarily helpful. She guided me through the labyrinthine Viennese officialdom. She set up meetings with the people I needed to call on to get anything done. She cautioned me not to get on the wrong side of the Vienna Representative Office. Dr Bock had also given me an introduction to Dr Brigitta Blaha, his successor. Her name would be inscribed in gold in my Book of Angels for bringing Vienna to Hong Kong, and more.

Apart from the cafes that Vienna is famous for – the art museums converted from once-grandiose palaces, the revered Musikverein, the omnipresent heurigers serving local wines and schnitzels, Mozart's face on just about everything, the Prater with its giant Ferris Wheel and the figure of Calafati that has been greeting fairground visitors for ages – there was a small cinema on the Opernring, showing an old black-and-white film called *The Third Man*.

You would've taken it for just another arthouse cinema frequented by arts students with their dates, and tireless film buffs, had you not noticed that only one film was on show and there's no other coming attraction. The movie posters and trailer photos in the foyer looked like they had been pinned up and forgotten to be taken down since the day they had stopped making black-and-white films. Written by Graham Greene and directed by Carol Reed, with Joseph Cotton, Alida Valli (Mussolini called her the most beautiful woman in the world), and Orson Welles, *The Third Man* is a film noir thriller set in post-war Vienna. Devastated by war, occupied and run by the armed forces from four Allied countries, the city was in a bad way. Vienna was on the brink of moral bankruptcy. It was preyed on by unscrupulous black marketeers personified by the character played by the viperous

Orson Welles. That's not the kind of memory a city wants to cherish and be reminded of all the time, but instead of sweeping it under history's forgetful rug, it's held up as a major tourist attraction for everyone to see.

On a cold and rainy afternoon, I found myself in the half-empty cinema, sitting through one hour and forty-four minutes of the film. The choppy projection and scratchy soundtrack were strangely hypnotic. So was the theme song strummed on the zither, and Orson Welles with his cobra eyes playing Harry Lime, the diabolical black marketeer. It took me back to a dark place. After the curtains had come down and the house lights were back on, I sat there brooding. Maybe this perpetual showing of the movie is some kind of Freudian therapy prescribed to heal the trauma of a troubled past. The treatment is to revisit the scenes, again and again, until people have become so used to them that they don't get freaked out the next time they're haunted by them.

Vienna has taken this even further. In 2005, the museum Dritte Mann or Third Man was set up in Pressgasses. It permanently houses and displays the manuscripts, photos, and memorabilia of the movie. I came across an essay by August Ruhs titled 'Living & Working in Vienna' and found this thesis-like quote that sheds some light on why the Viennese insist on doing this:

> *Creativity, going by Freud's useful distinction, involves an interaction with both the impulse and the object. Restructuring impulses would be sublimation while transforming the object would be idealisation.*

Another spin-off from the movie is a tour of the city's sewer system, where you can breathe in the excitement of the film's climactic chase scene and nostalgia for the bad old days.

Walking along the bank of the Danube I came across the Spittelau waste incineration plant. I wouldn't have recognised it if not for the smoke coming out of its tall bulbous chimney tower. It looked more like a museum building with a distinctive design. I was told that it had almost been burned down. The massive scarred structure had looked so dark and sinister that it reminded people of the incinerators used in the death camps of Auschwitz and Dachau. Even shorn of the macabre, it had been a veritable eyesore in the once-imperial and grandiose city. Yet, instead of removing it or rendering it less visible, the city council commissioned Austrian artist Friedensreich Hundertwasser – well known for his bold, colourful, and quirky style – to make an art piece of it that's got people talking, gawking, and giving their wildly different opinions.

The city also decided to tackle the famous blue Danube that had become very polluted. Factories had been dumping their chemical waste into it over the years. They cleaned it up and restored the river to its health. The municipal government declared that it's now safe enough to swim in and even built a Mediterranean-style seaside resort on its banks to prove their point.

I thought of our own harbour. Hongkongers see it as polluted and unfit for humans or marine creatures to swim in. I pictured a murky and dismal seabed littered with all kinds of discarded objects and evidence of unsolved crimes. I thought it'd make a great establishing shot for a film noir about Hong Kong.

Vienna is a musical city. No matter where you go, the *gemütlich* Vivaldi's *Four Seasons* or Mozart's *Eine Kleine Nachtmusik* follow you to every shop and street corner. And the Wiener Staatsoper and Musikverein, the opera house and concert hall, transport audiences to the pearly gates of musical heaven. I wanted to find out what young Viennese actually listen to when they're not listening to classical music. So, I went clubbing. They told me to check out Club Meierei, an all-night dance joint hosted by young DJs Heinz Tronigger and Meier Landsky, the rage of the club scene.

Vienna isn't a late-night city by any standards. After dinner, the streets are empty except for the few pedestrians hurrying home or lingering around tram stops. I found the club in a quiet street. A lone bouncer in a thin jacket was standing outside the door, huddling against the whipping cold night. I gave him a nod and he waved me past.

I expected to find a jam-packed, smoky den, playing mind-busting techno music. It was a large venue with spaced-out seating and not a whiff of smoke in sight. I got there between sets. A small crowd of mostly university students were chatting and waiting their turn at the bar to refill their drinks. When the next set started, people got up to dance, unhurriedly, like they knew they had all night and a life ahead of them to figure things out. They played Deep House, a combination of funk and electronic jazz with vocals to 'reach minds'. I picked out some lyrics from a remix of Madonna's *Nothing Really Matters*.

> *Nothing takes the past away*
> *Like the future.*
> *Nothing makes the darkness go*
> *Like the light.*

I was somewhat stirred by what I was listening to but felt this wasn't about us. Hong Kong was a young and sunny place and didn't have a troubled past to mess up its head. Whatever fears and doubts we might have about our future had already been patted down. Everything was going to be just dandy. Why get worried? Who cares what's going to happen in fifty years? We might not even be around anymore.

It's been years since I last listened to that song. Then I hear it again on Spotify. This time it's not just another Madonna MTV number to dance to. What really matters? I put the question to myself. It has to be hope. Hope is a good thing. For those who have fought and lost yet refused to 'go gentle into that good night'. Hope keeps you going for another round. The past never leaves; it only deepens.

DJs Heinz and Meier came for Spotlight Vienna in City Festival 2002. They brought along their own turntables and playlists to jam with top local DJ Joe Lai at the Fringe Club. It was a night that brought Deep House and Acid together. The gig lasted until dawn. The ear-throbbing bass rhythm lasted much longer.

The key cultural exchange programme was called *Re-Considered Crossing: Representation Beyond Hybridity*. It took up two double spreads in the guide to the City Festival to explain what it was about. Norman Jackson Ford came up with this puzzling event title. He was also the curator, with Susanne Gamauf and Klaus Pamminger from Fotogalerie Wien co-curating. In two parts, between Hong Kong and Vienna, some thirty artists, curators, and academics participating. It included exhibitions of lens-based media, symposiums, public lectures, and video screenings. The book, *Traversals* (*Map Book Publishers*, 2001), authored by Laurent Gutierrez and Valerie Portefaix, documented the entire event.

Norman, an art photographer from the US, was around the

Fringe a lot, and we'd come to know him quite well. We'd worked on a number of projects and once gone on tour to Seoul with him and other Hong Kong artists.

We introduced him to Esteban Antonio, a flamenco guitarist from London and frequent performer on the Fringe. Norman had taken some black-and-white photos of him to promote his coming world tour. Estaban, in a black leather jacket and open-front shirt, struck a pose that reminded me of some images I'd seen in Robert Mapplethorpe's *Perfect Moment* exhibition at the ICA in Philadelphia. Mapplethorpe's work created a big media scandal at the time for allegedly showing obscene images involving minors. Some years later, one early morning, the police came for Norman while he was still asleep in his flat. They arrested him and took away his computers to look for incriminating evidence. He was later charged and found guilty of possessing child pornography and sentenced to a prison term of eighteen months.

This could be a missed opportunity to look into subjects such as sexual perversity in art practices and start some serious discourse on what's taboo. After he'd been discharged, he packed up and left Hong Kong. He never explained or defended what he'd done. There's no chance to know if he was guilty as charged. Or, he had succumbed to the voyeuristic impulses of what Mapplethorpe perversely called perfect moments. We swept the whole unsavoury episode under the carpet of our minds. It seemed we didn't want to talk about these things either. Maybe we had problems bringing our repressed instincts into the open for fear of contaminating our arts. Who wants to expose what we keep in our own locked cabinets? I don't think anything as raw and challenging as Viennese Actionism will ever happen here. Frankly, we're much too decent and puritanical in our art making just as we are as a society. What would Freud find, if he tried to dig into our psyches?

There was a lighter side to our exchanges with Vienna: live jazz, a music film festival, a fashion show, and even a *heurigen* tavern to give a vinaceous taste of the city. I remember what W. H. Auden, the English poet, once said. He chose to live in Vienna for two reasons: concert tickets are affordable and so are the wines.

To mirror Vienna's attempts to trawl the bottom of things to extract the truth, I recruited the help of the Hong Kong Diving School. They went down into the murky depths of the harbour, took underwater photos, and picked up objects of interest from the seabed. We then showed the photos in an exhibition. Objects fished up, encrusted in barnacles, were handed over to artists to be made into sculptures which inspired a bunch of students from the Swire School of Design at Hong Kong Polytechnic to put on a fashion show.

Our harbour, we found out, is quite innocent of criminal activities, save for a few credit cards found on the seabed by our divers. These cards might have been discarded under suspicious circumstances, but we surmised that they had been hurled into the sea by people who had inadvertently reached their spending limits and regretted owning them. Other than that, it's nowhere nearly as polluted as the Danube used to be. Much to everyone's amazement, coral that only grows in relatively clean water was found in the sea not far from the Cultural Centre.

I'm not going to take my leave of Vienna – in parts disconcerting – without a bright note. I suggest the next time you visit Hong Kong Park, do look for a stone-and-bronze drinking water fountain. It's a gift from the City of Vienna, a bijou memento in Jugendstil design that serves as a reminder that, despite everything dark and brutal that happens in the world, time, like running water will eventually wash it off.

The other spotlight cities – Melbourne, Honolulu, Bergen, Singapore, Penang, San Francisco, Ho Chi Minh City, Kaiping, Guangzhou – all have their own stories to tell. As for me, Melbourne, whose rain and whipping wind that literally poured cold water on my first visit, has now become my second home and a city with open skyline, pockets of green gardens at every turn, unhurried coffee places, and foodies' treasure troves found in Prahran and South Melbourne markets.

Honolulu. Breathtaking scenery and protected volcanic craters where you can swim in clear aquamarine water among curious, frisky fish. The East-West Centre, with its vast collection of Asian American theatre scripts, was where I had an epiphany: I don't always have to make a mad dash into the theatre just before shows start like a sprinter on fire; I can allow myself time to savour the experience by arriving early, as Hawaiian theatregoers routinely do.

Bergen in Norway first caught my eye for a number of reasons. It was designated Cultural Capital of Europe that year in 2000, despite its small population size and relative anonymity. I'd also come across on the Internet an art space called Stiftelsen 3,14, fronted by Sigrid Szetu, whose surname sounded Chinese to me. On her website, she explains: 'Our whole *raison d'être* is the dialogue', so I wrote and started a dialogue with Sigrid.

I hadn't been to Norway and knew next to nothing about

LIFE ON THE FRINGE

Bergen. But the message on the Stiftelsen 3,14 website assured me that '[it is] moving away from the Euro-centricity in art and seeing that art is art wherever it is encountered, and there are more similarities than differences among different geographical regions.' I liked that and wanted to meet Sigrid, find out what the foundation was doing, and check out the city of Bergen.

In summer 2000, I took an evening flight from Stansted, an airfield outside London, to arrive in Bergen before midnight. I quickly cleared customs with a few Nordic passengers who had been enjoying the free alcohol to the maximum on the way. Sigrid was supposed to pick me up from the airport and take me to a hotel but mistakenly thought I was to arrive two days later.

By the time she got to the airport, she'd found out that there were no hotel rooms available that night. So she took me home instead. Her apartment, if I remember right, had bright multicoloured walls, children's things everywhere, and smelled of cigarette smoke. While we were chatting like old friends, she cleared out her daughter's room and made the bed for me to spend the night. Meanwhile, she asked Bjørn, her assistant, to push forward all my appointments. He also managed to book me into the Admiral Hotel by the port for a top-floor room facing postcard-perfect houses lined up neat rows along a narrow strip of harbour where fishing boats of all shapes and sizes berthed.

Bergen born, Sigrid studied painting at the Camberwell Art School, London and then lived in Borneo, where she married a Straits Chinese and acquired her non-Norwegian family name. She was slim, blonde, easy on herself and on other people. She ran me through the multicultural local arts world in the short while I was there, at the pace of speed dating. She also matched me up with Robert Sot, a multimedia artist from Poland, who took me everywhere. He later came with Spotlight on Bergen to Hong Kong. Robert gave me his perspectives on Norway, as an artist and outsider, with the kind of humour that downplays the misfortunes of life prevalent in Eastern Bloc countries under Soviet rule. When I said that people here seem to drink a lot of coffee, he replied: 'Do you know that Norway is the single largest importer of bad coffee in the world?' 'Can't be true,' I said, checking if he was serious. 'There are so few people here.' 'That's because they drink it non-stop,' he said. 'But surely not bad coffee?' I retorted. 'They don't care. They just drink it to stay awake, or they wouldn't even want to get out of bed in winter when it's night all day out there.'

He took me to check out Stiftelsen 3,14, located in the town square. It looked like a Florentine palazzo with a grand entrance and a marble staircase in the foyer. Downstairs were stores, crafts and souvenirs. The main hall upstairs displayed art by Jannicke, an ethnic Korean who had been adopted and raised by Norwegian parents, and whose boyfriend, a nightclub bouncer, had been shot dead by someone with a stolen gun eight years ago. In this show using firearms confiscated by the police to create everyday objects, Jannicke demonstrated how violence is made banal by our society.

Sigrid is a good connector. She knows everyone there is to know. She took me to the Artists' Union, the Cultural Capital Office, and the United Sardine Factory (USF). She also introduced me to Han Mei, an artist from Beijing, who introduced me to the Shu brothers from Hong Kong. 'They came here a few years ago. Now they're running a business empire. You might want to tap them for sponsorship.'

Whenever we went into meetings, everyone smoked and drank coffee, just as Robert described it. But for all the intake of caffeine, it didn't seem to have sped up their conversations, which were conducted at a Nordic tempo. Once someone started making a point, it had to be finished, even if it wasn't really necessary. So, meetings went on for quite a bit longer than they had to.

I was taken to the dockside to visit the USF. Previously a canning factory, when Bergen's main industry was in fishing, its many hangar-sized rooms are now rented to dancers, musicians, painters, and filmmakers. A jazz festival was going on. I met the USF manager, who was rightfully proud of what he was doing there. He told me the owner, who inherited the factory from his family, had been talked into doing this by a group of artists who needed space to work. He had been rather reluctant at first but now was very pleased because they had helped gentrify the neighbourhood and, therefore, added value to his properties.

He showed me the studio rooms for holding artists' residency: spacious and Nordically stylish with the sea lapping gently outside a spread of tall windows. We arranged for Victor and Mandy of Y-Space, a contemporary dance duo in Hong Kong, to stay there for a month, during which they devised and performed a breathtaking performance art piece. Victor wrapped himself up in bubble wrap, and Mandy rolled him down from the top of a slope. Later, when the artists from Bergen came to Hong Kong, Mandy and Victor took them around the city. Consul General Mr Rolf Hansen was a sponsor and kind host, and Espen, floor manager of M at the Fringe, originally from Norway, prepared a typical Norwegian soup, tasty and warming, that we served in our roof garden, throughout winter during the Festival.

The George Town Festival was our portal into Penang, an island situated in the Strait of Malacca on the north-western coast of Malaysia, and the only province governed by the Opposition Party in Malaysian Parliament. I first met Joe Sidek, the Director of the Festival, in Hong Kong during the Asia On the Edge symposium, the Fringe co-curated with Global Alliance from Singapore. Joe was among the seventeen delegates from ASEAN in attendance. You couldn't have missed him in a crowd; his enthusiasm for and pride in his hometown, George Town, was infectious.

George Town seems to have forgotten to wind its clocks. It looks almost unchanged from the day it had pictures taken for postcards, which have become vintage. I remember there was a time it neglected to keep up appearances. Those colonial, Peranakan, and traditional Chinese mansions that had seen better days looked like faded grande dames with no make-up on. Then they were given a head-to-toe makeover. In 2008, UNESCO declared George Town a World Heritage Site, and to celebrate, the city launched George Town Festival 2010, with Joe as Founding Director.

To bring Spotlight Hong Kong to Penang, we partnered with Joe and his capable associate, Gaik Cheng. Christy Chow, on our side, was a good match for Gaik, and both were adept at running the spreadsheets from their desks and deploying logistics in the field. On the ground, Joe had both local knowledge and the connections. He told us there was no purpose-built concert hall or drama theatre in George Town. Instead, performances, official ceremonies, public meetings, and film shows were held at the all-purpose town hall in the town square. That was the obvious choice but not what we were looking for. I always have my eye on buildings that are special and have their stories to tell.

The Eastern & Oriental Hotel (E&O) goes back to the time when George Town was a bustling financial hub in what was then Malaya, as well as a destination for passengers taking a deluxe train

LIFE ON THE FRINGE

journey to East Asia on the Orient Express, in the heyday of the British Empire. With its elegant bayside rooms with wide verandas, French windows with dark wooden shutters, and grand ballrooms with gilded corniced ceilings, you only have to say its name once and everyone knows where it is.

For our choice of venues, we either slum or glam it; anything in between is plain vanilla. We picked E&O Hotel, China House, Gurney Plaza, Blue Mansion, and MaCalister Mansion. All these buildings had been restored to their former glory, except Gurney Plaza, which was a new build.

China House used to be one of the many typical shophouses in George Town. It has a deceptively narrow frontage but inside it stretches to the full length of a street. The owner, Narelle, brought the café culture from Melbourne and turned China House into a hip food and arts joint, while retaining its local character and some of its original features. We installed the Saturday Night Jazz Quintet in its dimly lit inner sanctuary, where they played a memorable gig. Timeless.

Blue Mansion was the private residence of Cheong Fatt Tze, a Chinese merchant once compared to John D. Rockefeller in net worth. Cheong spared no expense, and the mansion was completed in 1904, after seven years of construction. The blue exterior walls, made from a mixture of lime and indigo dye, were supposed to be able to ward off evil spirits by making themselves invisible to them.

But as they say, inherited wealth usually doesn't last for more than two generations. By the 1980s, the last heir, presumably one of the long-lasting males, had run out of means for the upkeep of the thirty-eight-room mansion. Cheong Fatt Tze Mansion joined the skid row of the rundown, soon-to-be-knocked-down houses of George Town.

Laurence Loh told me how he walked past it one day to see greedy developers encircling it like vultures over a dying beast. He didn't know why, but he felt a calling to save and preserve it. Laurence asked his father for a loan to buy it; he has since become a well-known conservation architect. It took twenty years and more to painstakingly restore the building, transforming it into the gem of a boutique hotel that it is today.

That night, the Fringe Chair, Ms Wailee Chow, hosted a dinner in the Blue Mansion to honour Mrs Carrie Lam, then Chief Secretary of HKSAR, who joined the symposium as keynote speaker on heritage conservation and urban regeneration. It was a dinner prepared by a Michelin-star chef from Kuala Lumpur and served in exquisite antique chinaware. Laurence laid out a long hardwood table in the restored family dining room under soft ambient lights. It was an intimate event with a coterie of special guests.

Carrie seemed relaxed, even after a long day of speaking and rounds of official visits. She was a light eater who hardly touched her wine glass except to raise it for a toast. After dinner, Laurence showed us around and told us gripping stories of paranormal activity on the site over the years. He also presented Carrie with a coffee-table book about the Blue Mansion.

At the symposium the next morning, she shared her experience on the dismantling of Hong Kong's Queen's Pier and Star Ferry Pier, and the importance of communication with the conservation lobbyists in the process. During the intermission, she told me she had enjoyed the dinner, adding, 'I finished reading the book on Blue Mansion before bedtime. Very interesting. Glad I did that. I haven't read a book for a long time.'

A slim-faced man walked in. He had the eyes of someone who always knows what he wants and was dressed in a dapper tight midnight blue suit and a gleaming white, open-collared shirt. After the symposium, he introduced himself: 'I am Jimmy, Jimmy Choo.' A familiar name from the hit TV sitcom *Sex and the City*. His shoes, revered by the lead actress, also named Carrie, were legendary. Jimmy invited me to dinner. I felt like a Hollywood star.

'Bring anyone you like,' he said courteously. 'Just tell me how many are coming. I'll book the table.' We were all very excited to have dinner with Jimmy Choo. Cat even asked what she was supposed to wear for the occasion. Michael Morrison, one of the speakers, also the conservation consultant for Tai Kwan, asked to join. With a huge smile, he said, 'My daughter will be really impressed, more than anything else, if I tell her I'm having dinner with Jimmy Choo.'

That evening, Jimmy came to pick us up. We met him in the lobby of the hotel with his young assistant, also in a natty dark suit, looking as neat and smart as his boss. We were driven to our destination in the hotel limousine. It rode into the local quarter and came to a stop in front of a roadside hotpot place, laid out with low tables and clunky wooden stools. Two tables were reserved especially for our party. The place was filling up quickly. Jimmy introduced the patron to us, saying: 'This is the boss and a good friend. His is the best hotpot restaurant in Penang. He serves the best cuts of meat.'

He arranged our seatings as in a formal dinner. His assistant went around making sure everyone got their cold beers which, as the evening progressed, became a necessity. Temperatures were rising, as all the hotpots there were going full steam. We were shovelling down the boiled vegetables and meat like hot coal into a pizza stove. By the close of evening, we were dripping like a thatched roof in a tropical downpour. Jimmy, impeccable in his tight-fitting jacket, was cool as a cucumber. 'Now, for dessert, you must try our crispy poppan,' he said and took off with his assistant in his Mercedes Benz. They returned with bags of freshly baked, still warm-to-the-touch *poppans*. 'One each,' he said, handing them out. 'They're simply delicious.' He made sure that I got a large one all to myself and admonished my awestruck staff: 'If you coddle your boss, you can be sure he'll coddle you back.' I couldn't agree more with him.

We showed the film *The Way We Dance*, which has won enough awards to fill a shelf, at Gurney Plaza. We brought along the director, Adam Wong, and the cast to meet the audience. The hip hop dancers from the movie were also there to join in the finale with DJ FUNKB and rappers Big Sammy and Al Rocco. The outdoor party rocked the plaza that night.

This was all done with HKETO's Fong Ngai, head of the mission in Singapore, in the driver's seat. He belongs to a rare breed among Government's overseas appointees that prefer to stay active rather than sitting their time out trying hard to do no wrong. The following year, we brought Spotlight Penang to Hong Kong. Such a pity that we couldn't bring with it the mouth-watering aromas of its street food sizzling in the night market. The Chief Minister of Penang, the Honourable Mr Lim Guan Eng, came to officiate the opening. He was friendly and chatty and a Hong Kong vintage movie cinephile. We treated him to a super-hot dinner, at Coda Plaza, not for the meek and faint-hearted, which he tucked into, without breaking a sweat, much to our admiration. He rose in ranks to become Minister of Finance of Malaysia in 2018, for his business and political acumen, as well as his ability to take the heat.

LIFE ON THE FRINGE

There have been days in my life that I have subsisted on reading nothing but detective stories. Arriving in San Francisco late one night, I checked into a hotel on a terraced street, a garish neon light outside my window. The blanket of fog over the bay felt like a scene right out of detective fiction by Dashiell Hammett. Set against the backdrop of this iconic city, his stories always involve beautiful women who are in danger and then saved by Sam Spade, the gumshoe who speaks in clipped sentences and is hard on the outside but *moelleux* at heart.

As the sun came up, San Francisco became altogether different. This was my first visit. I was invited by the International Visitors Program 'to meet and confer with their professional counterparts and to experience the US first-hand.' They sent someone to take me around to meet people. Carl, I think, was his name, an African American, soft-spoken and very considerate. He had recently retired from a government agency. Since he had time to spare now, he wanted to do what he enjoyed most, to meet people from other countries.

Carl arranged for me to meet artists from the Bay Area at the Yerba Buena Center for the Arts. The YBCA came out of a deal with some land developers. It's a centre that serves the communities there. The artists who turned up that day were third- or fourth-generation Asian Americans. All of them had stories to tell about the terrible ordeals of their forebears who had come to Gold Mountain to build railways or labour in gold mines. These artists – Brenda Wong Aoki, Mark Isu, Jon Jang, Perla Ubungen, and Claudine Naganuma – tried to deal with the injustices of the past through the cathartic process of their arts in dance, music, and storytelling.

Claudine showed me around to Pier 39 and took me to the Stinking Rose on North Beach that served garlic in every dish, including ice cream. By the end of the day, we ended up at Top of the Mark, the penthouse bar in the Mark Hopkins Hotel, the city's tallest building. We sat down by the window and ordered two Old Fashioneds.

'We're in Weeper's Corner,' she told me, pointing out the Golden Gate Bridge to me in the distance against the blazing orange sunset. 'This was where the servicemen had their farewell drinks with their loved ones, before they were shipped out to fight in the war.'

Claudine was the artistic director of Asian American Dance Performances and was about to start her own company, dNaga, which is still running. Born of a Japanese father and a Chinese mother, she told me: 'I am their love child,' with a smile radiating from her beautiful brown eyes to the rest of her well-proportioned face.

'My father's family was put into a camp in Arizona during the war as nationals from a hostile country. They'd always thought they're born Americans fighting on the same side. So, what was done to them was really hurtful. He spent his childhood in camps, not the best places to grow up in. I want to do a piece based on what happened to him at Gila River Reservation.'

We talked about bringing that to Hong Kong as a spotlight programme. These Asian American artists seemed to have found their footing and unique voices. They were working more homogeneously here in San Francisco than elsewhere in America. I was curious how her Chinese and Japanese parents had met and got together at a time when the two countries were still smarting from the wounds of the war.

LIFE ON THE FRINGE

'My dad was a handyman,' she said. 'One evening he got an emergency call to fix a burst pipe from an address in Richmond. When he got there, Mom answered the door. She showed him into the family kitchen. That's how they met.'

It seemed that it was a *coup de foudre*, as the French say. 'And then they got married afterwards and had you as their love child?' I asked incredulously. 'No objections at that time from their families? Can't imagine what they'd gone through,' Claudine said. 'It's really complicated, messy, because they were both already married and had children of their own.'

We went on to talk about other things: her dance projects, works by other Asian American artists, and my next-day trip to the Napa Valley. Afterwards, I insisted on walking back to my hotel and taking a look at the bayside city by night.

Back in my room, resting my feet from a long day around town, I tuned in to the radio for some music. My notebook out, I tried to jot down my thoughts on the day but couldn't get my head around the story of this improbable romance between two strangers. The music channel was playing some American standards. Out of the blue, the voice of Frank Sinatra came on. It was a song by Rodgers and Hart:

> *I took one look at you . . .*
> *Though not a single word was spoken*
> *I could tell you knew*
> *That unfelt clasp of hands*
> *Told me so well you knew*
> *I never lived at all*
> *Until the thrill of that moment when*
> *My heart stood still.*

TURNING AROUND

I'm awestruck by the incomprehensible wonders of chance meetings. Time and again, on my life's journey, I've experienced them. They may not be as life changing as this one with Claudine's parents. In fact, they can be quite random and casual and not necessarily lead to anything special. But every time it happens, you feel there's something out there. You don't know what, and you can't see and touch it. But it's connecting you with a wider world, a presence and purpose of existence.

In traversing the world, I've met many people. Some I have kept in contact with and remained friends with. Some have passed by like ships in the open sea. Sometimes what I thought had been lost to the passage of time resurfaces with just a little probe. It seems that things happen for a reason. Nothing goes away for good; it's just lodged somewhere forever.

We presented the San Francisco ArXchange Showcase with YBCA two years later, in 1999. Brenda Wong-Aoki and Mark Izu, as a duo, did a narrative performance backed by live music called *Mermaid Meat*. I introduced them to the young Tang Shu Wing, who was then director of *No Man's Land*. Following that, we arranged a residency at YBCA for Shu Wing to work with Brenda and Mark. They'd found him lodging in a place within walking distance from YBCA, which was also a Sivananda yoga centre, for meditation and physical practice.

Shu Wing recalled in a conversation we had on a video call during the pandemic. I asked him about what he could remember of his time there. 'Almost monastic. Just right for me. I was going

LIFE ON THE FRINGE

through a spiritual phase.'

Two good things have come out of this. First, *Guan Yin, Our Lady of Compassion* (2001), a multimedia performance, was premiered at the New Vision Festival in Hong Kong and afterwards in *The Face Series* we presented at The Esplanade in Singapore. Second, following his brush with Sivananda yoga, Shu Wing went to an ashram in South India. After he returned in 2004, he was offered the post of Dean of Drama at the Academy for Performing Arts. He said, 'The training in the ashram had prepared me for my seven-and-a-half gruelling years at the Academy. You have to believe, in life, one thing leads to another.'

'My first memory of the Fringe was with the Theatre Workshop. It was started and run by Bill Poon and his girlfriend, Carmen Ling. I also took some classes from the Mime Lab. That was in 1985, or around that time. I helped Bill with a show staged in a carpark, a rather unusual place. Johnson Chang of Hanart Gallery was also involved. Soon after that, Bill passed away suddenly. It was a shock. No one had expected that. Very sad, especially for Carmen.'

'Around 1986, I left Hong Kong for Paris. Returning in 1992, I started Theatre Resolue with Kevin Ho. We created a show called *Two Civil Servants in a Skyscraper* (1993) and performed it in a festival in Kazakhstan, which got us some good press coverage when we re-staged it in Hong Kong. We produced several shows together, and then Kevin and I went separate ways.'

'Later I teamed up with Jim Chim. We did a two-hander called *No Man's Land* (1996), based on a bizarre case about two Hong Kong tourist guides in the Philippines. They were charged for some vague misdemeanour and detained until they paid a big fine to get off. We played it like slapstick comedy, very energetic.

The Fringe Theatre was just perfect for it.'

'In one of the scenes we popped up from the trapdoor. It's a cool contraption connecting the basement and the stage. It was rather crude, just a hole cut through the floor slab. We climbed up a wooden step ladder to get into the theatre. Then we ran out into the street through the fire exit door.'

'Outside, there were people waiting in the taxi queue. We gave them quite a shock. We pushed past them like two madmen in prison uniforms. At the end of the show, we asked the audience to play judge and give their verdicts. The show was very popular, and we did a long run.'

Jim, a drama graduate of the Academy, went on to become a successful comedian famous for his dorky TV commercials.

Between 1999 and 2002, we devised three shows – *Play the Old City, Once Upon the Time in Wong Uk*, and *Battle of Hong Kong* – with Shu Wing's newly formed company, No Man's Land.

In *Play the Old City*, we took the audience in a tourist bus to several heritage sites around Central, known in the past as Victoria City, for a dramatised guided tour. Besides the sightseeing, there was a subtext. We showed how Hong Kong was governed: how the church, schools, and law courts formed a trinity to hold sway over the mind, body, and spirit of the people.

The audience played camera-toting tourists. They disembarked at Man Mo Temple, the first stop, in Hollywood Road. It was the witching hour. While they were admiring the architecture in the forecourt of the temple and taking photos, some characters in period dress emerged from the dark and took the audience by surprise.

An angry-looking *tai tai*, wearing a fur-lined cheongsam and ostentatious gold ornaments, screamed like a banshee, while

LIFE ON THE FRINGE

dragging a scared scrawny girl by the arm to face a local dignitary in a robe and mandarin hat. He was flanked by two fearsome-looking uniformed policemen, playing threateningly with their batons at the girl, who was in tears.

'She stole my pearl necklace,' she called out in a shrill voice to catch everyone's attention. 'I did not, I did not,' the girl protested, wiping the tears off her face.

'Who are you?' one of the policemen asked the *tai tai* gruffly. 'She's my *mui tsai* [a maid who works only for room and board],' she cut in.

This episode continued to unfold. The mock tourist guide explained in an aside to the audience that this was how local people settled their disputes and grievances back then. They'd rather take their cases to street tribunals than to the law courts, which they believed would bring them bad luck.

After this, the tour bus moved on to visit four other sites. At each of them, a site-specific scene was played out. As with the gig at Man Mo Temple, we used local history and some personal stories culled from newspapers, the mosquito press, and history books to sketch a vignette. We fleshed it out with believable characters and vernacular dialogue, to give the audience a sense of time and place. To make it even more real, we used artistic licence to heighten the situations and facts. There may not have been an actual case of a stolen pearl necklace, but the injustices inflicted on poor people were common and real enough in those days.

One day, I came upon Wong Uk, literally House of the Wong clan. The greyish brick hillside house with a dark tiled roof once sat a stone's throw from the shoreline of Tide Cove in Shatin. It's now part of an attraction in a small park.

Shu Wing had become vegetarian. During rehearsal of *Once Upon A Time In Wong Uk*, he'd take out a chunk of hard cheese from his knapsack and munch on it while giving instructions to the actors. Once he caught me looking and offered me a bite. 'I started eating cheese in Paris,' he said. 'Plenty of calcium. Don't have to do any cooking either. So simple.'

Wong Uk was built in the style of a green brick Hakka house during the final year of the Qing Dynasty, in 1911. It has been restored as an example of indigenous architecture from that period, and Mr Tony Ma, Chief Manager of the Regional Council (now defunct), was keen to see it put to use. There's a courtyard in front of the house for family gatherings, sun-drying of laundry, and foodstuffs of all kinds. Inside there's an inner court open to the sky and a hallway to the main room – flanked by the kitchen and bedrooms – for dining and ancestor worship. I figured we could do some kind of re-enactment theatre there for a small peripatetic audience of about seventy people, showing the Wong family members engaging in daily activities and situations.

'Tableaux vivants,' Shu Wing suggested. 'Living pictures. The characters don't have to stay still or silent as in a painting. They can go about doing what they did back then.'

We knew very little about the people who'd lived there. Who were they? What did they do for a living? What were the things that worried them most? There was hardly any material to draw on for our research. Whatever had happened here wasn't considered important enough to be written down. We consulted Professor Shiu Kwok Kin, a local historian and scholar, who invited us to his apartment in Quarry Bay after dinner for a chat. Before we went, Shu Wing and I decided to grab a bite. It was the first time we shared a meal together, and we had known each other for over a decade.

'Let's go to Pizza Hut,' he said. 'I thought you didn't like this kind of food?' I said, surprised at his suggestion. 'No, I don't. I only go for the salad. We need fibre.' He must have come here a lot. He knew his way around. He showed me the salad bar, and after paying the cashier, we were each handed a plate. 'You can take as much as you like, but you're only allowed one helping,' he said and went on showing me how to pile up a mountain of vegetables, grains, and cut-up fruit on a small plate. I did as he'd done but far less impressively. We sat down with our vertical forests of greens in front of us and ate with a great deal of care for not spilling and concentration. Shu Wing wasn't one to waste time on eating; he went through his pile promptly and efficiently. I, by contrast, who had never had so much raw fibre at one go, was struggling.

Later, throughout our long conversation with Professor Shiu, who was most generous with his time mapping out the rural history of Hong Kong, I was making a real effort to keep the gas production of those natural greens in my shy stomach from going into overdrive. My face tightened into a permanent smile like the skin on a new drum, whereas Shu Win looked composed and collected and didn't even burp once.

From what we'd gathered from our chat with the professor and other sources, we drew up a sequence of domestic scenes we imagined could've happened. We wanted the audience to feel how it was living there and then. The Wong clan had been renting out their rooms to a stream of itinerant trades people passing through. Business had been good until a revolution broke out across the border and brought an end to the Qing Dynasty. The fighting and chaos had stopped the travellers from coming. It was during these turbulent times that the story begins. The brother, who's head of the clan, wants to marry his little sister off – so there will be one less mouth to feed – to some stranger from Nanyang, Malaya. He wants to buy himself a young and able-bodied bride to work in his general store.

'All for your own good,' the brother says to her. 'You'll have someone to care and provide for you.' The little sister wants none of this, at the risk of being kicked out of the family, if she's not doing as she's told. Torn between that and her own freedom, she turns to the womenfolk in the house for help and support.

To recreate the decoration and ambience, we decided against the use of stage props. We wanted to use authentic furniture and other fixtures to refurbish the entire house. We figured that the audience, who could walk around and get a close look at everything, might be put off by a staged setting.

Tony liked this idea. He put his shoulder behind it and helped clear the roadblocks of presenting site-specific theatre. He connected us with Mr S. Y. Yim, Chief Curator of Shatin's Heritage Museum that had just opened its doors to the public. We told S. Y. our concept, and the following afternoon, he took us to a warehouse: dim and musty; bunches of furniture, crockery, farming tools, and utensils covered in dust were corralled like cattle waiting to be slaughtered. He told us that the Museum had been given these antique items for keeps. 'They're not exactly art objects; they're quite commonplace. We're happy to loan them to you for your show.'

In the courtyard of Wong Uk, we set up a charcoal stove to roast sweet potatoes and boil peanuts with five spices. We sold them for snacks. Back in the days when life was wanting and village kids were always hungry, they would be drawn to them like monkeys to bananas. On that winter night, the aroma of peanuts, sweet potatoes, and a log fire put the audience in the mood. On entering the house, they were each given a rush Hakka hat to wear and pretend to be invisible ghosts.

The show opened with *tableaux vivants* of the menfolk sitting at a long, rough-hewn wooden table in the main room. They had just finished dinner and were now drinking tea from the rice bowls, cracking sunflower seeds, picking their teeth, and chatting away. The audience looked on with the guilty relish of voyeurs. After a while, some of the men wandered off into other rooms where the womenfolk were doing housework, while moaning audibly over the fate of their little sister. The audience is slowly piecing these scenes together to descry what's befallen the Wong clan.

Our next show was *Hong Kong at War – A City of Love & Betrayal*. It was staged the following year, in 2001, at an old marine fort that stands guard above Lyemun Pass – the sea entrance on the eastern side of Hong Kong Island. The Japanese army had landed there two weeks before Christmas of 1941. The fort, said to be impregnable, was under attack. A brutal combat ensued. Many defending soldiers were killed. The few who had been captured were bayoneted and thrown into the sea.

The old fort had only recently been converted into the Museum of Coastal Defence and hadn't yet opened to the public. Some nights, they say, you could still hear bloodcurdling cries rising from the echoey chambers. We couldn't have found a location more evocative for our show than this.

The story blends true stories with fiction, characters who got caught in historical moments during those three years and eight months of the Japanese occupation of Hong Kong. There's a young man who joined the Volunteer Defence Force (VDF) to fight in the Battle of Wong Nei Chong Gap and who made plans for a future he never got to see. Prime Minister Winston Churchill admitted confidentially that Hong Kong could not be defended, but in an official dispatch he ordered the VDF to fight to the last man, which this young man and many others did.

And there's the amicable and chatty Mr Suzuki, who went to every cocktail party, secretly drawing up maps to prepare for the military assault on the city. And the too-enterprising Colonel Doi, who led a successful surprise attack on the Shing Mun Redoubt and successfully broke through Gin Drinker's Line, yet he faced court martial for taking his own initiative and not following orders.

And then there's Emily 'Mickey' Hahn, the China correspondent for *The New Yorker* magazine. She was played by Lindzay Chan. As fate has it, Hahn met and fell for Major Charles Boxer: soldier, scholar, and top spy for British Intelligence. At the time, they were both married – Mickey to Zau Sinmay, a Chinese poet and dandy intellectual; Charles to Ursula Tulloch, an English rose lauded as the top beauty in the colony. Their affair caused a terrible scandal in colonial Hong Kong. To make matters worse, Mickey got pregnant. Instead of hiding in shame, she went public and took out a newspaper advertisement announcing the birth of her daughter, Carola, seven weeks before Japan invaded Hong Kong.

The play begins with Mickey alone in her Mid-Levels apartment, nursing her baby. There's the sound of shellfire and gunshots in the distance. She's just heard Charles has been shot in the Battle of Shouson Hill the night before. In her opening monologue, she's desperate to know if he's dead or alive.

I came across the name of Emily Hahn in her obituary in the *South*

China Morning Post. She'd led an amazing life – marching to her own drumbeat, never backing down from a chance for adventure, unafraid of controversy. I wanted to know more about her, so I started to follow her tracks, read her books and write-ups of her past exploits. Instead of fleeing from the war in Hong Kong when she had a chance, she stayed on, if only to make sure that Charles and others interned in prisoner of war (PoW) camps wouldn't die of starvation. She wrote about this in her two bestselling books, *China to Me* and *Hong Kong Holiday.*

Towards the end of the war, Mickey received news that Charles had been executed by the Japanese for the illegal possession of a radio in camp. It turned out to be false information. The two lovers reunited after the war, made good their promises to one another, and lived happily ever after. I'm always a sucker for fairy-tale endings.

To round out her character, I tracked down her younger daughter, Amanda Boxer, in London. A stage and film actress, Amanda invited me to her flat, best described as undomesticated. She cleared the clutter on her dining table to lay out photos from an album of her late mother. Engagingly, she took me through the stories behind each and every one of them though I suspect she might have been asked to do so many times before. I saw something of her mother in her – the outline of her intelligent face, the light in her eyes, the pleasure in spinning a good yarn.

She told me her parents had been living on different sides of the Atlantic. Charles Boxer had become a distinguished historian on colonial history of East Asia, taught in universities, and lived most of his later life in England. Emily settled back in New York, continued to publish her books and write for *The New Yorker.*

'We used to spend three months together every year,' Amanda

said. 'Mommy liked to say it was "an intimacy built around absence" that kept us together.' Emily Hahn passed away in February 1997, in New York, aged 93. 'How did your father receive the news?' I asked. 'He asked if she was in pain, and when I told him no, he was very relieved.'

Mickey was best known for her writings and adventures. What she was like as a mother? I was curious. But I didn't get around to asking Amanda. Instead, I found the pithy answer Mickey once gave in an interview: 'My younger daughter once rebuked me for not being the kind of mother one reads about. I asked her what kind that was, and she said, the kind who sits home and bakes cakes. I told her to go and find anybody who sits at home and bakes cakes.'

When everything was going our way, Shu Wing and I got into arguments over some production details I can't recall. We stopped talking, if we didn't have to, to one another. It was quite awkward. We needed to break the silence. Instead of turning on each other, we picked on the innocent young scriptwriter.

That year marked the sixtieth anniversary of the Japanese invasion of Hong Kong, and I conducted a guided tour as part of City Festival 2001. I took a group to see the remnants of the redoubts on Gin Drinkers Line. Scattered on the wooden slopes around Shing Mun Reservoir, these concrete bunkers had been built for defence and were connected by a network of tunnels. You can still read the names of London Tube stations inscribed above the tunnel entrances, a sad reminder of those soldiers who had died thinking of returning home to a normal life one day.

That day, a Saturday morning, our young writer was supposed

to present the first draft of his script. I asked him to meet us there so that he could also get a sense of the place. He turned up late, looking dishevelled and sleep deprived. He rummaged in his knapsack and took out some loose sheets of handwritten manuscripts from his knapsack and handed them over to us as though he'd been caught shoplifting.

Shu Wing took a quick look at them and rounded on him, saying: 'You really need to improve your handwriting. It's illegible.' I nodded in agreement. Then his phone rang. He sheepishly tried to answer. 'Look where you're going,' I cautioned him, as we walked up a steep climb. Shu Wing chimed in and said, 'Or you won't see what we've come to see.'

That couldn't be the best day of his life. I don't know if our young writer remembers any of this. But on that day, he got Shu Wing and me back on track again. For him, in later years – writing more legibly, no doubt – he's gone on to win major awards in theatre and film scriptwriting. His name is Loong Man Hong.

On the opening night of *Hong Kong at War* at the Coastal Defence Museum, I was sitting next to Susannah York. She had finished playing in another show that we presented at the City Hall and told me she'd like to see some local productions while she was here, so I'd arranged for her to come.

The year before, on my yearly pilgrimage to Edinburgh, I'd walked past the Traverse Theatre on Cambridge Street and caught her name on the billboard. The play was *Picasso's Women*. It's a series of monologues based on the lives of eight women in Pablo Picasso's life. She was the main draw of this new play by Brian McAvera that premiered on the Fringe.

In my wistful youth, I'd had a big crush on her. I remember the thunderbolt that struck me when I set eyes on her on the movie screen for the first time. She played Sophie, the ingenue and beautiful daughter of Squire Western, in Tony Richardson's movie, *Tom Jones*. I simply couldn't take my eyes off her. Now, so many years later, at our invitation she was appearing on stage in Hong Kong. She played Jacqueline, Picasso's widow in mourning, looking dishevelled in a crumpled housedress and contemplating suicide.

That night, we were sitting together in the front row of a makeshift theatre set up in the main hall of the Museum of Coastal Defence. We were watching Lindzay Chan play Emily Hahn in *Battle of Hong Kong*. Lindzay was speaking her lines in Cantonese.

'Could you tell me what's going on?' Susannah asked, sotto voce. Haltingly I made an attempt to translate for her. 'Stay close,' she said, pulling me gently to her side. 'It's alright. Let's just not be too much of a nuisance to anyone.'

Whispering in her ear, I felt the brush of her hair and the warmth on her face, as she smiled and nodded encouragement every time I faltered. At a stolen glance at her, in the soft dim light, she became for me, in a moment of displaced time, Sophie again, with her golden locks, cobalt eyes and blooming beauty.

Peter Wesley-Smith returned for a visit from Kangaroo Valley outside of Sydney, where he was now living, after retiring from teaching law in Hong Kong. It was a hot summer afternoon. I took him to the Central Police Station (CPS), to see where Ho Chi Minh, Founder of the Democratic Republic of Vietnam, had been kept prisoner. Few people knew anything about this historical episode. I'd thought CPS, the locals called Tai Kwun, dealt mainly with misdemeanours and other petty crimes.

'He was a wanted revolutionary on the run,' Peter said, 'and would've been deported back to Saigon [now Ho Chi Minh City]. They would've put him away; even executed him for attempting to overturn the French Colonial Government, if it hadn't been for Francis Loseby. He was the Hong Kong lawyer who defended and won his appeal case. He's become a big hero in Vietnam for saving the great man's life. I think there's also a bust of Loseby in the Foreign Correspondents' Club to commemorate him. Or is it in the Royal Yacht Club?'

A man in uniform was guarding the entrance to the vacated CPS compound. When we told him what we'd come for, he showed us around enthusiastically and later let us wander around on our own. We found our way into the magistracy's empty courtroom and cells that were used to hold prisoners awaiting trial. There I conjured up an avuncular Ho Chi Minh, lean and with a wispy grey beard, just the way he looks on those propaganda posters. I said to Peter that the historical court case could be turned into a gripping drama, and I'd like to commission him to write it.

I knew Peter before he became a law professor. He'd staged a satire piece at the Fringe called *Noonday Gun*, way back in 1986, which he wrote and put to music with Martin, his identical twin. Since then, other than writing books on Hong Kong law, he has written plays, an opera, and children's books. He called it his 'parallel career'.

He came up with a truthful rendition of the court case, ahead of schedule. But we felt that an injection of dramatic interest would add flavour to it. So, I asked Will Gluth, with whom we'd worked on several shows, if he could be the dramaturg, a sort

TURNING AROUND

of script doctor: someone who fact-checks, spots and fixes the discrepancies in the narrative, and makes the script reads better and more performable.

When I told Shu Wing about this project, he got excited right away. 'I know Peter.' he said. 'He taught me at law school. Cool guy.' By early 2007, the script was ready for a staged reading in front of an audience. We chose to hold it in the august Parliament Chamber at the Art House in Singapore. It's the venue where the cut and thrust of political debates took place. It has a special aura. Shu Wing even bought a Panama hat as prop to get in character. Peter also took the trouble of flying to Singapore to attend the reading.

Back in Hong Kong, I had a change of mind. I told Shu Wing that I needed him to be the director. He'd be perfect for it, but he said he was only interested in playing the Ho Chi Minh character. Time had become pressing. There were only five months left until showtime. Eventually, he introduced Peter Jordan, Head of Acting of the Academy, to direct. And I got Lee Chun Chow – everyone calls him C.C. – to step in for the title role. I've known C.C. from the days when we had him perform in Kuo Pao Kun's two black comedy plays, *The Coffin Is Too Big for The Hole* and *No Parking on Odd Days*, when he was a rookie at Chung Ying Theatre. He was brilliant. He's one of the few actors who can perform bilingually, in Cantonese and English, making it look easy and natural. *Ho Chi Minh in Hong Kong* (2008) ended up winning him the Best Actor Award for that year.

We decided to stage it in two venues, within walking distance of each other. The first half took place in the CPS compound. Before the show started, the audience was lined up at a side entrance on Old Bailey Street, just as prison visitors had been. A

LIFE ON THE FRINGE

couple of actors, dressed as prison guards, checked their names on a register book before letting them in. Once inside, they're herded across the courtyard like a band of surrendering soldiers.

Imagine it's getting dark. The place, enclosed in dull grey walls, feels grim and forbidding. All of a sudden, through the metal grilles of the prison cell windows come abusive shouts, punctuated by screams of pain. The audience, unsure of what's happening, is ordered by the guards to go down a flight of stone steps. In faint evening light, they could see, behind a barbed-wire iron gate, an inmate in tatty overalls being cudgelled repeatedly by someone in uniform.

The second half took place in the Fringe Theatre. By the time C.C. came on stage to tell his story as Ho Chi Minh, the audience that had walked from the old prison was ready for it.

Both brothers, Peter and Martin, were there to help with the production. They provided a rich backdrop: videos compiled from old newsreels, news clippings, and photos played to a soundtrack. There is a poignant moment in the play when our hero laments (by then he is supposed to be speaking from the dead) that despite his express wish not to be mummified and put on show in a mausoleum after his death, he can't escape the same fate met by other leaders to be gawked at for eternity.

We had a chance to pay our respects when we presented Spotlight Hong Kong in Ho Chi Minh City in 2008. We entered the mausoleum – built in the hybrid style of Greek Temple and local architecture – with a long line of foreign tourists and patriots from Hanoi. As we looked reverently on the embalmed waxen face of the great man, lying in state, I surreptitiously, under my breath, called on him to make our show a box-office and critical success.

Things work in mysterious ways. Everything was going

TURNING AROUND

as smoothly as we'd wished, except for the title of the show. Peter wanted it to be called: THE DETENTION AND PERSECUTION OF HO CHI MINH BY THE BRITISH AUTHORITIES IN HONG KONG AND THE TRIUMPH OF THE GLORIOUS RULE OF LAW. Not a word less. I can't remember how long the wrangle lasted between us to have it finally whittled down to just *Ho Chi Minh in Hong Kong*.

Peter is not one to bend his will easily, especially when he isn't in any way wrong. He must have put a lot of thought into it, too. It would make a suitable chapter title in a Henry Fielding novel. But for a play, not even Shakespeare could get away with one this long. Standing firm on this point, I put years of friendship with him on the line. In the end, he gave in, but sadly he no longer speaks to me.

After this production, there was a long silence between Shu Wing and me until one day I heard that he got married. I picked up the phone and called him.

Congratulations,' I said. 'Who's the lucky girl?'

'Eva, who else?' he said. Eva, his long-time girlfriend, kind and learned and wise, who's also author, professor, and social commentator.

'When did that happen?' I asked. 'We were in Las Vegas on vacation,' he said, guffawing. They're not the sort of people I can picture holidaying in Las Vegas. 'We didn't have much to do that day. We walked past one of those places where you can get yourselves married by an Elvis impersonator. That's what we did. So I'm married now.'

In 2010, we took the Saturday Night Jazz Orchestra to perform at the Shanghai Expo. Called SNJO for short, it's an eighteen-piece

LIFE ON THE FRINGE

Swing Band that's been led by Taka Hirohama since the 1990s. Taka, a musician and bandleader from Tokyo, was introduced to the Fringe by Kenny Matsuura, a Japanese jazz trumpeter, who later formed the Happy-Go-Lucky Big Band.

We were put on the stage of the Baosteel Theatre. It's huge and on that occasion was packed to the rafters. Some of the audiences were first-time listeners to the Big Band sound and Swing music. Elaine Liu was the vocalist. She sang a few numbers from the American Songbook, backed by Ted Lo on keyboards and Eugene Pao on guitar.

After the concert, as the musicians were clearing the stage, an old lady in a traditional Shanghai floral cheongsam and matching low-heeled, embroidered silk shoes made her way down the aisle. Stopping in front of the stage, she waved her hands, and a smile spread over her face. She said in a voice for all to hear: 'What I've just heard is the essence of happiness.'

chapter 14

VENICE CALLING

WE WANTED TO have a go at the Venice Biennale. It was something we had never done. Cat had never been surer that we should put in a bid for 2011. She might have had a prescience that it was now or never. It turns out that she got it right: this would be the last chance for independent curators to have a go at it. After that, M+ of West Kowloon Cultural District Authority (WKCDA) would take over and run it by themselves. There was no way of knowing what effect this might have on the overall arts development. It surely seemed to be going against the grain of equal opportunity and open competition. There's a saying in Chinese: 'Under a big tree, not an inch of grass can grow.'

We went ahead and did the first thing we had to do – select an artist. It had always been Frog King, even before we made up our mind to go after the prize. I've known him from the days when he was still known as Kwok Mang Ho, the bad boy in Master Lui Shou Kwan's Chinese painting class. Actually, he was more unwieldy than bad. He always treats artmaking as non-stop

LIFE ON THE FRINGE

play, oftentimes compulsive and can be like an engine that has gone rogue.

In Venice, I found out how relentless he is. We set him up in a nice little apartment near the Hong Kong Pavilion. But he hardly spent time there. In the middle of the night, waking up from his nap, he'd find his way back to the pavilion, sneak in, and work there until he was too tired to go on. Then he'd curl up behind his heaps of artworks and catch his forty winks. After the exhibition was dismounted, we found half-finished boxes of biscuits and drink cartons in his bolt hole. We figure that he never bothered to stop for a proper meal.

Once in our conversation he told me how he'd been brought up by his mother: 'Very strict and controlling. Now that I can do what I want, I'm doing just that.' In a way, he's overcompensating. The result of that is a phenomenal output of art. He likes to give it away. Cho Hyun Jae, a fellow artist and his partner, tries to drum some money sense into him but to no avail.

Frog King doesn't care about money. What he makes he spends on art materials and on the rents for his several art studios and storage spaces. So, he's always short. He kept a large studio in Cattle Depot that soon filled up with his artworks and things he collected from the neighbourhood junk vendors, such as unwanted personal belongings of the deceased. He bought the whole lot – furniture, photo albums, diaries, and whatnot. These memorabilia of a stranger's lifetime hold special meanings for him, and he hoards them. 'One day I'll show them in the Frog King Museum,' he said. 'Everyone's life should have a record. You can't just live and die and be no more.'

Cho Hyun Jae is a media artist from Seoul. It was in New York, the year was 1992, where she come across Frog King's work

VENICE CALLING

for the first time. In those days, he called himself Frog King Kwok and then dropped his surname to make it sound less of an expletive to become simply Frog King.

He was in a joint show held at a gallery in East Broadway called E-Flex. She liked the work so much that she wanted to meet the artist in person. But Frog King wasn't around. She picked up his name card from the reception counter and kept it. Three years later, at the Gwangju Biennale, where he was exhibiting, they met. She gave him her name card with her number on it and told him to call if he ever needed help.

'I never thought I'd hear from him again.' Cho said. 'But one night, he appeared at my door. I was living in Incheon at the time, with my mother. He arrived in a taxi with a suitcase and boxes filled with his artworks that he'd taken down from his exhibition.' 'He'd come all the way from Gwangju and didn't have enough wons to pay for the fare, so I paid for him. He had no place to stay for the night, so I put him up in the empty classroom next door – we were living in a school that had closed down. I was so afraid to wake up my mother. It was four o'clock in the morning. That's what happened. Not normal.'

Days before that encounter, Cho told me she had gone with her sister to consult a fortune teller, just for fun. He'd told her she was going to meet someone very special. 'I asked him how special? A painter, just like Picasso, and when he showed up like that, I thought he's the one!' she said and laughed.

Frog King had been living in New York before he met Cho. He went to the United States in 1980, enrolling at the Art Students League, an art school with a long history in the city. At the time, he was married to a music teacher from Hong Kong. 'I asked her to join me in New York,' Frog King told me. 'She wasn't sure what she would do there. She didn't follow me, so we separated.'

After that, he met Linda Pastorino in a crafts fair. She's a designer of fashion accessories. 'Her family has money,' he went on. 'I was a bum. I was sleeping in the boiler room of a restaurant in Chinatown. At night, after everyone was gone, I took food from the kitchen to feed myself. Alone, by myself, I played the tapes of Master Lui Sho Kwan's lectures, over and over again. I needed a place to make art and I became a helper in Ming Fei's studio.'

'I started making bracelets and necklaces. Linda's mother loved them. She put them in a special cabinet. She told Linda: 'You're sitting on a goldmine.' By that time, we were already married.

'We set up a gallery in Tribeca. I spent ten hours a day in the basement making custom jewellery. I worked with chemicals all day long, until my nails warped. Linda helped me sell them at trade fairs and big department stores. I was doing very well. I only needed to sleep four hours a day.'

'And Linda scolded me. She said, "Every time I turn my head around, you're sleeping. Why are you wasting your time like this?" You see, Linda only needs one hour of sleep,' he said, deadpan.

Leaving New York after fifteen years, he returned to Hong Kong. We invited him to do a warm- up act for Liu Sola's *Creative Rap RaRa* at the Convention Centre. A composer and performance artist from Beijing, Sola has a phenomenal vocal range and at the time was based in New York. Her performance, part of City Festival 2000, a box-office draw, took place in a long, rectangular auditorium with an end stage.

Frog King made a noisy, eye-catching entrance. He appeared in his Frog King costume that seemed to have been cut from the canvas of his dense, hieroglyphic paintings. Draped in strings of colour beads from neck to waist, bangles around the wrists, and wearing a pair of Froggy Glasses, he looked like a prop from a comedy store. He was lugging two large bags of musical toys: trumpets, curler-whistles, tambourines, and whatnot. He went down the long aisle, handing out these playthings to the audience, right and left. Then he went on stage.

At first, the audience seemed hesitant and self-conscious. After a while, like a voodoo doctor, he put a roomful of people into a trance-like state. Everyone joined in with gusto. Building to a crescendo, he took out stacks of loose white A4 paper and handed them out to the first-row audience. Then he made a feigned toss, and they followed. Sheets of white paper went up in the air and came down everywhere. The auditorium looked like a classroom on the last day of class. I don't think Sola was amused to see this when she turned up to start her show.

The Hong Kong Pavilion was set up on the ground floor of a tenement block facing the entrance to the Arsenale – former naval dockyard and armoury transformed into a vast and atmospheric exhibition site during the Venice Biennale. HKADC rented two of the mid-size rooms from the owners, who ran some cottage business there during off season. There's a recessed corner in the courtyard for boats from the canal to land. Also used as a makeshift outhouse for anyone who couldn't wait to go. It's slippery and dark even in daytime.

Frog King got his artworks ready for the Biennale in his Cattle Depot studio. He sent for our team – Ice, Simon, Tong, Peggy, and Claire – to pack them into a large container and ship them door-to-door, from To Kwa Wan in Kowloon to Campo

Work team (not full), *left to right*: Benny Chia (curator), Lee Wah Ming (builder), Ah Bay (Tech Manager), Claire Liang, Kith Tsang (curator), Catherine Lau, Kat Greer, and volunteers at the Hong Kong Pavilion, Venice Art Biennale, 2011

Posing with Picasso – Benny in the foreground
Photo by H.W. Wong

Action Painting by Frog King (Kwok Man Ho)
at Venice Art Biennale Opening, 2010

Zhujiajiao Frog King Boat Parade, 2012.
Shanghai–Hong Kong Cultural Exchange Project:
Frogtopia · Hongkornucopia II

LIFE ON THE FRINGE

Della Tana of Venizia. The packing was nothing short of a Zen exercise. The volume of a limited space can expand *ad infinitum* in Frog King's universe. Same with his artwork production, there's no such thing as enough. If the container hadn't been made of steel, it would have been bulging like a bodybuilder on steroids. When the container arrived at the Hong Kong Pavilion, it wouldn't fit through the entrance gate. We had to unload everything outside on the pavement in pouring rain to move them inside. It wasn't the welcome from Venice we'd expected.

From past experience, I know Frog King can be quite a handful. So, I rounded up Kith Tsang and WSK to join me as co-curators. Kith had exhibited at the Biennale, both as artist and curator. He and Frog King – as master and student – go back a long way. When he married Ger, Frog King had worked through the night to make an art installation for his rooftop wedding. Their mutual respect and love are touching.

As for WSK, he's a painter, curator, dean of an art school, museum director; he'd done it all by that time. He remembers that he and Frog King used to hang out when they were in New York: 'After he'd make a sale, high as a kite, he'd say, "I'm rich today. Let's have some fun." That was music to my ears. At that time, I was studying printmaking at Rutgers. Didn't have two coins to rub together.'

Frogtopia Hongkornucopia is the oddball title I'd come up with to grab some attention. Frog King thought it was cool. We consulted the Tung Shing, the Chinese Almanac, for a propitious opening date that's good for all kinds of activities. Our opening ceremony was to be held in the courtyard. It wouldn't be much fun if it rained, so we had our fingers crossed for a clear and cloudless sky. True to form, just as the Almanac predicts, the Venetian early summer morning brought out the sun, a cool sea breeze, and our Italian neighbours' washing of beddings and undergarments hanging from the clotheslines above us.

Meanwhile, journalists and crews from TV stations arrived, one after another, for shoots and interviews. My family and friends who had flown in from Hong Kong, Melbourne, Marseilles, and London the night before also showed up. All except Frog King. Everyone was asking for him. He was nowhere to be found. He was last seen putting up his weatherproof artworks in the courtyard.

Cho had installed a sculpture of hers above the entrance to the old boat landing, using knickers of different colours stretched over a bamboo frame. She also covered a half-submerged boulder at the edge of the canal in gold paint. Standing in the sun, it glittered eerily above the blue lagoon. Frog King took a photo when a seagull landed on it.

The main exhibition was set up in two separate spaces. One was showing videos of Frog King's artworks; the other was an installation of what he called *frog nest*. True to style, he filled it to the brim with artworks to let the viewers experience how tadpoles feel trapped in a puddle, gasping for air.

Frog King reappeared carrying a plastic aquarium filled with tiny sea slugs, a shopping bag of garish colanders and pails, and a bunch of lettuce from the market. He upended the colanders, put them on top of the pails and filled them up with water and shredded lettuce. 'That's breakfast for the slugs,' he explained. Then he made the sea slugs crawl all over the colanders. 'They're getting their breakfast,' he said. He went on to set up five of these pods in the courtyards. 'My artworks of the day. Call them crawling sculptures.'

Guests started to stream into the courtyard around noon,

LIFE ON THE FRINGE

unusually early for VIP previews. Our neighbours' washing had been taken down at our request. In their place, Frog King had spun his own web of clotheslines to hang up his drawings. As for Frog King, you couldn't miss him – all dolled up, from head to toe, in his signature gear - a larger-than-life totemic presence.

Some of the guests had flown in the day before. Jet-lagged and puffy-eyed, they stood around idly, after checking out the exhibits. It was a bit early for drinks, but the waiters in smart uniforms kept plying the guests with them. At this rate, we were somewhat concerned that the initial excitement would soon turn into suppressed yawns.

How did it start? I can't quite recall exactly how. But he soon got everyone going – chanting, beating on cans, body movement. All the racket drew a curious crowd of passersby, and soon the courtyard was filled with people joining in. Energy was mounting, and the crowd seemed to be getting into a group trance and a natural high. Whenever there were signs of flagging, Frog King would shout 'Action!' and the energy would pick right up again. This went on and on, until we lost track of time. I'm pretty certain we were the noisiest, most exuberant, and fun VIP preview on that day. None of the others came close.

The following evening, I treated family, friends, and my team to a surprise dinner party that Margaret had spent months arranging.

'In Venice,' she said, 'it's got to be the Danieli.' Hotel Danieli is vintage Venetian and sumptuous. The dining room has large windows looking over the lagoon. At sunset, it's every way as theatrical as a Canaletto painting of the eternal city that hasn't changed in a thousand years.

When the time came, Frog King and Cho, whom he calls Frog

Queen, descended on the hotel dressed up in their costumes. The doormen greeted them, without missing a beat, like two regulars. They went up the gilded, High-Renaissance staircase to our banquet room, taking their time, like two grandees.

For aperitivo, Bellinis were served; made with crushed white peaches in season, topped with well chilled prosecco. Frog King made us put on Froggy Glasses, Froggy breastplates, and strings of outsized plastic pearls, and took Polaroid photos of us. We could see how ridiculous we all appeared. Laughing with each other, we threw self-restraint out of the elegant Venetian glass windows and proceeded to thoroughly enjoy ourselves for the rest of the night.

We looked around Venice the following day. So much was going on. In every calle you turn into, there was at least one exhibition to catch your eye. To create some noise, we thought of hiring a gondola to let the Frog King parade down the canal. This proved to be more complicated than we'd imagined. The Venetian municipality has been honing their bureaucratic skills since the Middle Ages to frustrate frivolous requests such as ours. Eventually we had to drop the idea. But, later in Zhujiajiao – an ancient water town on the outskirts of Shanghai, a third of the size of Venice, with waterways and buildings preserved from Ming and Qing dynasties – where we'd chosen to repeat our exhibition, we revived this idea.

At the opening of the Return Exhibition of *Frogtopia Hongkornucopia* at Zhujiajiao's Himalaya Art Museum, he paraded down the canal in a long sampan, installing himself at the bow in full regalia, banging on a gong. This spectacle drew a curious crowd of bystanders watching from both sides of the Caogang River.

Later at the drinks reception, besides the usual phalanx of artists and distinguished guests, some forty kids in school uniforms showed up. They were from a nearby primary school where Frog

King had spent a month teaching, living, and playing with the kids. They were all over him. WSK, the then-director of the Himalaya Museum in Shanghai and Zhujiajiao, also hooked him up with Wang Nam Ming, a well-known art critic and performance artist from Shanghai, WSK's hometown. They did a kind of duet painting on the floor with mops as ink brushes.

This exhibition went on for six months in Venice and two months in Zhujiajiao. From the planning stage to finish, it took us three years and a bit more. To round up, we held an open session at the Fringe Club, to share with an audience of artists and curators who wanted to know what we had learned from the process and what the experience meant to us.

We had all worked tirelessly and selflessly to make this happen, especially those in the project team: Cat Lau, Claire Liang, Ice Chen, Simon Leung, Ah Bay, Wah Tsai, Kat Thomas. They are the unsung heroes behind the scenes. We couldn't have done what we did without their perseverance and expertise in logistics, budget control, and publicity. And in servicing Frog King and managing his expectations, we learned not to fit artists into preset curatorial modes or get in their way when they wish to express themselves optimally.

The maintenance part of an exhibition is often overlooked. After the bursts of fireworks at the opening in Venice, the sobering six months was a real test of purpose and consistency. We'd seen the way many exhibitions suffered slow deaths on the blank screens of malfunctioning videos, skewed hangings of artwork, the couldn't-care-less faces of the duty staff. We didn't want any of that. We wanted our docents there, keen as early birds, performing at their best. The humidity of the Venetian summer can be deleterious, so we took special care that our pavilion didn't languish in neglect.

We called for interns to be trained as docents. Some 150 candidates replied. After rounds of interviews, we selected Chan Wyn, Janice Leung, Christy Chow, Carmen Ho, and Matthew Wong. They would travel to Venice, spend a month there, take turns looking after the show and the pavilion, and be a part of the greatest art event in the world at the same time.

Zuraika 'Zu' Redo, a pixie-like denizen of Venice, was our local contact, trouble-shooter, and interpreter. She had been looking after the pavilion for three previous biennales in a row, serving as conduit for our day-to-day operations, especially during the change-over periods between interns.

'She scheduled gelato breaks in the afternoon for us,' Christy recalled fondly. 'And happy hour drinks at the end of day.' Refreshments administered to keep the spirit from sagging. Zu later came to Hong Kong, and we exhibited her art photography at the Fringe Gallery.

Matthew Wong was our fifth and last intern. A photographer and poet, he was a lanky lad, a bit gawky, kept to himself, and was never without a sketchbook during his stay in Venice. We asked him and the other interns afterwards if the internship had done them any good. Matthew wrote, 'Yes, it did meet my objectives and expectations, which were to gain first-hand exposure to a world-class art event. Perhaps in the future I will have another opportunity to achieve the same communication with audiences at such an event, this time as an artist.' We were not to know that he was only able to live up to half of that promise to himself.

After Venice, Matthew gave up photography and took up

painting. He left Hong Kong to return to Edmonton, Canada, and taught himself to paint – often large expressive works. Eight years later in 2019, when he'd gone back to Venice for a visit, he was on the brink of achieving international fame. His artworks had caught the attention of the New York art world. It appeared within reach to have his works on show at the Biennale.

Later that year, one evening he went out for a walk from his home in Edmonton. He never came back. He jumped. He took his own life, his mother Monita told us. His parents had flown back from Canada and called on us. They wanted to find out how he had lived this life in Hong Kong that they knew little about – this missing piece of puzzle for the gallery they're going to build to enshrine his works and memories. They didn't know Matthew used to come to the Fringe vault to read his poems with other poets in the monthly poetry gathering Outloud. He may have been suffering from Asperger's Syndrome, which made him socially awkward. For him to stand in front of an audience to recite poetry could be quite a challenge. 'But nobody seemed to have noticed he was any different,' Dave McKirdy, a fellow poet and Outloud regular, recalled. 'We were all a bit strange anyway. I think he felt he could be himself around this lot. Yes, I believe he was happy.'

Peggy Chan was among the four young artists who volunteered to fly to Venice to give Frog King a hand in taking down the exhibition. By that time, winter had set in, and the Biennale was winding down. Many of the shows were languishing like the stalls in a fun fair before closing time.

'I'm his fan,' Peggy said. 'I've always admired Frog King's work. This time we spent days with him, taking down the exhibits and packing. He was not his usual playful self; he was focused and serious. After clearing the rooms, he started to look for nails left on the walls – they were everywhere. He removed them all, one by one, with a pair of rusty pliers. After that he'd run his hand over the nail marks to make sure nothing was still sticking out.

'It was so cold that our fingers were frozen stiff. He cut his hand and was bleeding but didn't stop. I saw that. I was thinking: he doesn't have to do this. No one would notice if there was one more nail on the wall or not. Those rooms were pretty rundown anyway. He could have just found a warm place to put his feet up instead. I took it all in. That's what made me decide to become an artist like him.'

chapter 15

LEARN • PLAY • LEAD

I COULDN'T QUITE BELIEVE we received the Chief Executive's Community Project Grant for the second time. It felt like we had won the lottery, twice! It used to be called the 'Governor's Shopping List' when we had a Governor.

Every year around Christmas time, the government department heads would each compile a wish list of projects that were worthwhile but not necessarily meeting the criteria of urgent social needs. This would be delivered to the Governor in a large manila envelope marked 'On Her Majesty's Service', for his perusal. In a charitable and festive mood, the great man would pick out the ones that caught his fancy. He wouldn't have to check the price with the pesky Treasury Department. He just sent the bill to the Chief Steward of the Royal Hong Kong Jockey Club, who would ask no questions and settle it pronto with money made from the punters' bets on horses.

LIFE ON THE FRINGE

The reality was probably more prosaic, involving ineluctable red tape. These grants nowadays are given to bricks-and-mortar projects mainly, with the Jockey Club (now shorn of the Royal honorific) in full charge. We fit snugly into this category because, on the outside, we needed a good scrubbing and some tidying up, and the inside could use a change of clothes, in a manner of speaking. We didn't just have to fix the sagging doors, warped windows, and spalling walls; more urgently, we also had to install a sprinkler system in all our rooms to meet the fire safety codes.

When we were awarded the grant for the first time, we went blithely ahead to realise our dream plan. For all these years, we'd been fantasising what we'd do, if we had the money. Our wish list – a fairly long one – began with a well-lit, glass-fronted gallery at street level for all to see and admire the artworks on display. Then we would remove the bar and build a new theatre there. To make sure there's enough room, we'd take down the false ceiling and the two disused old columns, dig down and lower the floor slab by one metre, install a new lighting grid, set up a control room, and retractable seatings. Quite an ambitious undertaking. Why not? We'd always wanted to do this, hadn't we?

Then we would turn the original theatre into a New York-style jazz dive. Previously, it was the old Dairy Farm's general store. The first thing to catch your eye would have been the marble-topped counter, smooth and cool to the touch, running down the length of the room, filled with the soothing scent of cream, cold milk, butter, and ice cream. And the floor-to-ceiling windows with wooden shutters that looked out to the leafy Lower Albert Road on one side, and the long queue of traffic running down Wyndham Street on the other.

To shut off the traffic noise and light, instead of double-glazing the wraparound windows, we would lay bricks in them – a crude solution but very effective. We had kept it this way for twenty years. Now, having been given the chance, we wanted to ungag the windows and let the light back in again. That's a liberating and feel-good thing to do. Other than that, a list of must-do things: the fire sprinklers and central aircon system, rewiring all the electrics, upgrading the plumbing, and adding a few toilets. One of our standing jokes was: 'What's the most valuable thing in the Fringe Club?' The answer: 'Toilet, for we've only got one.'

It's a lot of work to be done all at once. But I didn't know better. And when Diana Wan - producer from Radio Television Hong Kong who wanted to make a documentary about this - asked me how long it's going to take, I answered breezily: 'Eighteen months at most.' My estimate was nowhere near the mark. It took us more than six years to get to the finish line.

What I hadn't anticipated was how long it would take to get the government departments – eight or nine of them in total – to give the green light for each item of work. They took their time, up to three months, separately, to come up with a no-object decision. In the middle of all this, the heritage status of the building was upgraded up from Grade 3 to Grade 1. What this meant was we had to comply with a stricter set of conservation standards and regulations.

One day, we calculated the number of years it'd take to complete the works. Longer than the lifespans of a cat and a dog. It was a sobering moment.

Work began to fall behind schedule. We were partly to blame, for we didn't want the renovation work to get in the way of our programmes, so we staggered them so as not to let our theatres go dark. We always believe, no matter what, the show must go on.

LIFE ON THE FRINGE

That's the ethos of show business, isn't it?

Ching Lee, our very experienced contractor, wasted no time in slapping us with a hefty legal claim. Our project manager and conservation architect didn't contest it, for fear that it might incur their wrath and cause the workers to drop their tools and walk out. That would be disastrous. We had to quicken the process, so we went to the government departments and pleaded with them to sit down and have a meeting together, but it fell on deaf ears. We began to feel desperate; toss and turn in our sleep. The impending claim was hanging like the mythical sword over our heads. Their claim was actually contestable, but we didn't know that until much later, after we'd been better advised.

Around that time, the Chief Secretary the Honourable Henry Tang and his gracious wife, Lisa, threw a garden party in their Peak residence. We were invited to attend. It was a clear and lovely day, and you could always trust them to serve only the best wines to their guests. On that day there were many. We wanted to bring our predicament to the Chief Secretary's attention and seek his help to resolve it. We came up with a tactic and teamwork worthy of a winning soccer team.

In order not to be diverted by other guests, I'd do the blocking while our Chairlady Wailee took Henry aside and let Cat make a lachrymose plea for our case. Henry turned out to be most sympathetic. Two days later, we got the various departments to sit down around the table, albeit somewhat reluctantly. We managed to bundle the tasks and speed up the decision process.

Looking back, if I had another shot with this project, of course I'd do it differently. To start, I wouldn't try to do quite so much. I'd bit off more than I could chew, as Ol' Blue Eyes sang. I would narrow the scope and focus on what's really important. I'd have the Antiquities and Monuments Office be there during the excavations, to identify the stairway to the long-lost ice vault. It so happened the workers on site discovered it by accident. There were some steps leading down to what might have been a basement. But there's no ready access – it could have been backfilled. Now the site is covered by a large steel plate for future investigation, if any.

Nothing could've prepared us for the sad, devastating news that Nick Ratcliffe, our structural engineer, had died of a stroke. It happened during the summer break when he was visiting family back home in the UK. Apart from the irreparable loss of a dear friend, I was at a loss as to how to deal with this situation halfway through the project. No other engineer would want to take up something like this. It would almost be like asking someone to finish a painting they hadn't started; extremely awkward. Thankfully, Wailee, who runs an architect firm herself, called in a favour. Another structural engineer stepped in to sort this out for us, to our great relief.

For me, before wading into the project, I would have definitely benefited from a Capital Works Management 101 course. Knowing how to manage the arts doesn't qualify me for managing a capital project such as this. At times, it'd felt like driving on a dirt track in the dark, not knowing when you'd hit a tyre-bursting bump. And there were many such bumps along the way.

With the money we received from our first grant, we'd done all the essential work items on our list. By the end, there was nothing left in the kitty for conservation works. To restore the old depot to its original condition would require us to patch up and smarten up. Take the facade, it was looking grimy and unwashed.

Learn · Play · Lead Youth Ambassadors gathering,
Jockey Club Cultural Heritage Leadership Project, 2016

Loose wires dangled from the walls. Old air conditioners perched on windows like rusty car parts. Window frames, some out of whack, had been painted in different colours over the years. Inside, some of the vintage handrails, wall and floor tiles, had gone missing. Door hinges creaked like old knee joints; so did the teakwood floorboards.

We wanted to restore the aesthetic symmetry to the building that had seen two generations of very different uses and adapt it to two disparate activities: selling milk and doing arts. It meant so much to us to complete this part of the restoration, so we applied for the grant (now called Chief Executive's Community Project grant) for the second time. This time, we proposed to do not only the capital works but also to take the opportunity to look into the past and present lives of the building, which had become integral parts of the everyday life of our city.

We titled our proposal the 'Cultural Heritage Leadership Project'. We made sure we ticked all the right boxes to get past the vetting board. It must have worked, for we eventually got the funding we asked for. After that, we decided to side-line the rather prim title and jazz it up to sound like the sequel to Elizabeth Gilbert's bestseller *Eat • Pray • Love*.

Learn • Play • Lead is what this two-year project has come to be known. It set out to take a good look at what cultural heritage is really about. It's not meant to be a theoretical study but to put into practice what we learned in the process. The first thing we tried to make sense of was that heritage isn't just about buildings and monuments, dates and names in history books; it's about you and me, and how we've lived our lives, and the stories we tell that matter most to ourselves.

We could see that we'd already become part of the story of the ice depot. Everything that happened since we arrived has become

LIFE ON THE FRINGE

a second-generation heritage of the place. The first generation belonging to the old Dairy Farm is recorded in the company's official publication *The Milky Way*. Penned by Nigel Cameron, it covers many business milestones but not much about the people involved. Since the company had changed hands a few times and expanded far beyond its original scope, corporate matters once of great importance had lost their significance to the successors who didn't quite get what all the fuss was about to begin with. However, for us, we treasured every scrap of news and anecdotes that would give us glimpses of how life was lived in those days. They help the old building explain itself, inanimate as it may seem. We realised that even the best-preserved rooms, with chock-a-block with architectural splendours, could still be lifeless and lonely without the people, the body warmth, communion among visitors, and stories to tell.

In the morning, we received the good news from Mr Vincent Fung, calling from the Home Affairs Bureau. I was beside myself with joy and disbelief. It must be how lottery winners feel when the last digit of their winning numbers is read aloud.

By pure coincidence, I was given a book to read days before; it's about those lucky people who had hit the jackpot and won big. Contrary to what one might think, they often don't end up happily ever after with their loot. The Wheel of Fortune invariably tips and turns south after reaching the top, and some of those 'lucky ones' end up worse off than before. A sobering thought which turned out to be not entirely groundless.

A call from Mr Sean Leung from the Jockey Club confirmed we had indeed been awarded the grant one more time. He also told us we were getting the full amount we had requested – for the capital works as well as the two-year Cultural Leadership programme. 'We normally only support the bricks-and-mortar part,' he said, 'not contents. Don't know how you managed it,' he went on, sounding somewhat resentful.

'Give me six hours to chop down a tree and I will spend the first four sharpening the axe,' Abraham Lincoln purportedly said. And I took that to heart even though the dictum conflicts with the urgings from Mr Leung to get things started pronto – something impatient Hongkongers tend to do.

Once we had signed the acceptance letter, we found our feet on the starting block, all ready to sprint off. The message we got from our sponsor was clear: get it done as quickly as possible, follow the rules, don't deviate from the written plan; it was also implied that as long as we deliver the numbers, there won't be many questions asked.

We began recruiting. The job market in 2016 was peaking: there were more job vacancies than available staff, especially in the service and arts sectors. Some polls estimated that there were no fewer than 30,000 unfilled posts in these two sectors alone.

We advertised to recruit a project director, project manager, and two coordinators. It turned out that there was no shortage of applicants, but many of them were coming from unrelated professions, probably taking pot shots at jobs paying more than what they were earning. In the end, we had to narrow it down to a few suitable ones. We didn't want to make any mistakes with our picks. Someone suggested using a graphologist for assessment, so during the job interview, we asked the applicants to write something on a given topic in their own handwriting. Afterwards, we sent the samples for analysis. We wanted to be sure they had the right qualities even if they didn't have the right job experiences. The result? Not only did we get a team of complementary skills, but we

LIFE ON THE FRINGE

also weeded out the lurking shirker and slacker. Or so we thought.

Catherine Liu came on board as the project director, the post hardest to fill. It's a senior management position, and people in the prime of their careers don't usually take on short-term contract jobs like this one. She had made a move from the Hong Kong International Film Festival as the Person-in-Charge of Film Awards. Tenacious, conscientious, and driven, she led the team from start to finish in the two-year race, without gasping for breath. We have given her the moniker of Cat Too.

Her number two was Erica Lam. Mercurial and one with lofty goals, she was put in charge of 'Learn' – the first word in our project title. Erica's background was in student liaison at a local university. The two coordinators, Sunny Hwang and C. Ting Chan, were both fresh out of university and belonging to a new breed: tech-savvy and laser-focused in front of a computer.

Sunny, who can subsist on a diet of juice and bubble tea, produced a record number of video clips – one every other day on average over two years that were put to use for online promotion and other uses – while researching the history of the old Dairy Farm shophouse and its surroundings. C. Ting put her design skills to the test, requiring her to grow ideas from seedlings to trees. She has documented this process and the extent of work in a book entitled *Creative Odyssey – The L.P.L Story*.

To kick off the capital work, we called for tenders to hire a team of professionals that included an Authorised Person (AP), Registered Structural Engineer (RSE), Conservation Architect, and Quantity Surveyor (QS). We knew we must choose smartly this time, so we formed a panel of interviewers who were in similar fields.

In the process we'd picked the AP, Mr Tom Yip, from the

eponymous architect firm that had been in business for many years, was well respected and a role model to young architects. The QS, Gary Hui, represented Bridgewater, another reputable firm. We were particularly impressed by the RSE, who introduced himself as Franky Chan of Be Frank, and who came across in the interview as energetic and in robust health. We were still haunted by the untimely passing of our dear friend Nick and didn't want that to happen to anyone in any circumstance. The conservation architect, Gabriel Lo, recruited by Tom, like the Archangel Gabriel of his namesake, often renders help to those caught between a rock and a hard place, a predicament in which we'd soon find ourselves.

We found the time to sharpen our axes, nevertheless. It felt incredibly luxurious to be able to do that. In this town, time is spent on doing things; we like doing things on the hop, not bothering too much to think things through. How many times have we done things because we've been told to do them? And not stopped to ask why and what for?

Now that we had a chance to sit around and talk, we asked ourselves some very basic questions, such as what does cultural heritage really mean? Do we have the same level of understanding? What are we hoping to achieve, and how are we supposed to do it? Meanwhile, we wanted to make sure everyone was on the same page, so we allowed time for a visual identity to fully evolve and express itself, instead of taking the usual shortcuts of piecemeal designs. I always believe we hear a message better if we can see it. This task had gone to C. Ting, whose studies included visual communication and design.

In our discussions, we all felt that cultural heritage is ultimately about people, their lives, their aspirations, their stories, and the stories passed down to them. This project would put us in touch with people who think their lives are ordinary and of no real significance; we'd show them that every one of us is unique, what has happened to us is every bit as important as what is written in the history books, and we're every bit Grade-1 heritage in the flesh.

My own self-realisation has been circuitous. It started years ago when I was young and impressionable. I was going through a religious phase. I was invited to a Bible camp on Lamma Island, attended by young proselytes like myself. I was brought up a Catholic and had always felt guilty about the sins I committed on a regular basis; despite the *mea culpas* and promises not to sin again made in the confessional, I hadn't really bettered my chances of going to Heaven when I died.

The year I started my matriculation at Diocesan Boys' School, I was taught English literature by Reverend Ellis, the school chaplain. He was the kindest person I'd encountered and a saint. That he'd written a thesis on D.H. Lawrence, known to us boys by his authorship of *Lady Chatterley's Lover* – probably the most-read book outside of our reading list – made us see him in a different light. When he knew from my essay writing that I often asked questions such as why we are here or do we all get snuffed out like candles in the end and are no more, he loaned me a book by Paul Tillich, a Christian existentialist thinker, who answered some of the questions that were bothering me. I was intrigued. That was what had brought me to the week-long Bible camp held on Lamma Island that summer.

It was very intense, talks and breakout group discussions scheduled throughout the day. Bernard Liu, a schoolmate, came for a visit. He sat in for a talk given by a well-known professor of space science, who spoke with conviction and authority about the universe and certainty of the existence of God.

Bernard stayed on after dinner. It was a warm mid-summer evening. We sat on the beach and chatted. I asked him what he thought of the talk. 'I'm agnostic,' he said. We'd made serious attempts to discuss matters of this nature before when we were not talking about girls. 'Do you believe God exists?' I asked Bernard. Then something extraordinary happened. A shooting star crossed the night sky. 'Show me another one,' he said nonchalantly,' and I'll believe.'

Seconds after he'd said that the sky was criss-crossing with them. Later, I found out that it was a meteor shower. But I've never seen anything quite like it since then. For Bernard, he remains an agnostic.

I came upon the name of George Ivanovitch Gurdjieff in Peter Brook's memoir, *The Threads of Time*, that I'd picked up from a book tent at the Edinburgh Book Festival. Peter Brook is my theatre idol. That he'd brought back to life a rundown comic opera house called Bouffes du Nord – situated in an unfashionable quartier of Paris near Gare du Nord known as 'Little Turkey' – and turned it into a theatre Mecca has always struck a deep chord in me. I hung on to his every word. I wanted to find out more about this spiritual guide, Gurdjieff, that had such a profound influence on him.

Originally from Transcaucasia, a region between Eastern Europe and Western Asia, Gurdjieff was a mystic and teacher, a composer and choreographer. In his teachings, he says that we are asleep and go through life sleepwalking; that we are wind-up automatons, unable to break out of our patterns of thought and behaviour. He advocates that we need to be awakened from our sleep to become fully conscious beings; otherwise, whatever we do carries no real meaning and value to ourselves.

At that point, I was feeling like a wound-up automaton. My life was patterned on my addictions to work, nicotine, alcohol, and a load of negative emotions. They led me into a kind of hellish karmic cycle. Once my mind was in the grip of powerful emotions such as fear, anger, and remorse, I lost control and couldn't escape from them. They would drag me into a maelstrom and give me sleepless nights. In the morning, waking to a searing headache, I'd pop a couple of Panadol to squelch the pain and go back to work. My smoking habits, my family doctor told me, were turning my heart into stone: part of it had calcified. I didn't want to go on this way; I couldn't go on this way.

Gurdjieff wrote about self-remembering, using a system of knowledge he had devised for body and mind training. I began to look into what he had to say. My bookshelves were filled with books by his followers: P. D. Ouspensky, Margaret Anderson, John G. Bennett, and Jane Heap, who taught his method to Peter Brook. And finally, writings by the master himself. I read *Meetings with Remarkable Men* with great interest, including what the translator wrote in the introduction: 'He calls to us to open our eyes. He asks us why we are here, what we wish for, what forces we obey. He asks us, above all, if we understand what we are. He wants us to bring everything back into question . . . and compels us to answer.'

Above the entrance to the Temple of Apollo, they say, was the inscription announcing to all who take heed: Know Thyself. This set me on my quest, through which I've come to know my crippling shyness, terror of appearing in front of a crowd, speaking or social-ising, the dysphasia that has made it hard for me to memorise even a snatch of song lyrics or poetry.

Gurdjieff uses the analogy of a horse-drawn carriage. The carriage represents our physical body, the horse is our emotional body, and the driver is our thinking mind. When the driver is asleep, the horse takes the carriage to wherever it trots, often following the same trodden paths. If the horse is agitated, it can go wild and crash the carriage. Only if the driver is fully awake and aware can the carriage be directed to where it's meant to go.

Gurdjieff's method, called The Fourth Way, says that to become conscious beings we need to work on ourselves at all times. We have to be self-vigilant, and that takes a lot of effort. To start, the carriage has to be in good condition to go on any journey. I was aware that my body wasn't in good shape. I had to do something about it. I had to stop smoking, stop taking painkillers, and get medical attention for my heart.

Ancient esoteric knowledge is a rare substance, Gurdjieff believes. Knowing isn't enough; you have to live what you know. Two branches of ancient knowledge in Chinese culture that I know of superficially are Taoism and Traditional Chinese Medicine (TCM); they are intertwined in theories and practices in many ways. I wanted to know more. I conjecturally believe that cosmos plays no favourites in disseminating knowledge and wisdom to the world - they're randomly tossed out to those who seek them.

I went to a cardiologist. He took a scan of my defective heart and showed me the part that had been calcified. 'Any medication for this condition?' I asked. He was very forthcoming: 'Nothing I can prescribe.' I asked if doing exercise could help. 'Not much,' the doctor said, 'It's degenerative.' I began to sound desperate. 'Is there anything I can do?' He said with finality, 'Nothing.' If nothing can be done here, I thought, maybe I should look elsewhere. That's when I started to look into Taoist practice and TCM.

There is a Taoist saying that we, not some higher power, are ultimately responsible for our own lives and well-being. I took it to mean that we only have ourselves to blame if we fuck up. Smoking was the cause of my ailment: I had to put a stop to it. I'd tried many times to kick the habit but failed. I believed seek and ye shall find. That is, if we look for help, ultimately, we'll find it, because we keep our eyes open when we're looking for something that's really important to us.

I came across some pointers in Martin Seligman's positive psychotherapy books. He says we must stop being such a sourpuss who always thinks of what can go wrong. Instead, we can look on the bright side of things and focus on what can go right. He says we learn to feel helpless, like a constantly frustrated lab rat: we think we can't change anything, with the bad hand we've been dealt.

I'd been thinking a lot about all the bad things that smoking was doing to my health. My rational mind told me to quit, but my body wasn't listening. This time, I decided to change tack and think about all the good things it would bring, if I stop. I'm very sensitive to scent, so I told myself: 'Each time you open your wardrobe, everything smells fresh and clean, unlike the smoker's breath. And your favourite foods taste so much better.' I kept telling these things to myself, until my body started to respond and conform.

I kicked the habit for good in three months. I would be lying if I said it was easy. I found out first-hand just how addictive nicotine is. We tell ourselves anything just so we won't have to stop, even if we know it's killing us. That's how dangerous it is.

Yet once you've chosen to take a path, you'll meet other seekers who are keen to share their knowledge with you. That's what happened. I was at the Kee Club (no longer here) for lunch and by chance ran into Christian Romberg. I've known Christian from the days we ran the Fringe Club from his hip joint 1997 in Lan Kwai Fong. He was now the boss of this stylish club in Central. While waiting for my guests to arrive, I wandered into an alcove where he kept sacred objects and books on Tibetan Buddhism. Christian is from Austria. I never asked him about how he had come to be interested in Tibetan Buddhism or whether he had read Heinrich Harrer's Seven Years in Tibet and his life-changing encounter with the young Dalai Lama. That day he gave me a familiar quick smile and said with some urgency, 'Have you heard of Bruce Lipton?'

I told him I hadn't. 'You must read his book,' he said, writing the name down. A developmental biologist, Dr Lipton has a specialty in epigenetics, and the gist of his book *The Biology of Belief* is that genes do not predetermine everything; environmental factors and our self-beliefs also have a big influence on our mental and physical condition. His claims are often mocked as New Age babble and are not taken seriously by mainstream medical science, but I felt there was a message for me.

I wanted to do something for my defective heart. I consulted other heart doctors, cardiologists, as they're called. They all recommended taking statin drugs as a way to prolong my life. It's a known fact that once you start taking statins, you can't quit – it is pretty much for the rest of your life. They don't actually cure you but just keep your readings within a normal range. In fact, people often find themselves losing strength and vitality from taking them over a long time. I felt statins would make me dependent; that's not what I wanted, so I decided to look elsewhere for better solutions.

I went ahead and enrolled in adult education classes in TCM. My mother used to make me drink Chinese herbal tea when I was unwell, and while I didn't like the pungent smells or the bitter taste,

LIFE ON THE FRINGE

I always felt better afterwards. She even made me believe that an itinerant TCM doctor had cured me of diphtheria – once a potentially fatal disease – when I was a baby.

TCM has been passed down through the ages. Essentially, it is a healing system made up of four parts: herbal treatment, acupuncture, body massage, and breathing exercises. It sees the human body as an interconnected organism instead of independent parts as in specialist Western medicine practice. There are enough texts written about TCM to fill a whole library. Most of these are written in classical Chinese that's archaic and requires decoding. All that felt very daunting. I wouldn't have ventured in if a fellow seeker hadn't appeared on the scene. Together, we made it over the threshold, seven years of studies, mostly in the evenings. And, even so, we had just skimmed the surface.

We were lucky to have found a teacher who taught the important principles – that our body can heal itself, a good diet is the first line of defence, the use of medicine is the last resort, find treatment before you get sick, and the best option is to lead a healthy body-and-mind life. That may sound like platitudes that everyone knows and talks about but not so easy to put into practice.

I learned that some TCM practitioners had become masters because they themselves had suffered from chronic illnesses. To save their own lives, they practised the medicine on themselves and some had lived to tell their stories and passed their knowledge and skills down the generations. Nowadays, we'd call them self-experimenters.

I was looking for medicinal herbs that would be good for my heart. This gave me a focus and purpose I'd never had at school. Eventually, it paid off: I found two herbs, *sanqi* (Panax notoginseng) and *danshen* (Salviae Miltiorrhizae Radix et Rhizoma), made out what I thought to be the right dosage, and used it on myself like a lab rat. After a time, I felt my heart pumping like normal again. No more heaving, puffing and breaking out in sweat climbing stairs and walking up slopes; other symptoms also disappeared. When I went for my check-up months later; the numbers were all within the *normal* range.

Some TCM masters are also practising Taoists. I tried this on my own, yet as keen as I was, I was making little progress. I knew I'd need a teacher, a guru. As they say, the teacher appears when the student is ready, and for me, my Taoist master showed up while I was browsing in a bookshop, of all places, at Oslo airport where I was in transit.

The book caught my eye because we have the same surname. How I tracked him down in a village in Thailand is another story. The journey of a seeker is never on a straight path. Mine had started with Peter Brook's memoir, which brought me to Gurdjieff, meeting fellow seekers, my TCM teacher, and now to my Taoist master and spiritual guide. I am awake, present and, the fact that I am still alive and kicking (at the time of writing and God willing), and my heart is pumping with mucho gratitude and happiness, never ceases to amaze me.

The Learn • Play • Lead project played out like the title of Gurdjieff's book *Meetings with Remarkable Men*, encounters with people who had most influenced him on his spiritual journey. His definition of a 'remarkable' person is someone who is resourceful of mind, able to respond to situations either as sheep or wolf and exercise self-restraint over coarser instincts; and is tolerant towards others' shortcomings.

Over the two years of our project, we encountered our fair share of remarkable men and women. Their names – making for a long and impressive list – have come to mind along with their friendly faces. Among them: K. J. Wong, concert pianist; Wilson Ng, orchestra conductor; Patrick Mok, social historian; Elaine Liu, jazz musician and photographer; Hanison Lau, mixed-media artist; Laurence Loh, conservationist and architect; Kevin Tan, conservation activist; Andy Wong, dancer and choreographer; Wang Shouzhi, art historian and urban designer; Yan Pat To, playwright and theatre director; Rico Wu, theatre director; Indy Lee, educator; Jinhua Tan, conservationist; Lee Hoyin, conservation architect; Michael Wolf, photographer; Yip Kai Chun, visual artist; Susi Law, exhibition curator; Chan Cho Kiu, artist; Jess Lau, artist; Raymond Pang, artist and exhibition designer; Tang Hoi Chiu, curator. Also, Fiona Chang, Henry Lee, Raymond Yuen, Martin Chan, Iczza Wong, and many others on our long honour roll.

Like thumbprints, none of them is the same or duplicable. 'Most of us don't think our stories are anything special,' Dr. Patrick Mok was telling me in *Naked Dialogues,* a series of frank talks in front of a live audience that I hosted. 'We don't think they are worth listening to by the public, or important enough to be written down as records.'

To prepare the guests for the dialogues, I made a point of asking each of them to tell us beforehand what is most important to them and write it down in no more than six words. This isn't as easy as it sounds. Sometimes it'd take days for them to come up with a response; what we were looking for was essentially a motto that they could live by. I asked Patrick for his and he came up with two words: 'Embrace Ordinariness'.

As a social historian, Patrick helped with the set-up of an oral history archive at Hong Kong University. 'We interviewed some 120 people for random samples. Some of them were elderly; some were from a working-class background. Not everyone was articulate. They'd start by saying – I don't know, there's nothing to tell, just do the same things every day, nothing special.

'But after a while, with some prompting, they'd start telling their stories. Each time they repeated them, more details would come out. At this point, they started to think what had happened to them actually meant something.'

With some satisfaction, Patrick concluded: 'An ordinary life doesn't mean it's nothing.'

Happiness is what we all go after in life; it's what matters most. Wasn't it Alexander Pushkin, the swashbuckling Russian poet, who said at the end of his exceptionally adventuresome and colourful life that *there's no happiness outside of the ordinary?*

Andy Wong teaches dance to the elderly and those with disabilities. He's also a healer; his medium is dance. He uses the body to communicate and express emotions that are difficult to put into words. Those emotions may be the joy you find in dancing, or they may have come from a dark place inside, causing pain.

We didn't do the entire series sitting on our bums! Andy brought along what he calls his Dancing Angels. There were some twelve to fifteen of them. He introduced them to the audience, saying, 'They're not professional dancers. But they have one thing in common: they all love to dance.' Then he led them in a simple dance.

Andy speaks in a soft hypnotic tone. We soon got into some very intimate topics. I had asked him beforehand if there were any taboo subjects he would prefer not to go into.

LIFE ON THE FRINGE

'I'm ready to go all the way,' he said. In his prime as a lead dancer in a contemporary dance company, he was an Adonis, adored by his audience. Some years ago, he celebrated his betrothal to his long-time partner, in a party held at the Fringe. He's very open about his gender orientation. 'We experience ups and downs, like any other couple. We struggle with temptations; we feel lonely and the need to be loved. We're all the same under the skin.'

He opened up – his body and words in complete synchronicity – and the audience reciprocated. Their own experiences resonated with the personal stories Andy was sharing. The life of a dancer can be harsh and even unforgiving. It allows little room for slip-ups and errors. Those nights of self-blame often see no dawn. His advice, after all that he has been through, is to be kind. To ourselves, and to others. It was an emotional session. As in Gurdjieff's allegory of the carriage, driver, and horse, Andy gave a masterclass in how to harness one's emotions and heal one's wounds.

One of the Project's deliverables, as they're called, was to produce a theatre show with a cultural heritage theme. Yan Pat To had just won a playwriting award from Theatertreffen Stückemarkt in Berlin. It was Cat Too who spotted him.

A versatile talent – not only does Pat To write plays, but he also wants to direct them. In fact, it was perfect timing, for he was looking for an opportunity to try his hands at doing both, on his return from Berlin.

I hadn't met or worked with him before. My previous experience with theatre directors was not exactly a stroll down the garden path, more like crossing a minefield. Pressure, real or imaginary, is inevitable. This time the conditions were even less favourable: we had a minuscule budget and a *full-Nelson* stranglehold deadline. Everything had to be done within three months: writing the script, auditions, rehearsals, and going into production. Naturally, I was anxious and wary. Instead of sugar-coating the deal, I decided to throw Pat To some curveballs. He'd have to be creative, not only with the dry, obligatory theme on the ice depot in the play, but also in finding solutions to overcome the site-specific limitations.

'Let's do something different, shall we?' I started airily in our first production meeting held in the Fringe Vault over coffees and Pandan cakes. 'Let's not do the show in a theatre. Let's take the audience around like they do in a guided tour of a historical building. We take them into the rooms. We play the scenes there. This way we don't even have to build sets; we use the building for backdrops.'

I took a look at him while he was busy jotting down notes in the notebook he brought with him. Bespectacled in the black-rimmed glasses he'd probably been wearing from school days, he took everything in. He has the complexion of someone who doesn't see much of the sun; eats whatever put in front of him and laughs at his own jokes.

'Do you think you could do this without interfering with our day-to-day operations?' I kept going while drawing his attention to the roomful of people around us. 'So that we could still let our club members take their coffees and drinks as usual?'

Without batting an eyelid, Pat To made it into what he called immersive theatre with a peripatetic audience following after the actors as the drama unfolds. In one scene, two actors playing a couple were in deep conversation sorting out a relationship crisis. They're seated at a table by themselves; around them were club members chatting and enjoying their coffee, unaware that there was theatre going on in their midst. Meanwhile the dialogues between the actors were piped into the headphones worn by the audience; it created the effect of putting another layer of reality above that of the quotidian.

We took time to sharpen our axes for this play, over many cups of coffee at the Vault cafe which had been converted from a basement with white-tiled walls once used to store ice slabs shipped in from some faraway cold countries. We drew references from two books I'd brought to the table – Alain Fournier's *The Grand Meaulnes* and John Fowles's *The Magus* – novels about reality-bending experiences that took place in secret domains. In a way, I saw Pat To as some sort of magus who could conjure things and situations up in his play. He played with fragments of Hong Kong wartime stories and anecdotes about the building; threaded them into a doomed, tragic romance of two modern-day long-distance lovers. It was his first attempt at immersive theatre; he entitled it *He & She: Flow of Time*.

The audience, on entering, was given a blue-coloured drink made from butterfly pea flowers. According to Chinese mythology, when we pass from this life into the next, we have to drink a magic potion to forget who we are and what we've done. To dramatise this experience, production designer Hanison Lau, known as Shing Shing to his friends, dimmed the lights and laid out the drinks in neat rows on a long wooden table in the middle of the lobby.

Hanison used to tell us he could see into the spiritual world; and every time he came to the Fringe Club, he'd run into ghosts there. He said he saw them loitering on the stairs or lounging in the back rows of our empty theatres. 'Never an empty seat in the house when you do a show here,' he liked to joke.

An artist working in mixed media, Hanison surrounds himself in his studio with antique furniture, art objects, old books, and photo albums of people long gone. At night, when he's done his day's work, he'd burn a stick of incense, don an old gown, and transport himself back to a time he once lived in grace and harmony. During the day, he finds himself increasingly dissatisfied with the modern world and the new social order.

According to him, he traverses from one world to another, following the change of time in the day. This was later used as the curatorial concept for the exhibition he was commissioned to do for us called *Between Art and the Other Worlds*. The centrepiece was a black tent for the viewer to enter and, perchance, make contact with an unknown presence. Inside, a fixed-point video played non-stop on a screen, accompanied by a sound tape of crackling static. Viewers were supposed to sit and watch intently until they got drawn hypnotically into it. There's a likelihood that they might detect something paranormal on the screen or sense it and freak out. So, we made everyone sign a safety clause before letting them into the tent; that effectively raised the level of excitement of the event.

Hanison claims that sometimes he can catch glimpses of the other world through half-closed doors and by a sudden turn of his head. I couldn't resist asking him what he'd seen. He liked to tell the scary bits – catching sight of a falling body in a window at night or a woman who disliked people drinking in her presence and would make them break their glasses down in the Vault café where wines were served. Much of what he told us didn't sound that much scarier than what's happening in our material world, maybe a bit gloomier and more skulking in dark corridors.

LIFE ON THE FRINGE

For me, I much prefer the world that we have created within these watermarked windows and flaking brick walls. It's not always visible to people passing by who get so wound up in their heads or their handheld devices to notice that there's a door to the secret domain and it's always open.

'This building,' I once told three young artists I'd met for the first time, 'if you look at it long enough, you might see it as a cargo ship with its bow towards Victoria Peak. It looks as though it's about to sail up the ravine of the mountain.' I show them the porthole windows on the North Block, occupied by the Foreign Correspondents' Club. On the South Block where we're housed, it looks like the forward part of the ship. This image must have stuck, for it later resurfaced in the exhibition *Passengers' Anecdotes*, curated by Susi Law. After a long time getting to know the lie of the land, the artists Jess Lau, Bunchi Chan, and Yip Kai Chun came up with three narratives: *Lost & Found*, *Slope*, and *I've Seen It All*.

Kai Chun, before developing his concept for his work, brought his sleeping bag and stayed overnight at The Fringe Club. He wanted to hear what the old building had to say to him. The night he spent there alone, he chose different spots to put his head down. He says he didn't sleep much; in case he'd miss something. From this nocturnal experience, he created his artwork *I've Seen It All*.

The Outlier: Placemaking of the Fringe, a mixed-media exhibition, brought the The Learn • Play • Lead project to a close. It was not an event to chronicle and enumerate our achievements but to reinterpret the past from the perspective of the present. We liked to have a chance to tell our own story. In some ways, we've deposited our memories among objects we kept for sentimental reasons.

Memories, we've found out, instead of carved in stone, are more like wet clay that can remould and remix by the passage of time.

A Tarkovsky-inspired image of nostalgia had found its way into C. Ting's poster design; the ice depot, appearing as a floating island engulfed by fog, is suggestive of how rootless and insubstantial life can be.

What better way to start a story than: Once upon a time, we found ourselves standing in front of the chained-up gate of the abandoned ice depot, key in hand? From an old metal filing cabinet, Cat pulled out a large manila envelope which she had kept for almost forty years. Inside, bunches of keys, some still with their key tags attached. They no longer served their purpose, because all the locks had either been lost or changed. One tag had '18th floor' written in blue ink. This gave rise to all kinds of conjectures, because our building has only two storeys.

Although we were pinched for space, we had tried not to throw anything away. We had tucked items into filing cabinets or stacked them in a corner in the basement – keys, broken window frames, loose floorboards, door panels, old Fresnel snout lanterns, out-of-service IBM PCs, and a fire-engine red Olivetti typewriter – just in case they'd be called back to life by the trumpets of the Archangels one of these days.

Six of these *treasures* were selected by the poet Liu Wai Tong. We commissioned him to compose six *haikus*, each accompanied by a black-and-white still-life photograph he'd taken.

Mixed-media artist Raymond Pang used our ancient window frames to create an art installation. He made fossil-like sculptures with our vintage PCs and the Olivetti typewriter. What's more, he also designed the exhibition space. Raymond has a rare gift for spatial arrangement of exhibits.

LIFE ON THE FRINGE

We paid homage to Andy Warhol's *Time Capsules*. We deposited our programme guides, handbills, old photos. and press clippings collected over the years into thirty-five cardboard boxes. That's what Warhol had done with bills, ticket stubs, invitation cards, and other titbits of his life from each year and labelled them Time Capsules. We year-marked them with the acrylic blue paint favoured by museums.

I went through a slew of old photos – records of past events and happy moments long gone. Many of the faces I couldn't put a name to. Many of the occasions that once meant the world to me had become only vaguely familiar. Those memories, I could vouch for, hold true. But like all things in life, they don't stay still any more than we do. We change, our moods and circumstances change, and so do they. Those photos have faded and aged, so do the people in them. I recognised some of them who are no longer with us, their smiling faces forever preserved in that happy moment. I felt lost and vaguely sad. Chet Baker's singing came on, plaintive and insistent like falling rain on a sleepless night:

> *Almost blue*
> *Almost doing things we used to do*
> *Almost you*
> *Almost me*

Almost Blue thus became the theme song and colour tone of the exhibition.

We came up with a ritual for viewing, such that the experience wouldn't be reduced to rummaging for old things in a box. We wanted the viewers to get a frisson in anticipation of travelling back in time to when everything about the Fringe was first-pressed and fresh.

We partitioned a corner in the gallery with walls of brown boxes. To make it look like an alcove in a library, we laid out a long table with benches and concentrated overhead lighting for the viewer to sit and look through the contents. The docent would also mention that the table and benches were made from the original garage door and floorboards. They were over one hundred years old and very much a part of our history.

Another area in the gallery was made to resemble the reception lobby of a talent agency. On the two walls, it showed some seventy portrait photos of artists who had either performed or exhibited at the Fringe. There was a black leather settee framed by a square rug, and a coffee table upon which you'd find several folders of artists' bios. The viewer could go through the folders, pick one out to call and have a two-way conversation about what they could remember of their first encounters at the Fringe. K J happened to be high on the call list.

K J – KaJeng Wong – is a classical pianist. Classical pianists, especially local ones, don't get featured on the big screen, at least not as readily as sociopaths or felons do. So, when I heard that the documentary film *K J: Music & Life* about a young concert pianist was showing at Broadway Cinematheque in Kowloon, I went and checked it out. It was a Sunday matinee, playing to a full house of local fans.

It says in the publicity that the film was shot over a six-year period on a shoestring budget by a young director who used to play the cello in a symphony orchestra. It traces the coming of age of a music prodigy by the name of K J. There's a moment in the movie when, as a precocious nine-year-old, he asks his father why we bother doing what we do, if we all end up dead anyway. When he doesn't get an answer to his liking, he bawls.

339

In screen time, he turns from a cute, smart child into a brash, exasperating teenager, but still has the audience rooting for him, probably because we see him struggle with growing pains, especially with the unexplained break-up of his family. This has so traumatised him that he drops out of school. It also causes his body to turn against him, something I only found out after meeting him in person for the first time.

It was early in the morning. We were about to fly out to join the Sing50 Programme for the celebration of Singapore's 50 years of Independence. K J turned up at the check-in counter, looking flushed in the face. He was lanky and stood a full head taller than I had seen him in the movie. In my mind, he would always be that nine-year-old boy with a cheeky smile, but here in front of me was a handsome young man with delicate features. He was dressed in a well-pressed blue cotton shirt and greeted me with a big smile. Taking another look at his face, I got a bit wary and wondered if he had been drinking and partying all night.

It turns out that except for the sake of keeping up appearances on social occasions, K J doesn't really touch alcohol. The skin condition was caused by his body rebelling against the dashing of a dream once held dear and sacred to his younger self: that the home is a safe place to cocoon with everyone in it with unconditional love. He felt betrayed and to this day hasn't really moved beyond his anger and disillusionment. The slow-burning rage manifests itself subcutaneously, on his face and body. He seems to be in constant disquietude, except when he sits in front of the piano to play. Then the inner turmoil subsides, leaving him in peace.

K J would be a good one to call on the list. He always speaks his mind, holding nothing back. 'When I think of the Fringe,' he once said in an interview, 'I always smell delicious food.'

He came back from abroad for a visit during COVID. I took him to see the Be40 exhibition that we put on to celebrate our 40 years on the Fringe. I told him this might be our swan song.

'I must've played here over twenty times,' he said, looking around the familiar space. 'You know what, this was where I first met her.' He was talking about the girl he almost married. 'But we're not together anymore' He sounded heartbroken. He played two more concerts for us, perhaps for the last time, before flying back to Amsterdam.

Our Chairlady Wailee, once brought along a *feng shui* master for a reading of the Fringe Club. He came with his compass and other tools of his trade and walked around the premises a few times to feel the *chi*, the energy. 'Your building,' he said, sounding judiciously certain of his findings, 'is like a stealth fighter jet. It's sitting right here in front of you, but you can't see it; it's fallen under an invisible spell.' Or what I recall him saying.

How could we make it more visible? We deferred to his wisdom. The master closed his eyes and made a hand gesture to invoke some mysterious power for answers. In awe, we held our breath and waited. Then, as if coming out of a trance, he announced: 'Lay down some red door mats at the entrance, so people know where to find their way in.'

Wailee had taken over from Ronald as our third Chairperson. She couldn't be more different from her two predecessors: young, single, female, with a wacky sense of humour. Though she, too, was born into wealth. An entrepreneurial professional, she was unfailingly humble, courteous, and well mannered. She had graduated from Oxford University, went on to finish her master's at the

LIFE ON THE FRINGE

University of Washington, and upon her return to Hong Kong, set up her practice as a design architect in her own firm, WDA.

Full of new and bold ideas, Wailee wasn't afraid to put them to the test, including her sartorial style and her bachelorette apartment where she entertained clients and Fringe sponsors. It was in a low-rise built on a private terrace, with a front porch and high ceiling that echoed a more leisurely lifestyle from a past era. The centrepiece in the living room was a stand-alone bathtub, installed next to a baby grand piano, with a floor-to-ceiling installation of toilet rolls like a Yayoi Kusama artwork. There couldn't be a better fit for the Fringe than this. For the many years of our association, her freewheeling spirit had prevailed, until her circumstances changed.

We were there throughout, bearing witness to the big events in her life. The quick and decisive courtship and modern-day fairy-tale marriage: two young, smart professionals with means of their own, and a future of great promise, tying the knot. Her wedding reception was held at the Fringe: she'd chosen our Arte Povera concrete floor-slab rooftop over the glitzy hotel ballroom.

For the next two decades, she helped us steer in calm and choppy waters. In turn, we were in step with her, as she journeyed through trying times during the breakdown of her marriage, the contentious divorce, and the final years with her father. It can't be a straightforward matter to keep life's big moments away from the workplace, especially when you get so caught up with it over a long time.

Everything seemed to be fine as we wrapped up the second round of our renovations. Except one thing: our grant covered neither the purchase of kitchen equipment nor the refurbishment of our two catering facilities. They were not considered part of heritage conservation, we were told by our sponsor. This got us into a tight spot, for we had to use food and beverage to generate much-needed income to sustain our operation.

In our negotiation with GPA for our lease, we had an understanding that we would take care of the building's maintenance and provide for ourselves and not to rely solely on public funding for our continued existence. All these years, we had managed to hold up our end of the bargain, but the protracted renovations took the wind out of our sails and slowed our operations down to half-capacity. The money held in reserve to shore up any shortfall in the budget had been drained. Yet, we believed this was no more than just a dip on the chart; we could overcome this, once we had everything back in place. We decided to ask the Board for help to tide us over.

One of the main functions of an arts board is to look after the fiscal health of the organisation and help it fundraise if necessary. But in this situation, down to the last person, they had their eyes off the ball. Maybe they thought we, as veteran players, could win this match on our own. Or maybe they'd been counting on Wailee, captain of the team, to do the heavy lifting. Time and again, she had come through for us, so why should this time be any different? Or maybe, everyone had other things to care about.

I was looking all over for help like a forager in the woods. A piece of kitchen equipment in fire-engine red caught my eye when I was at the opening of Vessel, a new art space in East Kowloon created by the very capable Ruby Yeung with shipping containers. It was displayed on the counter of an outdoor booth like a trophy. I asked Ruby about it. Always generous with her contacts, she introduced Sandra Wong to me over lunch, and several days later, we met at her vast showroom of kitchen units and equipment in Wong Chuk

Hang. After showing us around, she sat me down and told me to write out our wish list.

'Anything you need,' she said, explaining that they were returned goods, that they couldn't sell them, so we could have them for free. They could also fit out the ovens and fridges for us, but that we'd have to build our own service and back counters. We would also have to install the plumbing and wiring.

I thought this was too good a deal to pass up. I sent out a round of emails to board members, but no one came back with an offer to help. At this point, in my eagerness to do what I thought was necessary, I made out a personal loan to the Fringe. I was confident that this would give us a better chance to turn things around. Nobody raised any red flags to tell me not to, so I went ahead. I shouldn't have done it, I know, even though I meant well. Anxious to do the right thing, I had overstepped the boundary of management.

And when things started to take a downturn, beginning with the tremors of social unrest in Central, I doubled down. In order to keep the operation going, both Cat and I decided to withhold payment of salaries to ourselves, so that our staff could get paid. It didn't seem like such a big sacrifice at the time. We believed this would be temporary, just a bad patch to ride over. Very soon, things would soon be back to normal and we'd be repaid the salaries as backpay. What we couldn't have expected was that we were going down a long fault line, and we would be shaken, one quake after another, by street protests turning violent, the city undergoing a sea change, and then years of living in the shadow of COVID. By mid-2020, we couldn't hold out any longer.

It was an agonising moment when we finally accepted that there was no way we could go on. Some of our staff had been with us twenty or thirty years, working shoulder to shoulder, through thick and thin. After getting everyone to agree, we worked out the money side of things, and we all stepped down. How did that feel? It felt like having your fingers chopped off, one by one.

There were still some months before our lease was up. Not to let the place go dark and look forlorn, some of us volunteered to stay on with no pay or part-time. And then Wailee resigned. We knew she was facing her own challenges. It wasn't an easy time for her. For us, still reeling from other blows, it was a roundhouse to the head. To follow suit, two board members also resigned; no longer having enough members to form a quorate group, the Board fell into disarray.

If we look back and ask what had brought this on, those extreme external circumstances were certainly major factors. They caught everyone by surprise and there was no way to prepare for them. Another factor could well be that of the management: in a desperate attempt to salvage the sinking ship, we made the wrong judgement calls. There's a big bag of questions for members of the Board, too: Have they done their best to fulfil their fiduciary duties in looking after the fiscal health of the company, instead of letting it slide to a tipping point? Shouldn't someone have spoken up when meetings were reduced to chat sessions while we waited for a habitually tardy member to show up? When this member in question finally showed up, he would talk through the meetings on his mobile phone in a voice worthy of a football coach on the pitch. Why was this kind of behaviour tolerated? When the ground rules for a functioning board were ignored, the game was as good as lost. The remaining Board did make a last-ditch attempt, roping in one more member to form a quorum in an attempt to salvage the expiring lease.

LIFE ON THE FRINGE

The garden on the roof continues to thrive. Sheryl and Osbert, a wife-and-husband team of urban farmers, came every Saturday afternoon to prune and take care of the garden that they'd planted. Osbert has been here from the start. He was a commercial photographer in those days. He took the first set of colour photos of the nascent Fringe. There was Lorette van Heteren performing by streetlight through the broken windows, followed by others whose names we haven't forgotten. Now, eons later, their faces and bodies caught by his soft lens could still be seen, preserved in sumptuous colour, and undimmed by time.

Those of us who were still around would occasionally go to the rooftop oasis to harvest the tomatoes, the odd cucumber and aubergine, cabbage, all kinds of mint, dill, fennel, tarragon, thyme, rosemary, parsley, sweet and Thai basil, candy leaf, lemon grass, vanilla grass, calendula and chamomile, and other edible flowers.

From the herb garden, I created my own recipe to emulate the tisane Marcel Proust had been served with *petite madeleines*, evoking pages of memories in his epic novel *In Search of Lost Time*. I served this infusion brewed in a clear glass teapot to guests who came to bid us farewell and retrieve their own memories of the place.

At the same time those planters doubled as safety barriers to prevent visitors from falling over the parapets. It was made into a freely planted garden which the French call *le jardin sauvage*.

A wild garden was what we'd been cultivating all along. Like those disorderly plants we let grow, the arts thrive best in less than ideal conditions, just like the grapevines that have to survive hostile elements and infertile soil to produce a good vintage crop. They all vie to get more of the sun, water and nutrients, but first of all, they must be allowed to bloom free, unafraid, and at no one's bidding.

As for the wild garden, where would it go next? Will another rooftop such as ours be found? The long shot is a bit fuzzy, like looking into the distance from a rain-swept window. I don't know for certain what is going to happen next. We've had a good run. We've met our fair share of remarkable people and done our fair share of interesting things. We've got knocked back enough times going down the wrong paths to learn our lessons.

In the end, no one knows where life is taking us and the surprises it brings. No one really knows, no matter how wise or important they think they are. You may as well go your own way. If you make mistakes, they're yours; no one else's. If you've done well, the kudos is all yours too. No one's life journey goes the same way. If you find yourself at a crossroads, always take the right turn; that is, do what you love. You can't go wrong.

Let me end here by sharing with you the song I always go back to when things are getting tough. Composed by Michel Legrand, written in French by Jacques Demy, lyrics in English by Marilyn and Alan Bergman, vocals by Tony Bennett and Bill Evans on piano, *You Must Believe in Spring* ends with the lyrics that say it for me:

> *... in a world of snow*
> *Of things that come and go*
> *Where what you think you know*
> *You can't be certain of*
> *You must believe in Spring and love*

EPILOGUE

I TOLD WONG KAJENG, the concert pianist, in a WhatsApp chat that I had written about him in my memoir. He asked me what it's called. I told him, 'A Life on the Fringe', or something just as bland. He said tongue-in-cheek: 'Your next book should be called "Dreaming of Food and Sex". That would be a best-seller, I promise you.'

I'm not so sure about the sex part. Don't think I'd be up to it. I'm no Norman Mailer or D. H. Lawrence. Nowhere near. But I love to talk about food, for I always believe food is an art. These days with time to spare, I do dream and talk rather a lot about it. Maybe also to compensate for something I didn't get enough of when I was growing up.

I won't forget for lunch it was always the five slices of white bread – Mother bought from the corner store every morning – split down the middle with my brother Joe. We'd spread Dairy

LIFE ON THE FRINGE

Farm butter on them like a couple of dedicated bricklayers intent on getting it even and right. There was never any jam around, so sometimes we'd sprinkle white sugar on it to add sweetness and extra texture to break the monotony. We'd then gobble them up and wash them down with a sweetened condensed milk called Longevity. That's why I love buttered toast to this day. Given the choice now, I'd choose French butter on sourdough bread. Add a dab of lavender honey on toast to make it a treat to die for (*A Very Long Engagement*, the movie).

Since then, I've made quite a food journey of discovery. But I've never lost my love for the kind of food Mother cooked for every Chinese festival, such as sticky rice dumpling, steamed turnip cake covered in chopped Chinese sausage and coriander, crispy sweet sesame ball, and a mean beef brisket curry that she'd learned to cook to perfection from her days spent in Ipoh of old Malaya.

On those occasions Mother would take over the tiny, shared kitchen in the crumbling tenement we lived in at that time and cook up a storm, over a small kerosene stove and wood fire. The intense aromas of the cooking would call a temporary truce in our decade-long feud with our landlady and her hostile clan and make everyone swoon for life's simple pleasures.

On weekends, Mother would treat us to some Hokkien (Fujianese) mee in this hole-in-the-wall restaurant on Lyndhurst Terrace, after the movies at Queen's or King's Theatre in Central. We would savour the noodles – seasoned by sweet dark soy and oyster sauce with shrimps and cabbage fried in lard – in the after-glow of those feel-good MGM dance musicals.

This was among the first epiphanies that manifested on my palate. The next one happened during a long school summer holiday. I was preparing for my matriculation exam. My buddy

350

EPILOGUE

Philip's dad – who ran the Macau Ferry Service that plied between Hong Kong and Macau; a four-hour sea journey on board a small passenger ship – treated us to a weekend in Macau. There were four of us. He put us up in the Bella Vista Hotel atop a promontory overlooking the Praya Grande; there was a wide and colonnaded balcony where they served a five-course dinner in Macanese style (Portuguese-influenced local cuisine). Placed on our table were silver-plate cutlery, crystal wine glasses on white, and embroidered placemats that we took special care not to leave food stains on.

An elderly gentleman took us through the dinner menu. The items were all unfamiliar to us. After taking our orders, he asked if we'd like some wine to go with them. That's how I was introduced to the first bottle of Mateus Rosé wine. When the effervescent pink drink was poured into the wine glass, it misted over. The bottle-green flask had a label on it that evoked the idyllic Portuguese countryside. This and the whole setting transformed us instantly from a clutch of gawky adolescents into sophisticated men-about-town.

Young and foolish, I was also intrepid when it came to putting food I hadn't tasted before in my mouth. I told myself I'd try anything at least once for the experience and to challenge my taste buds. That's how I developed a taste for stinky cheese and French food.

I was on a visit to Rouen – a French city an hour and a half drive from Paris – famous for its imposing Gothic cathedral. Margaret and I were invited to lunch at Pierre's apartment near his workplace. Pierre is a French Lebanese building engineer. He had a copain at work, Francis. Pierre and Francis worked and had lunch together. On this day, they'd prepared a simple lunch for us – crudités (a cut salad of fresh vegetables) and navarin d'agneau (lamb

351

stew). They also prepared some cakes for dessert. They had two whole hours for lunch, so we ate at a leisurely pace. To bring the meal to a nice finish, Pierre surprised us by taking to the table a small block of runny, yellow-brown rind cheese with an overpowering ammonia smell.

'This is probably too strong for your taste,' Francis said. And Pierre said with a wink and a smile, 'not everyone can eat it. But they say if you could, you'd be allowed to live in France for as long as you want.'

If there was one thing I wanted very much at that time, it was to live and die on the Left Bank of Paris. Without a moment's hesitation, I sportingly cut up a big piece and chucked it all in. That's how I sealed my fate, with my first taste of *Pont-l'Évêque* – its aroma or stench, love it or loathe it – and didn't stop there. To this day, I have no fear of cheese, no matter how strong.

'You got very hungry when you did not eat enough in Paris because the bakery shops had such good things in the windows and people ate outside tables on the sidewalk so that you saw and smelled the food,' wrote Ernest Hemingway in *A Moveable Feast*, as he recalled the days when he had a big appetite but no money. 'He ordered a humble potato salad and apotheosised thus in his terse trademark prose:

'The *pommes à l'huile* were firm and marinated and the olive oil delicious. I ground black pepper over the potatoes and moistened the bread in the olive oil. After the first heavy draft of beer I drank and ate very slowly.'

To replicate the experience, I went to Brasserie Lipp on Boulevard St-Germain and picked the spot on the banquette where the great man had ensconced himself, and I ordered the famous *pommes à l'huile* on the menu. I remember this vividly

EPILOGUE

because it was the day that I'd received a cheque from *She* magazine in Singapore for a story I'd written for them. One of the proudest days of my life.

It was approaching lunch hour and the place was filling up, and the Parisian waiter had expected me to order more than a measly potato salad and was typically dismissive in his manner. There, munching on the boiled potato I had a revelation that hunger might have improved Hemingway's appreciation of Cézanne's geometric landscapes, but it did nothing of the kind for me; only made me salivate at menus displayed in clear glass and shiny copper cases outside restaurants where I fancied eating but couldn't afford to.

How did we start serving food at the Fringe Club? It started with lunchtime concerts. It was in the early days. It drew a small but keen audience. Cat, who liked to look after the well-being of those coming through our door, saw to it that no one had to give up lunch, not even for art's sake. She roped in her mother to help. They got hold of two large electric rice cookers, one for cooking rice, the other for a simple meat and vegetable dish. To advertise this to passers-by, she and our pixie curator, Lisa Cheung, would sit by the window and eat with feigned gusto.

Come the Festival, we got really busy. One of the performers volunteered to help in the kitchen when she wasn't performing on stage. She was a proselytising vegetarian. Soon we all merrily munched on sprouts, green leaves, nuts, and beans, generally feeling good about ourselves.

As the Festival was coming to an end, our green cook had to return to her UK home, and Kim showed up. She used to be chef on a luxury yacht and was taking six months' shore leave which she wanted to spend exploring the clubbing scene in Hong Kong.

LIFE ON THE FRINGE

Somehow the name Fringe Club popped up on her online search, though it wasn't exactly the kind of club she was looking for. She ended up landing herself a half-day job, doing what she's good at and, the rest of the time, doing what she liked doing most.

Kim would go from all-night clubbing to her early morning swim, before turning up for work. A bit hung over but sober. Then one day she came in late, her left arm in a sling. She said she'd slipped and fallen and broken her arm. It's really awkward to work in the kitchen with only one arm. Sally Barnett, our intern from New Zealand, ever so kind and helpful, came to her aid. Kim, despite her disability, was very professional and could whip up vegetarian dishes that were not only healthy but also taste good, with her one good hand. That's how our legendary vegetarian buffet lunch got started and kept going for more than thirty years.

Kim rejoined the crew of her yacht after spending six months with us. As we were wringing our hands over what to do next, Joe Pumin Porndit showed up. He was the line cook of the Thai food section in the Furama Hotel. His mother, Jen Jer, was our cleaning lady at the time. She volunteered to cook us a Thai meal that turned out to be a scrumptious feast. I was impressed. I suggested she take over our kitchen and do a Thai version of what Kim had been doing. She demurred saying, 'My son is a better cook. I'll get him to come and talk to you. He can show you.'

What happened was the Furama had sold its business and would soon close down. Jen Jer's son Joe was therefore freed up. He came to take over the running of our kitchen. For over twenty years, up until COVID-19, when we had to face closure ourselves, he took care of our vegetarian lunch buffets, bar snacks, opening reception cocktail canapés, and managed to spice up the salads and pasta dishes with a plethora of Thai flavours – his secret recipes

EPILOGUE

of satay sauce, mushroom soup, tom yum kung, and pesto paste remain secret to this day – adding another layer of memories of the Fringe for someone like KJ.

While we were getting to grips with our catering, Michelle Garnaut from Melbourne made her debut with a restaurant called *M at the Fringe*. Deco-inspired by the bohemian eclecticism of Miettas' on Alfred Place in Melbourne, it served standard Western as well as Mediterranean dishes such as souvlaki, falafel, and tagine. It was unlike any others and soon became very popular.

I was taken with the idea of having a place right above our theatre where you could get a drink or a main course before a show and come back for dessert afterwards, like the trattorias on Broadway in New York to attract theatre-goers. I asked Michelle to create a special menu and set the price in keeping with our affordable shows.

Eventually *M* and the Fringe parted ways after being together for twenty years; the separation, as these things go, caused hurt and pain on both sides. The head-to-toe renovation of the Fringe building had taken way more time to complete than expected. We couldn't sit around and wait. Michelle subsequently moved her business to Shanghai and Beijing. After a long hiatus, Circa 1913, a restaurant serving a fusion of Japanese and French cuisine, took over. It was the brainchild of Alen Ng, a production designer and builder for luxury products launches. He was introduced to us by Kathy Chan, our Club Manager. His slight build and mild manners belied his unshakeable self-belief and single-mindedness. He did his own design and took his time to source fabrics and other materials. He wanted an understated, elegant backdrop for his signature dish that we called *La cage aux folles* behind his back. Instead of serving sashimi on a simple plate, Alen used an ornate

LIFE ON THE FRINGE

Chinese bird cage to create a wow effect. 'You always feed your eyes first,' he liked to say. Truth is, not everyone likes to eat from a birdcage. Maybe once was enough. But Alen was unfazed and kept marching to his own drumbeat. He kept Circa going from 2016 until 2019, when COVID-19 disrupted food business and the habit of eating out; he had to throw in the towel.

At this juncture, Andrew Sun, food writer and a super connector, introduced Julia Bombana to me. Julia is married to Chef Umberto Bombana. His flagship restaurant, *Otto e Mezzo*, is the only Italian restaurant outside of Italy recognised with three Michelin stars. I'd pictured Julia as a version of Hermès handbag-toting *tai tai* on Jimmy Choo heels. Andrew assured me she's nothing of the kind.

He proceeded to set up a meeting for us to meet in a small dim sum restaurant called *Nove* – number 9 in Italian – tucked in a side-street in Central. To get to it, you have to squeeze past stalls selling ladies' undergarments, stockings, and knick-knacks displayed in heaps. A narrow passageway opened to a burst of gold and red lanterns suspended from the ceiling. Wrapping round the walls were the rich details from the reproduction of a Chinese classical painting entitled *One Hundred Horses* by Lang Shining (a.k.a. Giuseppe Castiliglione, Jesuit court artist to three Qing emperors).

Julia, in a faded T-shirt and black jeans, greeted me with a big smile. She got to her feet, gesturing to the theatrical surroundings, and said, 'This is all Albert's [Albert Kwan, design architect] ideas. He used to work a lot with David Tang. Does it remind you a bit of the China Club?' She quickly sat me at a booth and got down to business.

'These days there are so few good *dim sum* places left,' she said.

356

EPILOGUE

'Once those old *sifus* (masters of *dim sum*, in this case) retired, it's very hard to find someone to replace them.'

At this point, Julia went and fetched *sifu* Bal Gor 波哥 from the kitchen. He showed up in his smart chef's uniform. We chatted. He said he was way past his retirement age. But he looked to me like he could easily do a few more laps without gasping for breath. Julia said he's a master of traditional Cantonese *dim sum* with sixty years of experience.

'These days nobody bothers to learn the trade, too hard,' she explained. '*Dim sum* is mostly mass produced in central kitchens – food factories.' She wanted a place where you could taste authentic *dim sum* and Cantonese dishes, and sip *pu'er* tea all day. 'Just like the Hong Kong we used to know, back in the good old days.' So, once she'd heard of Bal Gor's intention to hang up his toque, she made him an offer.

She made a bid for the space vacated by Circa 1913. It wasn't exactly the best time to open a new restaurant during the COVID-19 pandemic, as people didn't feel it safe to eat out. I asked her why she wanted to take the risk.

'There's never a right time,' she said. 'You do it when the conditions are there. Besides, Chef [Bombana] loves old buildings. He says they have deeper flavours.'

It had always been my dream to have a tea house at the Fringe. But never thought it possible because, for one thing, our kitchen space was rather small and the floor was leaky. We couldn't figure out where those leaks were springing from. On a bad day they'd drip down to the theatre below. Also, the air-conditioning system had a way of conking out at a time when you could die from heat stroke. These and other nagging problems came with a century-old building. Julia and her team didn't just patch them

LIFE ON THE FRINGE

with sticky tape and hope for the best. They did thorough repairs for the long haul.

I had a chance to sit down for a chat with Chef Bombana after he got off work in Otto e Mezzo. The COVID-19 pandemic was still raging and nobody knew when it'd be over. 'Is this the right time to do this?' I asked again. 'Now is always good,' he said. 'I only want one restaurant [of my own in life]. Now I have more than one. I'm happy.'

The restaurant Nove at the Fringe opened to business on time. Albert, who designed the interior, was on site to supervise the works throughout. Due to the pandemic, everything slowed down, but he was able to get the help he needed to get the job done in time.

When I told Eugene Pao, best-known jazz guitarist in Hong Kong, that we had a Cantonese tea house and we'd like to name a dim sum after him, the way they had done with Peach Melba, the famous dessert, for the celebrated opera singer, Dame Nellie Melba, he was amused and said, 'Why not?' Julia also liked the idea.

'You must name one after Ted, too,' Eugene played along and said blithely, 'or he'll be jealous.' Ted Lo, an equally well-known jazz pianist of Hong Kong, is his buddy and they often performed together. Chef Bal Gor went ahead and created the *Eugene bao and Ted Lo shou* for the Nove menu at the opening.

Looking back, the struggles that we'd gone through, during those seemingly endless pandemic years, have become things of the past. No one could've guessed that it would end as abruptly as it started. I hope we've learned our lesson this time not to take things in life too seriously. What we think can't be changed will change. What seems hopeless will eventually turn a corner. What was thought to be just a fun and frivolous act

EPILOGUE

of naming a dessert or *dim sum* dish for you, could be your shot at immortality.

'As above, so below,' the Taoists like to say.

The world is a mirror of ourselves. In the end, we create the kind of society we live in. Let's tread lightly into the future. There's no telling where it's going to take us. Like the punchline of a good joke, it only works if it catches us by surprise.

THE END

ACKNOWLEDGEMENTS

I AM DEEPLY INDEBTED to many people for the writing and production of this book, and I would like to thank in particular Mary Chan of MCCM Creations and Michael Duckworth of Hong Kong University Press, for their support, trust and belief in me as a writer who has yet to make his mark. Madeleine Slavick for her skilled and sure-handed editing of my shambolic first draft. Peter Suart for his endearing designs and the Suartesque humour of his drawings. Victoria Finlay for her expert advice generously given, and her unflagging optimism that kept me going. Cat Lau for her steadfast, custodial care of Fringe Club history and fact-checking my manuscript. See Ting Chan for her technical support. The very capable MCCM team: Lie Fhung, Anna Koor and Sunny Pang for his translations. And Shirley Wong, for her inspirational touch on the book title.

I am immeasurably grateful to Marissa Fung-Shaw, for her evocative preface; Tseng Sun Man, Victoria Finlay, Lynn Yau, and G.C. for their time and kind endorsement of my novice attempt at writing.

My boundless appreciation to all the artists whose works sustained and brought to life the Fringe Club through the years. Without them, it would be a soundless gong and empty shell. They are, by cursory head-counts, numbered in the thousands. In the limited length of my narrative, I could only have skimmed the surface and brought up only a handful of them. The rest have taken up a special place in my heart and are never far from my memory.

It is to the far south I have come to roost in my dotage. For this I am much indebted to my adopted country on the land of the

ACKNOWLEDGEMENTS

First Nations people and the Australian Consulate-General, their past and present Consul Generals, in particular, Jocelyn Chey, Julie Chater, Paul Tighe, Elizabeth Ward, and Gareth Williams – the host of my book launch reception – and Joanna Bayndrian, Public Affairs Director, and her predecessor, Gavin McDougall, and Candy Leung, the indispensable perennating link; to them my deep gratitude for their staunch support over four decades.

And I salute the remarkable people I have come across along the way: Camilla Hale, Simon Evans, Peter Tregilgas, Kaitai Chan, Carrillo Gantner, Wayne Harrison, Jill Smith, Will Gluth, Aubrey Mellor, Matthew Aylmer of Red Door, oenophile and culinary explorer, and all the others whose names have temporarily slipped my mind. And those at the British Council in the antediluvian days: Oliver Siddle, Tom Buchanan, Maria Ho, and the peerless Estella Tong. Also the colleagues-in-arms, through the ages, at Cultural Presentations Office of LCSD (formerly part of the Urban Council), Hong Kong Museum of Art, Alliance Francaise, Goethe Institut and a long list of consulate-generals in Hong Kong, in particular, of Austria, Spain, US Information Agency and Asian Cultural Council.

I could not have gone the distance without the support and participation of generations of audiences and club members; all the writers and editors of the media – Zelda Cawthorne, Alice Cairns, Cherry Barnett, Vernon Ram, Petra Hinterthur, Elven Ho, Mary Loh, Victoria Finlay, Kevin Kwong, Andrew Sun, Fionnuala McHugh, to name but a few.

All the past Board and Committee members, in particular the

LIFE ON THE FRINGE

late Keith Statham, Barrie Wiggham, Patrick Williamson, Rachel Cartland, David K.P. Li, Ronald D.B. Leung, Wailee Chow – for steering the Fringe at sea to terra firma. And to each and every member of staff for their hard work and dedication in keeping the Fringe in the race and its engine running.

Above all, I would like to thank my family in Australia, Singapore and France – Margaret, Poyang, Chikay, Elaine, Annie, Liana, Holly, Damian, Micah, Thomas; Lydia, Tony, Hawk, Hannah, Sarah; Terry, Agnes, Diana, Bruno – for their love and care at all times.

INDEX

Abbas, Akbar, 22

Adelaide Fringe, 66, 71, 139–140, 175

A Midsummer Night's Dream, 49, 50

Art Resource & Information Centre, 227

Artist Commune, 119, 238–239, 240–241

Arts Administrators Association, 226

Arts Council (of Australia), 191, 223

Arts Council (U.K.), 57, 193

Arts Fair, 72, 78–79, 84, 112

Asialink, 207, 209, 219–220

Asian Cultural Council, 157

Astbury, Brian, 82

Avignon Off Festival, 174, 248

Bailey, Bill, 56

Battle of Hong Kong, 277, 287

Bennet, Richard Rodney, 82

Berger, Helga, 31, 41, 44–45

Berkoff, Steven, 179

Between Art and the Other Worlds, 335

Beyond, the rock band, 126, 168

Billy Bishop Goes to War, 102–103

Block, Liz, 93

Blue Mansion, 268–269

Bock, Helmut Dr, 255

Boston Ballet Company, 51–53

Brook, Peter, 59, 148, 323–324, 329

Bryceland, Yvonne, 75, 82

Burdett-Coutts, William, 179

Cable & Wireless, 32, 127

Cameron, Nigel, 318

Chan, Flora, 57

Chan, Kaitai, 140–141, 144–145, 195–196, 205, 207, 221–224

Chan, Lindzay, 144–145, 204, 283, 287

Chan, Rupert, 49–50

Chapman, Peter, 45

Cheng Pik Yee, 113, 128

Cheung Tat Ming, 49

Cheung, Dominic, 49

Cheong, Leen Hilton, 105

Chey, Jocelyn, 207

Chief Executive's Community Project Grant, 311, 317

Chinese Theatrical Arts Festival, 115, 195

Cho Hyun Jae, 294–295

Choo, Jimmy, 270, 356

Chow, Sherman, 49

Chow, Wailee, 269, 314, 341–342, 345

Chow, Yvonne, 33

Chow, Winsome, 137–138, 195

Chrysalis, 124

Chung Ying Theatre Company, 49–50, 68, 128, 146, 289

Circus Oz, 194

City Contemporary Dance Company, 207, 221

Cinderella, 51, 54

City Festival, 119, 212–213, 241–242, 246, 260, 285, 296

Clarke, Martin, 49, 51

363

LIFE ON THE FRINGE

Council for Performing Arts
(CFPA) , 113, 191, 226, 228
Culture, Sports, and Tourism
Bureau, 65

Dairy Farm, 13, 68, 70, 74, 86, 88,
90, 135, 150, 153, 312, 318, 320
Dancing Angels, 331
Davies, Jennifer, 83
Day, Peter, 48
Death in Hong Kong, 118, 119, 241
Decroux, Etienne, 112
Demarco, Richard, 178–181
Dindo Paola, 135, 150
Dingwall, Brian, 151
Doyle, Christopher, 117, 171, 222
Duncan, Neil, 31, 41, 43–44, 51, 56
Durham, Greg, 166

Edinburgh Fringe, 74, 175, 178, 181,
251
Eldon, David, 232
Emily on Emerald Hill, 251
Endgame, 103

Festival Fringe, 10, 61–62, 65, 67,
72–79, 90, 100–101, 104, 106,
115–117, 152, 167, 168, 171– 172,
174–175, 238, 242, 248
Festival of Asian Arts, 116, 202
Findlay, Scott, 151
Fisher, Rodney, 116, 203
Flagstaff House, 59–60
Foley, Daniel, 100, 102-103
Fok, Philip, 81, 84, 112, 124–129, 222,
237
Fontyn, Margot, 52
Foreign Correspondents' Club, 62,
91, 288, 336

Fournier, Pierre, 54
Frager, Malcolm, 54
Fringe Mime Lab, 120, 139, 195, 276
Fringe Rooftop Studio, 132, 135–136,
149
Fringe Vault, 308, 315, 333–335
Frog King, 293–297, 301–306, 308
Frogtopia Hongkornucopia, 301–302,
305
Fung, John, 204
Furama Hotel, 53–54, 354

Gantner, Carrillo, 207 , 209-210,
220-221
Garnaut, Michelle, 149–150, 152, 355
Garrison Players, 45
Garrison, Douglas, 246
George, Colin, 49
George Town Festival, 266–267
Glass, David, 120, 178
Gluth, William, 211, 219
Goh, Colin, 250, 252–253
Goss, Bernard, 49–50
Government Property Agency, 136
Great Expectations, 116, 196,
202, 227
*Guan Yin, Our Lady of
Compassion*, 276
Gurdjieff, George Ivanovitch, 323,
324, 325, 329

Hale, Camilla, 68–69, 120– 121, 125
Halley, Bernard, 88–89
Hardy, Charles, 61
Harley, Michael, 49
Harrison, Wayne, 198, 201
Harry Odell Productions, 20–21, 54
He & She: Flow of Time, 334
Hellman, Daphne, 171, 184–186

INDEX

Heteren, Lorette van, 130, 131, 346

Hobson's Choice, 49

Ho, Carmen, 307

Ho Chi Minh in Hong Kong, 289–291

Ho, Kevin, 205, 276

Ho, Patrick Dr, 246

Ho, Tao, 30

Home Affairs Bureau, 318ß

Hon, Josh, 132, 135

Hong Kong at War – A City of Love & Betrayal, 282 , 286

Hong Kong Academy for Performing Arts, 34, 146, 204, 226, 276

Hong Kong and Shanghai Bank, 59

Hong Kong Arts Centre, 9, 28–31, 33–34, 44, 46–47, 49, 52, 56–57, 68, 102, 120, 122, 227

Hong Kong Arts Development Council, 230, 233, 235

Hong Kong Arts Festival, 45–47, 61–62, 179, 202, 246

Hong Kong City Hall, 21, 30, 50, 52, 54, 112, 114, 138–139, 142, 144, 147–148, 189, 195, 222, 225, 286

Hong Kong Cultural Centre, 202, 225, 262

Hong Kong Diving School, 262

Hong Kong Fable, 113, 128–129, 137–139

Hong Kong Jockey Club, 188, 311–312, 318

Hong Kong Players, 45

Hong Kong Standard, 45, 48, 95

Hotung, Joseph Sir, 231

HSBC Charitable Foundation, 110

Husserl, Edmund, 26

I am Hong Kong, 50, 128

I Club, 106–107

I Don't Wanna Play House, 218

Impromime, 112

Inspired by Ancient Rock Carvings, 238

Jockey Club Cultural Heritage Leadership Project, 316–318

Jockey Club Studio Theatre,135

Jones, Desmond, 81, 112, 113, 125–129

Koo, Colette, 166–167, 169

Kuo Pao Kun, 250, 289

Kwan, Sean, 204–205

La Fille mal gardée, 51

Lai, Orlean, 246

Lament of Sim Kim, 115, 148, 195

Lam, Osbert, 80, 116, 135, 171, 346

Lanier, Richard, 157, 160-161

Last Tango in Hong Kong, 102

Lau, Benny, 246

Lau, Catherine, 84, 169, 171, 181-183, 293, 299, 306, 314

Lee Chun Chow (aka C.C.), 49, 289

Lee, Lena, 146, 195

Lee Owen, 196

Lee Theatre, 52

Legere, Phoebe, 172, 183-184

Leigh, Andrew, 48

Leong, Gregory, 28, 30–32, 34, 39, 41, 44, 51, 55–56

Les Sylphides, 51

Leung, Ronald Ding Bong Dr, 105-106, 163-164

Li K. P., David, 96, 105, 147, 163

Li, Jacqueline, 111

Lianne & Chuck, 221, 223

Lily, Peta, 120, 178
Ling, Carmen, 112, 276
Liu Wai Tong, 337
Lo, Carmen, 49
Lodders, Hans, 167
London's Old Vic Theatre, 48
Loong Man Hong, 286
Lourey, Simone, 219–220
Lui, Mabel, 95

Ma, Tony, 227, 229, 279
Made in Hong Kong, 207
Maisky, Mischa, 54
Mak, Antonio, 73, 132, 135
Mandarin Oriental, 55
Manson, Patrick Dr, 69
Marble Mime, 112
Marceau, Marcel, 81, 84, 112
Melbourne International Comedy
Festival, 220–221

Naganuma, Claudine, 272
New Vision Festival, 276
Nickelodeon, 125
Night & Day Entertainment Guide,
153–156
No Man's Land, 275–276
No Parking on Odd Days, 250
Noonday Gun, 142, 288
Nove at the Fringe, 178

Odell, Henry, 20–21
Oil Street Artist Village, 240
One Extra Dance Company, 143, 198
Once Upon the Time in Wong Uk,
277–279
Outhwaite, Michael, 37
Outloud, 308
Owen, Nick, 49, 51

Parliament Chamber at the Art
House, 289
Passengers' Anecdotes, 336
Performance Exchange, 99, 100
Phan, Mingyen, 250
Play the Old City, 277
Poon, Bill, 112, 124, 276

Ratcliffe, Nick, 93, 151, 315
Rauschenberg, Robert, 106
*Re–Considered Crossing:
Representation Beyond
Hybridity*, 260
Recreation and Culture, 65
Romberg, Christian, 326
RTHK Radio 3, 146

Salon Films, 111
Sanctuary, 211, 268
Schulman, Martin, 227
*Second Spring – A Letter to My
Daughter*, 211, 219
Senior Civil Servants' Association,
88
Seoul Fringe 2004, 247
Servotte, Herman, 27
Sham Shui Po POW Camp, 47
Shih, Pan, 171, 187
Shih, Yen, 187–188
Shum, Jim, 75
Shouson Theatre, 49, 52
Sir Frederick Ashton's *Cinderella*, 51
Six Chapters of a Floating Life, 114,
140, 144
Smith, Jill, 210
Soar Like a Bird, 75
So Hau Leung, 33, 56
Soirées, 59, 137, 182
South China Morning Post, 45, 48,

67, 129, 182, 283
Spotlight Bergen, 263–265
Spotlight Ho Chi Minh City, 249, 263, 290
Spotlight Hong Kong, 216, 217, 246–247, 249, 252–253, 267, 273, 290
Spotlight Singapore, 216, 217, 249, 253–254, 263
Spotlight Penang, 216, 249, 263, 267, 271
Spotlight Vienna, 255, 260
Spring Fever Hotel, 49
Sridhar, Krishnamurti, 121
Statham, Keith, 61, 62–63, 65–67, 75, 178
Stolen, 211, 215, 218
Sydney Theatre Company (STC), 116, 198, 202–203, 206–207
Sunbeam Theatre, 52, 54
Swire School of Design, 262
Sze Suk Ching, 42
Szetu, Sigrid, 263–265

Tai Kwun, 287
Tang, Melvin, 54
Tang Shu Wing, 275–276, 279–280, 285–286, 289, 291
Teatro. Dom Pedro V, 137–138
The Absolutely Fabulous Theatre Connection, 47
The Arts Policy Review Report, 228
The British Council, 48, 71, 113, 120, 125, 127, 178, 228, 243–244
The Coffin Is Too Big for the Hole, 250
The Creative Nation, 191-192
The Guise, 82

The King and I, 19, 45
The Milky Way, 318
The Outlier: Placemaking of the Fringe, 336
The Playbox Theatre, 209–211, 215, 218, 220
The Press Club, 100
The Star, 48
The Substation, 250
The State Theatre, 21
Theatre Royal (Plymouth), 57
Thomson, Katherine, 206
Tobias, Mel, 95
To, Raymond Kwok Wai, 50, 128
To Love & War: The Mickey Hahn Story, 202
Tong, Estella, 178, 229
Tregilgas, Peter, 66–67
Trethowan, Hugh, 50
Tsang, Kith, 76, 298, 302
Tseng Sun Man, 226–227, 229
Tsoi, Hardy, 49–50
Traverse Theatre, 179–180, 286
Twelfth Night, 47, 49
Two Civil Servants in a Skyscaper, 276

United Arts, 52–53
Urban Council, 105, 114, 155, 163, 167, 190, 202, 221

Venice Biennale, 293, 297, 301–307
Vessel, 343
Victoria Barracks, 45, 60, 243

Walford, Glen, 49
Warhol, Andy, 107, 338
Wear, Eric, 154
Welch, Andrew, 34, 57, 58, 66–67
Wesley-Smith, Peter, 142, 287–288

West Kowloon Cultural District,
198–200, 240, 293
Wiggham, Barrie, 65–67, 91, 98–99,
104–105, 170
Wild Rice Theatre Company, 220,
252
Williamson, David, 211
Williamson, Patrick, 104, 110
Wong, Alan, 31
Wong, Andy, 330–331
Wong Chau San, Anthony, 205
Wong KaJeng, 339, 349
Wong, Matthew, 307–308
Wong Shun Kit, 118, 237–239, 302,
306
Wong, Yank, 132, 135
Wong Uk, 277–279, 281
Wraight, Anthony, 229

Yau, Lynn, 47
Yerba Buena Center for the Arts,
277
Yeung, Elaine, 111
Yeung, Ruby, 343
Yeung Tong Lung, 132, 135–136
Yio, Chiu Ming, 123
Youde, Edward Sir, 127

Zhujiajiao's Himalaya Art Museum,
305–306
Zuni Icosahedron, 75